Lecture Notes in Computer Science 2696

Edited by G. Goos, J. Hartmanis, and J. van Leeuwen

T0238476

Springer

Berlin
Heidelberg
New York
Hong Kong
London
Milan
Paris
Tokyo

Joan Feigenbaum (Ed.)

Digital Rights Management

ACM CCS-9 Workshop, DRM 2002
Washington, DC, USA, November 18, 2002
Revised Papers

 Springer

Series Editors

Gerhard Goos, Karlsruhe University, Germany
Juris Hartmanis, Cornell University, NY, USA
Jan van Leeuwen, Utrecht University, The Netherlands

Volume Editor

Joan Feigenbaum
Yale University
Department of Computer Science
P.O. Box 208285, New Haven, CT 06520-8285, USA
E-mail: joan.feigenbaum@yale.edu

Cataloging-in-Publication Data applied for

A catalog record for this book is available from the Library of Congress.

Bibliographic information published by Die Deutsche Bibliothek
Die Deutsche Bibliothek lists this publication in the Deutsche Nationalbibliografie;
detailed bibliographic data is available in the Internet at <http://dnb.ddb.de>.

CR Subject Classification (1998): E.3, C.2, D.2.0, D.4.6, K.6.5, F.3.2, H.5, J.1, K.4.1

ISSN 0302-9743
ISBN 3-540-40410-4 Springer-Verlag Berlin Heidelberg New York

Springer-Verlag Berlin Heidelberg New York
a member of BertelsmannSpringer Science+Business Media GmbH

http://www.springer.de

© Springer-Verlag Berlin Heidelberg 2003
Printed in Germany

Typesetting: Camera-ready by author, data conversion by Olgun Computergrafik
Printed on acid-free paper   SPIN: 10927984   06/3142   5 4 3 2 1 0

Preface

Increasingly, the Internet is used for the distribution of digital goods, including digital versions of books, articles, music, and images. This new distribution channel is a potential boon to both producers and consumers of digital goods, because vast amounts of material can be made available conveniently and inexpensively. However, the ease with which digital goods can be copied and redistributed makes the Internet well suited for unauthorized copying, modification, and redistribution. Adoption of new technologies such as high-bandwidth connections and peer-to-peer networks is currently accelerating both authorized and unauthorized distribution of digital works.

In 2001, the ACM initiated an annual series of workshops to address technical, legal, and economic problems posed by the digital distribution of creative works. The 2002 ACM Workshop on Digital Rights Management (DRM 2002), held in Washington, DC on November 18, 2002, was the second in this annual series. This volume contains the papers presented at that very well attended and stimulating workshop.

The success of DRM 2002 was the result of excellent work by many people, to whom I am extremely grateful. They include Sushil Jajodia, Charles Youman, and Mary Jo Olsavsky at George Mason University, the members of the Program Committee, my assistant, Judi Paige, and my student Vijay Ramachandran.

April 2003   Joan Feigenbaum
New Haven, CT, USA   Program Chair, DRM 2002

Program Committee

Organization

DRM 2002 was held in conjunction with the 9th ACM Conference on Computer and Communication Security (CCS-9) and was sponsored by ACM/SIGSAC.

Table of Contents

ACM DRM 2002

A White-Box DES Implementation
for DRM Applications[*]

Stanley Chow[1], Phil Eisen[1], Harold Johnson[1], and Paul C. van Oorschot[2]

[1] Cloakware Corporation, Ottawa, Canada
{stanley.chow,phil.eisen,harold.johnson}@cloakware.com
[2] School of Computer Science, Carleton University, Ottawa, Canada
vanoorschot@scs.carleton.ca

Abstract. For digital rights management (DRM) software implementations incorporating cryptography, *white-box* cryptography (cryptographic implementation designed to withstand the *white-box attack context*) is
more appropriate than traditional *black-box* cryptography. In the white-
box context, the attacker has total visibility into software implementation and execution. Our objective is to prevent extraction of secret keys
from the program. We present methods to make such key extraction difficult, with focus on symmetric block ciphers implemented by substitution
boxes and linear transformations. A DES implementation (useful also for
triple-DES) is presented as a concrete example.

1   Introduction

In typical software digital rights management (DRM) implementations, cryptographic algorithms are part of the security solution. However, the traditional
cryptographic model – employing a strong known algorithm, and relying on the
secrecy of the cryptographic key – is inappropriate surprisingly often, since the
platforms on which many DRM applications execute are subject to the control of
a potentially hostile end-user. This is the challenge we seek to address.

A traditional threat model used in *black-box* symmetric-key cryptography is
the adaptive chosen plaintext attack model. It assumes the attacker does not
know the encryption key, but knows the algorithm, controls the plaintexts encrypted (their number and content), and has access to the resulting ciphertexts.
However, the dynamic encryption operation is hidden – the attacker has no
visibility into its execution.

We make steps towards providing software cryptographic solutions suitable in
the more realistic (for DRM applications) *white-box* attack context: the attacker
is assumed to have all the advantages of an adaptive chosen-text attack, plus full
access to the encrypting software and control of the execution environment. This
includes arbitrary trace execution, examining sub-results and keys in memory,
performing arbitrary static analyses on the software, and altering results of sub-
computation (e.g. via breakpoints) for perturbation analysis.

---

[*] This research was carried out at Cloakware.

J. Feigenbaum (Ed.): DRM 2002, LNCS 2696, pp. 1–15, 2003.

Our main goal is to make key extraction difficult. While an attacker controlling the execution environment can clearly make use of the software itself (e.g. for decryption) without explicitly extracting the key, forcing an attacker to use the installed instance at hand is often of value to DRM systems providers. How strong an implementation can be made against white-box threats is unknown. We presently have no security proofs for our methods. Nonetheless, regardless of the security of our particular proposal, we believe the general approach offers *useful* levels of security in the form of additional protection suitable in the commercial world, forcing an attacker to expend additional effort (compared to conventional black-box implementations). Our goal is similar to Aucsmith and Graunke's split encryption/decryption [1]; the solutions differ.

White-box solutions are inherently (and currently, quite significantly) bulkier and slower than black-box cryptography. These drawbacks are offset by advantages justifying white-box solutions in certain applications. Software-only white-box key-hiding components may be cost-effectively installed and updated periodically (cf. Jakobsson and Reiter [8]), whereas smart cards and hardware alternatives can't be transmitted electronically. Hardware solutions also cannot protect encryption within mobile code. While white-box implementations are clearly not appropriate for all cryptographic applications (see [4]), over time, we expect increases in processing power, memory capacity and transmission bandwidth, along with decreasing costs, to ameliorate the efficiency concerns.

In black-box cryptography, differences in implementation details among functionally equivalent instances are generally irrelevant with respect to security implications. In contrast, for white-box cryptography, changing implementation details becomes a *primary* means for providing security. (This is also true, to a lesser extent, for cryptographic solutions implemented on smart cards and environments subject to so-called side-channel attacks.)

In this paper, we focus on general techniques that are useful in producing white-box implementations of Feistel ciphers. We use DES (e.g. see [11]) to provide a detailed example of hiding a key in the software. DES-like ciphers are challenging in the white-box context since each round leaves half the bits unchanged and the expansions, permutations and substitution boxes are very simple (and known). We propose techniques to handle these problems.

We largely ignore space and time requirements in the present paper, noting only that white-box implementations have been successfully used in commercial practice. In the present paper we restrict attention to the embedded (fixed) key case; dynamic-key white-box cryptography is the subject of ongoing research. The motivation for using DES is twofold: (1) DES needs only linear transformations and substitution boxes, simplifying our discussion; and (2) our technique readily extends to triple-DES which remains popular. We outline a white-box implementation for AES [5] elsewhere – see Chow et al. [4], to which we also refer for further discussion of the goals of white-box cryptography, related literature, and why theoretical results such as that of Barak et al. [2] are not roadblocks to practical solutions.

Following terminology and notation in §2, §3 outlines basic white-box construction techniques. §4 presents a blocking method for building encoded networks. §5 provides an example white-box DES implementation, with a recommended variant discussed in §5.3. Concluding remarks are found in §6.

2   Terminology and Notation

We follow the terminology of Chow et al. [4]. A major concept used is the encoding of a transformation. In our work, examples of transformations include a *substitution-box* (S-box or lookup table) as well as the overall DES function. Input/output encodings are used to protect these transformations as follows.

Definition 1 (encoding) *Let X be a transformation from m to n bits. Choose an m-bit bijection F and an n-bit bijection G. Call $X' = G \circ X \circ F^{-1}$ an encoded version of X. F is an* input encoding *and G is an* output encoding.

$\langle v_1, v_2, v_3, \ldots, v_k \rangle$ is a k-vector with elements v_i; context indicates whether elements are bits. v_i is the ith element; $v_{i..j}$ is the sub-vector containing elements i through j. $_k v$ denotes explicitly that v has k elements. $_k\mathbf{e}$ is any vector with k elements (mnemonically: an *entropy*-vector); $_k\mathbf{e}_i$ is its ith element, and $_k\mathbf{e}_{i...j}$ is the subvector from its ith to its jth element. $x\|y$ is the *vector concatenation* of vectors x, y. $x \oplus y$ denotes their bitwise *xor*.

Transformations may have wide inputs and/or outputs (in the DES construction, some are 96 bits input and output). To avoid huge tables, we construct encodings as the concatenation of smaller bijections. Consider bijections F_i of size n_i, where $n_1 + n_2 + \ldots + n_k = n$. Having used $\|$ for vector concatenation, we analogously use $\|$ for *function concatenation* as follows.

Definition 2 (concatenated encoding) *The* function concatenation *$F_1\|F_2\| \ldots \|F_k$ is the bijection F such that, for any n-bit vector $b = (b_1, b_2, \ldots, b_n)$, $F(b) = F_1(b_1,\ldots,b_{n_1})\|F_2(b_{n_1+1},\ldots,b_{n_1+n_2})\| \ldots \|F_k(b_{n_1+\ldots+n_{k-1}+1},\ldots,b_n)$. For such a bijection F, plainly $F^{-1} = F_1^{-1}\|F_2^{-1}\| \ldots \|F_k^{-1}$. Such an encoding F is called a* concatenated encoding.

Generally, output of a transformation will become the input to another subsequent transformation, which means the output encoding of the first must match the input encoding of the second as follows.

Definition 3 (networked encoding) *A* networked encoding *for computing $Y \circ X$ (i.e. transformation X followed by transformation Y) is an encoding of the form: $Y' \circ X' = (H \circ Y \circ G^{-1}) \circ (G \circ X \circ F^{-1}) = H \circ (Y \circ X) \circ F^{-1}$.*

P' denotes an encoded implementation derived from function P. To emphasize that P maps m-vectors to n-vectors, we write $_m^n P$. For a matrix M, $_m^n M$ indicates that M has m columns and n rows. (These notations naturally correspond, taking application of M to a vector as function application.)

$_m^n\mathbf{E}$ (mnemonic: *entropy*-transfer function) is any function from m-vectors to n-vectors which loses no bits of information for $m \leq n$ and at most $m - n$ bits for $m > n$. A function $_n^n f$ which is *not* an instance of $_n^n\mathbf{E}$ is *lossy*.

An *affine transformation* (AT) is a vector-to-vector function V defined for all $_m\mathbf{e}$ by $_m^n V(_m\mathbf{e}) = {}_m^n M_m\mathbf{e} + {}_n d$ (concisely: $V(\mathbf{e}) = M\mathbf{e} + d$). M is a constant matrix, and d a constant *displacement vector*, over GF(2). If A and B are ATs, then so are $A\|B$ and $A \circ B$ where defined.

3   Producing Encoded Implementations

DES consists of permutations, S-box lookups and *xor* operations, as is well known (e.g. [11]). Our approach is to apply encodings to each of these steps. For S-box lookups and *xor* operations, encoding each operation (along with its input and output) seems to increase security adequately within our context. For the various permutations (bit re-orderings), the problem is more difficult.

As these permutations are, by nature, very simple, it is difficult to hide the information being manipulated. To access more tools, we find it convenient to change the domain from bit re-orderings to linear algebra. We first express each of the DES permutations and bitwise *xor* operations as ATs. While the resulting ATs are still very simple and fail to hide information well, the idea is that subsequent use of non-linear encoding (see §4) significantly changes the situation.

3.1   Techniques for Tabularizing Functions

We produce implementations of conventional ciphers as networks of substitution boxes (lookup tables). Since ATs are easy to compose or decompose, we obfuscate even subnetworks representing affine subcomputations by using non-affine substitution boxes. In this section we describe several building-blocks useful for such implementations. We will use all of these except **Combined Function Encoding** in our DES example.

Partial Evaluation. If part of the input to P is known at implementation creation time, we can simply input the known values to P' and pre-evaluate all constant expressions. For example, in the fixed-key case where the key is known in advance, pre-evaluate all operations involving the key. For DES this essentially means replacing the standard S-boxes with round-subkey-specific S-boxes.

Mixing Bijections. We diffuse information over multiple bits as follows.

Definition 4 (mixing bijection) *A mixing bijection $_n^n V$ is a randomly chosen $n \times n$ bijective AT.*

In DES, for example, the permutations, represented as ATs, have very sparse matrices (i.e., contain mostly zero entries): one or two 1-bits per row or column. To diffuse information over more bits, rewrite such a permutation P as $J \circ K$

where K is a mixing bijection and $J = PK^{-1}$, replacing a sparse matrix by two non-sparse ones with high probability. This is advantageous in subsequent de-linearizing encoding steps (see §4).

I/O-Blocked Encoding. For large m, encoding an arbitrary function $_m^n P$ as a substitution box for $P' = G \circ P \circ F^{-1}$ takes too much space (box size varies exponentially with m). For large n, the same problem arises for P''s successors. We must therefore divide P's input into a-bit blocks ($m = ja$), and its output into b-bit blocks ($n = kb$). Let $_m^m J$ and $_n^n K$ be mixing bijections. Randomly choose encoding bijections for each input and output block: $_a^a F_1, \ldots, _a^a F_j$ and $_b^b G_1, \ldots, _b^b G_k$. Define $F_P = (F_1 \| \cdots \| F_j) \circ J$ and $G_P = (G_1 \| \cdots \| G_k) \circ K$, and then $P' = G_P \circ P \circ F_P^{-1}$ as usual. (See §4 for methods used to represent wide-input ATs such as J, K above by networks of substitution boxes.)

This permits us to use networked encoding (def. 3) with a 'wide I/O' linear function in encoded form, because as a preliminary step before encoding, we need only deal with J and K (i.e., we replace P by $K \circ P \circ J^{-1}$), using the smaller blocking factors of the F_i and G_i. That is, if the input to P is provided by an AT X, and the output from P is used by an AT Y, we use $J \circ X$ and $Y \circ K^{-1}$ instead. Then the input and output coding of the parts can ignore J and K – they have already been handled – and deal only with the concatenated non-linear partial I/O encodings $F_1 \| \cdots \| F_j$ and $G_1 \| \cdots \| G_k$, which conform to smaller blocking factors easily handled by substitution boxes. This easily extends to non-uniform I/O blocked encoding (where blocks vary in size).

Combined Function Encoding. For functions P and Q that happen to be evaluated together, we could choose an encoding of $P\|Q$ such as $G \circ (P\|Q) \circ F^{-1}$. Essentially, we combine P and Q into a single function, then encode the combined input and output. The encoding mixes P's input and output entropy with Q's, ideally making it harder for an attacker to determine the components P and Q. Note that this differs from concatenated encoding (def. 2) in how the encoding is applied. Here, the encoding applies to all components as a single unit.

By-Pass Encoding. Generally, an encoded transform implementation should have a wider input and/or output than the function it implements, to make transform identification difficult. For example, for $_m^n P$ to have a extra bits at input and b extra bits at output, $a \geq b$, encode $_{m+a}^{n+b} P'$ as $G \circ (P \| _a^b \mathbf{E}) \circ F^{-1}$. $_a^b \mathbf{E}$ is the *by-pass* component of P'.

Split-Path Encoding. To encode a function $_m^n P$, use a concatenation of two separate encodings: for a fixed function R and all $_m \mathbf{e}$, define $_m^{n+k} Q(_m \mathbf{e}) = P(_m \mathbf{e}) \| _m^k R(_m \mathbf{e})$. The effect is that, if P is lossy, Q may lose less (or no) information. We sometimes use this technique to achieve *local security* (see §3.2.)

3.2   Substitution Boxes and Local Security

We can represent a function $_m^n P$ by a substitution box (S-box) or lookup table: an array of 2^m n-bit entries. To compute $P(x)$, find the array entry indexed by the binary magnitude x. The exponential growth in S-box size with its input width limits S-boxes to the representation of narrow input functions.

When the underlying P is bijective, the encoded S-box for P' is *locally secure*: it is not possible to extract useful information by examining the encoded S-box alone, since given an S-box for P', every possible bijective P is a candidate. (This is similar to a Vernam cipher $c = m \oplus k$, where given ciphertext c, every plaintext is a candidate m because for each, some key k exists whose *xor* with m yields c.) This means only that successful attacks must be non-local.

The lossy case is not locally secure. When a lossy encoded function f is represented as an S-box, its inverse relation f^{-1} relates each output element to a *set* of bit-vectors, thus locally partitioning f's domain. Leaking this partition can provide enough information to allow subsequent non-local attacks such as the one in the **Statistical Bucketing Attack** subsection of §5.4.

4   Wide-Input Encoded ATs: Building Encoded Networks

Constructing an S-box with wide-input, say 96 bits (or even 32), consumes immense amounts of storage. Thus in practice, a wide-input encoded AT cannot be represented by a single S-box. *Networks* of S-boxes, however, can be constructed to do so. The following construction handles ATs in considerable generality, including compositions of ATs, and for a wide variety of ATs of the form $_m^n A$ encoded as $_m^n A'$. A network's form can remain invariant aside from variations in the bit patterns within its S-boxes.

For an AT A, we partition the matrix and vectors into blocks, yielding well-known formulas using the blocks from the partition which subdivide the computation of A. We can then use (smaller) S-boxes to encode the functions defined by the blocks, and combine the result into a network using techniques from §3.1, so that the resulting network is an encoding of A.

Consider an AT A, defined by $_m^n A(_m\mathbf{e}) = _m^n M _m\mathbf{e} + _n d$ for all $_m\mathbf{e}$. Choose partition counts $m_\#$ and $n_\#$ and sequences $\langle m_1, \ldots, m_{m_\#} \rangle$ and $\langle n_1, \ldots, n_{n_\#} \rangle$, such that $\sum_1^{m_\#} m_i = m$ and $\sum_1^{n_\#} n_i = n$. The m-partition partitions the inputs (and columns of M); the n-partition partitions d and the outputs. Block (i, j) in partitioned M contains m_i columns and n_j rows; partition i of the input contains m_i elements; and partition j of d or the output contains n_j elements.

At this point, it is straightforward to encode the components (of the network forming A) to obtain an encoded network, by the methods of §3.1, and then represent it as a network of S-boxes (see §3.2.) In such a network, *no* subcomputations are linear; each is encoded and represented as a non-linear S-box.

A naive version of this network of S-boxes is a forest of $n_\#$ trees of binary 'vector add' S-boxes ($m_\#(m_\# - 1)$ 'vector add' nodes per tree). At the leaves are $m_\#$ unary 'constant vector multiply' nodes. At the root is a binary 'vector add' node (for no displacement), or a unary 'constant vector add' node. These constant unary nodes can be optimized away by composing them into their adjacent binary 'vector add' nodes, saving the space for their S-boxes.

A potential weakness of this entire approach is that the blocking of A may produce blocks (e.g. zero blocks) which convert to S-boxes whose output contains none, or little, of their input information. This narrows the search space for an attacker seeking to determine the underlying AT from the content and behavior of the network. However, such blocked implementations appear to remain combinatorially difficult to crack, especially if the following proposal is used.

ADDRESSING THE POTENTIAL WEAKNESS. Encode $_m^n A$ via $_m^n A_1$ and $_m^m A_2$, with mixing bijection (see def. 4) A_2 and $A_1 = A \circ A_2^{-1}$. Encode A_1, A_2 separately into S-box networks using this matrix and vector blocking method, connecting outputs of A_2''s representation to inputs of A_1''s, thus representing $A' = A_1' \circ A_2'$.

While this helps, in general it is not easy to eliminate $m \times n$ blocks which lose more bits of input information than the minimum indicated by m and n. For example, if we partition a non-singular matrix $_{kn}^{kn} M$ into $k \times k$ blocks, some $k \times k$ blocks may be singular. Therefore, *some* information about an encoded AT may leak in its representation as a blocked and de-linearized network of S-boxes when this blocking method is used.

5   A White-Box DES Implementation Example

We now construct an embedded, fixed-key DES implementation. We begin with a simple construction having weaknesses, in both security and efficiency. These are addressed in §5.3.

DES is performed in 16 rounds, each employing the same 8 DES S-boxes (DSBs), $\mathbf{S}_1, \ldots \mathbf{S}_8$, and the same ATs, sandwiched between initial and final ATs (the initial and final permutations). Each DSB is an instance of $_6^4 \mathbf{E}$ (see e.g. [11]). Fig. 1(a) shows an unrolling of 2 DES rounds. The round structure implements a Feistel network with a by-pass left-side data-path ($\mathbf{L}_r, \mathbf{L}_{r+1}, \mathbf{L}_{r+2}$) and active right-side data-path (everything else in the figure). $\mathbf{K}_r$ is the round-r subkey.

5.1   Replacing the DES SBs

Fig. 1(b) shows the modified implementation of the two rounds. Each round is represented by 12 'T-boxes' (see **Preparing**... below). (Each such group of 12 is denoted by an $_K^r \mathbf{T}$ in Fig. 1(c).) Between rounds, the left and right sides are combined into one 96-bit representation. Each round's $^r \mathbf{M}_2$ transform subsumes the P-Box, round-key *xor*, side flip and **Expansion** after the round-r S-box step (for details, see **The Transfer Functions** in §5.2).

As shown in Fig. 1(c), a transform $\mathbf{M}_1$ is needed for an initial input expansion from 64 to 96 bits. Likewise a transform $\mathbf{M}_3$ is needed to reduce the final output size. ($\mathbf{M}_0$ and $\mathbf{M}_4$ are discussed in §5.3: **Recommended Variant**.)

Eliminating the Overt Key by Partial Evaluation. In each round, a DSB's input is the *xor* of 'unpredictable' information (i.e. data), and 'predictable' in-

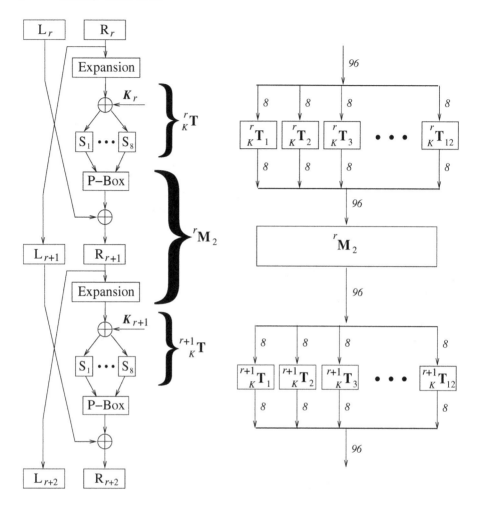

(a) Two Rounds of DES

(b) Two Modified DES Rounds Before
De–Linearization and Encoding

(c) Modified DES Before De–Linearization and Encoding

Fig. 1. Original and Modified DES

formation (from the algorithm and the key). We can merge the 'predictable' information and the DSBs into new S-boxes dependent on the key and round. The new S-boxes are identified as $_K^r\mathbf{S}_i$. Here K is the encryption key, r is the round number, and i is the corresponding DSB number, such that, for any given input, $_K^r\mathbf{S}_i$ yields the same result as $\mathbf{S}_i$ would produce in round r if the DES key were K, but the xors of the inputs of the original DSBs have been eliminated (see **Partial Evaluation** in §3.1). Each of the $16 \times 8 = 128$ $_K^r\mathbf{S}_i$'s is still in $_6^4\mathbf{E}$ form (6 input bits, 4 output bits).

At this point, the overt key K has disappeared from the algorithm: it is represented in the contents of the $_K^r\mathbf{S}_i$'s. This permits us to remove the xors ("$\oplus$") with the inputs to $\mathbf{S}_1, \ldots, \mathbf{S}_8$ shown in Fig. 1(a).

Preparing the Modified DSBs for Local Security. In *grey-box* (smart card) implementations of DES, the DSBs are now known to be effective sites for statistical attacks. To make such attacks more difficult in a white-box implementation, we prefer to employ S-boxes which are locally secure (see §3.2). This implies replacing lossy S-boxes with something bijective. We convert the lossy $_K^r\mathbf{S}_i$'s into $_8^8\mathbf{E}$ form using split-path encoding (see §3.1) as follows. Define

$$_K^r\mathbf{T}_i(_8\mathbf{e}) = {_K^r}\mathbf{S}_i(_8\mathbf{e}_{1..6}) \| R(_8\mathbf{e})$$

for all $_8\mathbf{e}$, fixed key K, rounds $r = 1, \ldots, 16$, and S-box number $i = 1, \ldots, 8$. Here we also define $R(_8\mathbf{e}) = \langle\, _8\mathbf{e}_1, {_8}\mathbf{e}_6, {_8}\mathbf{e}_7, {_8}\mathbf{e}_8 \,\rangle$ for all $_8\mathbf{e}$.

The first six bits of the input of a $_K^r\mathbf{T}_i$ will be the 6-bit input to DSB i in round r. We then add two extra input bits. The left 4-bit half of the output of a $_K^r\mathbf{T}_i$ is the output of DSB i in round r, and the right 4-bit half contains the first and last input bits of DSB i in round r followed by the two extra input bits. That is, the right half of the output contains copies of four of the input bits.

Each $_K^r\mathbf{T}_i$ is a bijection, as the function $F_{a,b,c,d}$ defined for any constant bits a, b, c, d by $F_{a,b,c,d}(_4\mathbf{e}) = {_K^r}\mathbf{T}_i(\langle a\rangle\|_4\mathbf{e}\|\langle b, c, d\rangle)$ is a bijection. (Every row of every DSB contains a permutation of $\langle 0, \ldots, 15\rangle$, with the row selected by the bits corresponding to a, b above. The xor with the relevant bits of key K effectively re-orders this permutation into a new one. The output of $F_{a,b,c,d}$ is therefore a bijection mapping the $_4\mathbf{e}$ according to a 1-to-1 mapping of the input space determined by a permutation. Since $_K^r\mathbf{T}_i$ simply copies the bits corresponding to a, b, c, d to the output, $_K^r\mathbf{T}_i$ preserves *all* of its input entropy, i.e. is a bijection.)

Providing 64 Bits of By-Pass Capacity. In our construction, we wish to hide the difference between the left and right Feistel data-path sides, so each $^r\mathbf{M}_2$ expects more than just 32 bits of S-box outputs. Both the left and (unchanged) right sides are needed. We refer to this as needing 64 bits of by-pass.

As converted above, each $_K^r\mathbf{T}_i$ carries 8 bits to the next $^r\mathbf{M}_2$: 4 bits of S-box output, 2 bits from the right side and 2 bits that can be chosen to be from the left. This means 8 T-boxes will carry only 16 bits from the left and 16 from the right. Thus the by-pass capacity of the $_K^r\mathbf{T}_i$'s is deficient by 32 bits.

Therefore we add four more S-boxes per round, designated $_K^r\mathbf{T}_9, \ldots, {_K^r}\,\mathbf{T}_{12}$. Each is a bijective AT of 8 bits to 8 bits. These extra S-boxes are AT's to make it easier to access the bypassed bits for subsequent processing. (Subsequent steps will de-linearize *every* S-box, so use of ATs for these by-pass paths need not compromise security.) These extra S-boxes provide the remaining 32 bits, 16 bits each of right-side and left-side by-pass capacity.

5.2   Connecting and Encoding the New SBs to Implement DES

Data-flow for our DES implementation just before AT de-linearization and S-box encoding (§3.1, §3.2) is shown in Figs. 1(b,c). After de-linearization and encoding, M_0 and M_4 are composed with their diagrammatically adjacent transforms and all M's and T's are replaced with corresponding M''s and T''s. Except for this composition and addition of "*′*" characters (indicating de-linearized, encoded functionality, including, where required, the 'anti-sparseness' treatment in **The Transfer Functions** below), the figures are unchanged.

Data-Flow and Algorithm. Before de-linearization and encoding, each M_i or $^r M_i$ is representable as a matrix, with forms $^{96}_{64} M_1$, $^{64}_{96} M_3$, and, for each round's $^r M_2$, $^{96}_{96} M_2$. (See §5.1, and for more details **The Transfer Functions** below.)

In Figs. 1(b,c), arrows represent data-paths and indicate their direction of data-flow. The italic numbers *8, 64,* and *96* denote the length of the vectors traversing the data path arrow next to them. The appearance of rows of $^r_K T_i$'s in order by i in Fig. 1(b) does not indicate any ordering of their appearance in the implementation. The intervening $^r M_2$ transformations can handle any such re-ordering.

The Transfer Functions. In constructing M_1, $^r M_2$'s, and M_3, we must deal with the sparseness of the matrices for the ATs used in standard DES. The bit-reorganizations, such as the **Expansion** and **P-box** transforms in Fig. 1(a), are all 0-bits except for one or two 1-bits in each row and column. The *xor* operations ("⊕" in Fig. 1(a)) are similarly sparse. Therefore, we use the method proposed for handling sparseness in §4's ADDRESSING THE POTENTIAL WEAK-NESS: doubling the implementations into two blocked implementations, with the initial portion of each pair being a mixing bijection. We will regard this as part of the encoding process, and discuss the nature of the M_i's prior to this 'anti-sparseness' treatment.

The following constructions are straightforward, all involving only various combinations, compositions, simple reorganizations, and concatenations of ATs.

M_1 combines the following: (1) the initial permutation of DES; (2) the **Expansion** (see Fig. 1(a)), modified to deliver its output bits to the first six inputs of each $^1_K T_i$; combined with (3) the delivery of the 32 left-side data-path bits to be passed through the by-pass provided by inputs 7 and 8 of $^1_K T_1, \ldots, ^1_K T_8$ and 16 bits of by-pass provided at randomly chosen positions in the four 'dummies', $^1_K T_9, \ldots, ^1_K T_{12}$, all in randomly chosen order.

$^r M_2$ for each round r combines the following: (1) the **P-box** transform (see Fig. 1(a)); (2) the *xor* of the left-side data with the **P-box** output; (3) extraction of the original input of the right-side data-path; (4) the round's **Expansion** (which was provided by $\mathbf{M}_1$ for the first round); and (5) the left-side by-pass (provided by $\mathbf{M}_1$ for the first round).

$\mathbf{M}_3$ combines the following: (1) ignoring the inputs provided for simultaneous by-pass; (2) the left-side by-pass (provided by $\mathbf{M}_1$ and $\mathbf{M}_2$ for the previous rounds); (3) inversion of the **Expansion**, ignoring half of each redundant bit pair; (4) swapping the left- and right-side data (DES effectively swaps the left and right halves after the last round); and (5) the final permutation.

Blocking and Encoding Details. We recommend 4×4 blocking for the $\mathbf{M}_i$'s. As a result of the optimization noted in §4, this means the implementation consists entirely of networked 8×4 ('vector add') and 8×8 ($^r_K\mathbf{T}'_i$) S-boxes.

Aside from $\mathbf{M}_1$'s input coding and $\mathbf{M}_3$'s output coding, both of which are simply 64×64 identities (appropriately blocked), all S-boxes are input- and output-coded using the method of §3.1 in order to match the 4-bit blocking factor required for each input by the binary 'vector add' S-boxes.

5.3   Recommended Variant

The above section completes a *naked* variant of white-box DES. The *recommended* variant applies input and output encodings to the whole DES operation. Referring to Fig. 1(c), we modify our scheme so that $\mathbf{M}_1$ is replaced by $\mathbf{M}_1 \circ \mathbf{M}_0$ and $\mathbf{M}_3$ is replaced by $\mathbf{M}_4 \circ \mathbf{M}_3$, where the $\mathbf{M}_0$ and $\mathbf{M}_4$ ATs are $^{64}_{64}\mathbf{E}$ mixing bijections. As part of our encoding, we combine $\mathbf{M}_1 \circ \mathbf{M}_0$ and $\mathbf{M}_4 \circ \mathbf{M}_3$ into single ATs. When encoded in 4-bit blocks, they become non-linear.

One issue that arises is whether this recommended variant of DES (or other ciphers) is still an implementation of the standard algorithm. Although it employs an encoded input and output, we can pre- and post-process the input to this computation by the inverses of the pre- and post-encodings, to effectively cancel both. One might refer to this as operating on *de*-encoded *intext* and *outtext*. The de-encoding process can be done in any one or a combination of several places, for example: the software immediately surrounding the cryptographic computation; more distant surrounding software; or ideally, software executing on a separate node (with obvious coordination required). The pre- and post-encoding itself can be folded into the component operations of the standard algorithm, e.g., DES, as explained under I/O-Blocked Encoding per §3.1. Taking into account the de-encodings, the overall result is again equivalent to the standard algorithm.

The overall result is a data transformation which embeds DES. By embedding the standard algorithm within a larger computation we retain the (black-box) strength of the original algorithm within this embedded portion (which does implement the standard algorithm). Furthermore the encompassing computation provides greater resistance to white-box attacks. By using pre- and post-encodings that are bijections, we have in effect composed 3 bijections.

WHITE-BOX 'WHITENING'. It is sometimes recommended to use 'pre- and post whitening' in encryption or decryption, as in Rivest's DESX [9]. We note that the recommended variant computes *some* cipher, based on the cipher from which it was derived, but the variant is far from obvious. In effect, it serves as an aggressive form of pre- and post-whitening, and allows us to derive innumerable new ciphers from a base cipher. Essentially all cryptographic attacks depend on some notion of the search space of functions which the cipher might compute. The white-box approach increases the search space.

WHITE-BOX ASYMMETRY AND WATERMARKING. The recommended variant has additional advantages. The effect of using the recommended variant is to convert a symmetric cipher into a one-way engine: possession of the means to *encrypt* in no way implies the capability to *decrypt*, and *vice versa*. This means that we can give out very specific communication capabilities to control communication patterns by giving out specific encryption and decryption engines to particular parties. Every such engine is also effectively watermarked (fingerprinted) by the function it computes, and it is possible to identify a piece of information by the fact that a particular decryption engine decrypts it to a known form.

5.4   Attacks on Naked Variant DES Implementation

The attacker cannot extract information from the $_{K}^{r}\mathbf{T}'_i$'s themselves: they are *locally secure* (see §3.2). Consequently all attacks must be global in the sense of having to look at multiple S-boxes and somehow correlate the information. We know of no efficient attacks on the recommended variant.

By far the best place to attack the naked variant of our implementation seems to be at points where information from the first and last rounds is available. In round 1, the initial input is known (the $\mathbf{M}_1$ input is not coded), and in round 16, the final output is known (the $\mathbf{M}_3$ output is not coded). Both known attacks (see below) on the naked variant exploit this weak point.

The Jacob Attack on the Naked Variant. The attack of Jacob et al. [7] is a clever DFA-like [3] attack, inducing a controlled fault by taking advantage of the unchanged data in the Feistel structure, thus bypassing much of the protection afforded by the encodings. However it requires that the input (or output) be naked (i.e., unencoded), and simultaneous access to a key-matched pair of encrypt and decrypt programs, a situation unlikely with an actual DRM application using white-box DES. It is not obvious how to relax either of these requirements. It is also not clear how this attack can apply to ciphers that are not Feistel-like.

Statistical Bucketing Attack on Naked Variant. This attack is somewhat similar to the DPA attacks [10]. In the DPA attacks, keys are guessed and differences in power profiles are used to confirm or deny the guesses. Our statistical bucketing attack also involves guessing keys, but guesses are confirmed or denied by checking if buckets are disjoint.

Attacks should be focussed on the first and final rounds. Cracking either round 1 or round 16 provides 48 key bits; the remaining 8 bits of the 56-bit DES key can then be found by brute-force search on the 256 remaining possibilities using a reference DES implementation. For ease of explanation, we discuss only attacking round 1 of the encryption case.

Consider S-box $^1\mathbf{S}_i$ in round 1 of standard DES. Its 6 bits of input come directly from the input plaintext, and it is affected by 6 bits of round 1 sub-key. Its output bits go to different DSBs in round 2 (with an intervening xor operation). We focus on one of these output bits, which we denote b. $^2\mathbf{S}_j$ will refer to (one of) the round 2 DSBs affected by b. That is, we pick $^1\mathbf{S}_i$ in round 1 which produces bit b, which is then consumed by $^2\mathbf{S}_j$ in round 2. Potentially, bit b can go to two different S-boxes in round 2 (either one will suffice).

Make a guess on the 6 bits of sub-key affecting $^1\mathbf{S}_i$, run through the 64 inputs to it, and construct 64 corresponding plaintexts. The plaintexts must feed the correct bits into $^1\mathbf{S}_i$ as well as the xor operation involving b. For convenience, fix the left side to all zeros. This effectively nullifies the xor operations. The other 26 bits in the plaintexts should be chosen randomly for each plaintext. Using any reference implementation of DES, divide these 64 plaintexts into two buckets, I_0, I_1, which have the property that if the key guess is correct, bit b will have a value of 0 for the encryption of each plaintext in the I_0 set; similarly, for each plaintext in the I_1 set, if the guess is correct, b will have a value of 1.

Next take these two buckets of plaintexts and run them through the encoded implementation. Since the implementation is naked, one can easily track the data-flow to discover which $^2\mathbf{T}_{z_j}$ encodes $^2\mathbf{S}_j$. Examine the input to $^2\mathbf{T}_{z_j}$ to confirm or deny the guess. The encryption of the texts in I_0 (resp. I_1) will lead to a set of inputs I_0' (resp. I_1') to $^2\mathbf{T}_{z_j}$. The important point is that if the key guess is correct, I_0' and I_1' must necessarily be disjoint sets. Any overlap indicates that the guess is wrong. If no overlap occurs, the key guess may or may not be correct: this may happen simply by chance. (The likelihood of this happening is minimized when the aforementioned 26 bits of right hand side plaintext are chosen randomly.) To ensure the effectiveness of this technique, we would like the probability that no *collision* (an element occurring in both I_0' and I_1') occurs in the event of an incorrect key guess to be at most 2^{-6}. Experimentally, this occurs when $|I_0| = |I_1| \approx 27 - 54$ chosen plaintexts in all – so the 64 plaintexts mentioned above are normally adequate.

The above description works on one S-box at a time. We can work on the 8 S-boxes of a round in parallel, as follows. Due to the structure of the permutations of DES, output bits $\{3, 7, 11, 15, 18, 24, 28, 30\}$ have the property that each bit comes from a unique S-box and goes to a unique S-box in the following round. By tracking these bits, we can search for the sub-key affecting each round 1 DSB in parallel (this requires a clever choice of elements for I_0 and I_1, because of the overlap in the inputs to the round 1 DSBs). Experimentation shows that fewer than 2^7 plaintexts are necessary in total to identify a very small set of candidates for the 48-bit round 1 subkey. The remaining 8 bits of key can subsequently be determined by exhaustive search.

This gives a cracking complexity of 128 (chosen plaintexts) × 64 (number of 6 bit sub-keys) + 256 (remaining 8 bits of key) $\approx 2^{13}$ encryptions. This attack on the naked variant has been implemented, and it successfully finds the key in under 10 seconds.

5.5   Comments on Security of the Recommended Variant

While we are aware of no effective attack on the recommended variant, we also have no security proofs. The assumed difficulty of cracking the individual encodings leads us to believe the attack complexity will be high. The weakest point appears to be the block-encoded wide-input ATs. We note it is not merely a matter of finding weak 4×4 blocks (ones where an output's entropy is reduced to 3 bits, say, where there are only 38,976 possible non-linear encodings). The first problem is that the output will often depend on multiple such blocks, which will then require some power of 38,976 tries. Of course, as previously noted, *part* of such encodings may be guessed. However, the second, apparently much more difficult problem, is that once the attacker has a guess at a set of encodings, partial or otherwise, for certain S-boxes, how can it be verified? Unless there is some way to verify a guess, it appears such an attack cannot be effective.

Whether the recommended variant herein is reasonably strong or not remains to be seen. However, even should the answer be negative for this particular variant, we believe the general approach remains promising, due to the many variations possible using the multiplicity of approaches discussed.

5.6   Supplementary Notes on Cardinality of Transformations

For a given m and n, there are 2^{mn+n} m-input, n-output ATs, but we are primarily interested in those which discard minimal, or nearly minimal, input information – not much more than $m - n$ bits (cf. *lossy* in §2 and *locally secure* in §3.2). If $m = n$, then there are $2^n \prod_{i=0}^{n-1}(2^n - 2^i)$ bijective ATs, since there are $\prod_{i=0}^{n-1}(2^n - 2^i)$ nonsingular $n \times n$ matrices [6]. It is the latter figure which is of greater significance, since we will often use ATs to reconfigure information, and changing the displacement vector, d, of an AT, can at most invert selected output vector bits: it can't affect the AT's redistribution of input information to the elements of its output vector.

We note that while the number of bijective ATs is a tiny fraction of all bijections of the form $_n^n P$ (there being $2^n!$ of them), the absolute number of bijective ATs nonetheless is very large for large n. This ensures a large selection space of bijective ATs which we use, e.g. for pre- and post-encodings.

6   Concluding Remarks

For DES-like algorithms, we have presented building blocks for constructing implementations which increase resistance to white-box attacks, and as an example proposed a white-box DES implementation. The greatest drawbacks to our approach are size and speed, and as is common in new cryptographic proposals, the lack of both security metrics and proofs. Our techniques (though not using

DES itself) are in use in commercial products, and we expect to see increased use of white-box cryptography in DRM applications as their deployment in hostile environments (including the threat of end-users) drives the requirement for stronger protection mechanisms within cryptographic implementations. While the current paper addresses fixed-key symmetric algorithms, ongoing research includes extensions of white-box ideas to the dynamic-key case, and to public-key algorithms such as RSA.

References

1. D. Aucsmith, G. Graunke, *Tamper-Resistant Methods and Apparatus*, U.S. Patent No. 5,892,899, 1999.
2. B. Barak, O. Goldreich, R. Impagliazzo, S. Rudich, A. Sahai, S. Vadhan, K. Yang, *On the (Im)possibility of Obfuscating Programs*, pp. 1–18 in: Advances in Cryptology – Crypto 2001 (LNCS 2139), Springer-Verlag, 2001.
3. Eli Biham, Adi Shamir, *Differential Fault Analysis of Secret Key Cryptosystems*, pp. 513–525, Advances in Cryptology – Crypto '97 (LNCS 1294), Springer-Verlag, 1997. *Revised*: Technion – Computer Science Department – Technical Report CS0910-revised, 1997.
4. S. Chow, P. Eisen, H. Johnson, P.C. van Oorschot, *White-Box Cryptography and an AES Implementation*, Proceedings of the Ninth Workshop on Selected Areas in Cryptography (SAC 2002), August 15–16, 2002 (Springer-Verlag LNCS, to appear).
5. J. Daemen, V. Rijmen, *The Design of Rijndael: AES – The Advanced Encryption Standard*, Springer-Verlag, 2001.
6. Leonard E. Dickson, *Linear Groups, with an Exposition of Galois Field Theory*, p. 77, Dover Publications, New York, 1958.
7. M. Jacob, D. Boneh, E. Felten, *Attacking an obfuscated cipher by injecting faults*, proceedings of 2nd ACM workshop on Digital Rights Management – ACM CCS-9 Workshop DRM 2002 (Springer-Verlag LNCS to appear).
8. M. Jakobsson, M.K. Reiter, *Discouraging Software Piracy Using Software Aging*, pp.1–12 in: Security and Privacy in Digital Rights Management – ACM CCS-8 Workshop DRM 2001 (LNCS 2320), Springer-Verlag, 2002.
9. J. Kilian, P. Rogaway, *How to protect DES against exhaustive key search*, pp.252–267 in: Advances in Cryptology – Crypto '96, Springer-Verlag LNCS, 1996.
10. Paul Kocher, Joshua Jaffe, Benjamin Jun, *Differential Power Analysis*, pp. 388–397, Advances in Cryptology – Crypto '99 (LNCS 1666), Springer-Verlag, 1999.
11. A.J. Menezes, P.C. van Oorschot, S.A. Vanstone, *Handbook of Applied Cryptography*, pp. 250–259, CRC Press, 2001 (5th printing with corrections). Down-loadable from http://www.cacr.math.uwaterloo.ca/hac/

Attacking an Obfuscated Cipher by Injecting Faults

Matthias Jacob[1], Dan Boneh[2], and Edward Felten[1]

[1] Princeton University
{mjacob,felten}@cs.princeton.edu
[2] Stanford University
dabo@cs.stanford.edu

Abstract. We study the strength of certain obfuscation techniques used to protect software from reverse engineering and tampering. We show that some common obfuscation methods can be defeated using a fault injection attack, namely an attack where during program execution an attacker injects errors into the program environment. By observing how the program fails under certain errors the attacker can deduce the obfuscated information in the program code without having to unravel the obfuscation mechanism. We apply this technique to extract a secret key from a block cipher obfuscated using a commercial obfuscation tool and draw conclusions on preventing this weakness.

1 Introduction

In recent years the advent of mass distribution of digital content fueled the demand for tools to prevent software and digital media from illegal copying. The goal is to make it harder for a malicious person to reverse engineer or modify a given piece of software. One well known technique for preventing illegal use of digital media is watermarking for audio and video content [1] which had only limited success. Another common approach is to only distribute encrypted content (see, e.g., CSS [2], Intertrust [3], MS Windows Media Technologies [4], Adobe EBooks [5]). Users run content players on their machines and these players enforce access permissions associated with the content. In most of these systems the software player contains some secret information that enables it to decrypt the content internally. Clearly the whole point is that the user should not be able to emulate the player and decrypt the content by herself. As a result, the secret information that enables the player to decrypt the content must be hidden somehow in the player's binary code. We note that hardware solutions, where the decryption key is embedded in tamper-resistant hardware [6,7,8], have had some success [9,10], but clearly a software only solution, assuming it is secure, is superior because it is more cost efficient and easier to deploy.

This brings us to one of the main challenges facing content protection vendors: is it possible to hide a decryption key in the implementation of a block cipher (e.g. AES) in such a way that given the binary code it is hard to extract the decryption key. In other words, suppose $D^k(c)$ is an algorithm for decrypting

J. Feigenbaum (Ed.): DRM 2002, LNCS 2696, pp. 16–31, 2003.

the ciphertext c using the key k. Is it possible to modify the implementation of $D^k(c)$ so that extracting k by reverse engineering is sufficiently hard? If hiding the key in a binary is possible, it has a crucial advantage over alternative key hiding techniques: in order to decrypt content the binary needs to be executed, and efficient access control mechanisms exist in the operating system in order to prevent unauthorized execution, whereas hiding a stored key in memory is difficult [11]. Key obfuscation is a very old question already mentioned in the classic paper of Diffie and Hellman [12].

Code obfuscation is a common technique for protecting software against reverse engineering and is commonly used for hiding proprietary software systems and sensitive system components such as a cipher. Commercial obfuscation tools often work by taking as input arbitrary program source code, and they output obfuscated binary or source code that is harder to reverse engineer and thus to manipulate than the original software [13,14,15,16,17]. However, it is unclear whether obfuscation techniques can be strong enough to protect sensitive software systems such as a cipher implementation.

In this paper we investigate a commercial state-of-the-art obfuscated cryptosystem [18] that hides a secret key. An *ideal obfuscation tool* turns program code into a black-box, and therefore it is impossible to find out any properties of the program. In practice however, obfuscation tools often only *approximate the ideal case*. When obfuscating a cryptosystem the obfuscator embeds a secret key into the program code and obfuscates the code. It should be hard to figure out any properties about the key by just investigating the code. However, we show how to extract the secret key from the system in only a few cryptographic operations and come to the conclusion that current obfuscation techniques for hiding a secret key are not strong enough to resist certain attacks.

Our attack is based on differential fault analysis [19] in which an attacker injects errors into the code in order to get information about the secret key. The impact of this attack is comparable to an attack on an RSA implementation based on the Chinese Remainder Theorem that requires only one faulty RSA signature in order to extract the private key [20].

Fault attacks are a threat on tamper-resistant hardware [9], and in this paper we show that an adversary can also inject faults to extract a key from obfuscated software. Based on our experience in attacking an obfuscated cryptosystem we propose techniques for strengthening code obfuscation to make fault attacks more difficult and make a first step in understanding the limits of practical software obfuscation.

2   Attacking an Obfuscated Cipher Implementation

In this section we describe our attack on a state-of-the-art obfuscator [18] illustrated in Figure 1. We were given the obfuscated source code for both DES encryption and decryption of the iterated block cipher. Our goal was to reverse engineer the system only based on knowledge of this obfuscated source code. For the given obfuscated code the attacker does not learn more properties about the

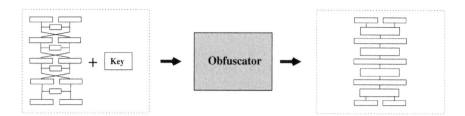

Fig. 1. Operation of the obfuscator on the round-based cipher: It transforms the key and the original source code into code that implements every round as a lookup table of precomputed values. The intermediate results after each round are encoded

program by investigating the obfuscated source code than by just disassembling the binary because most of the program is composed of lookup tables.

In this particular approach the obfuscation method hides the secret key of a round-based cipher in the code. Because a round-based cipher exposes the secret key every time it combines the key with the input data of a round, the obfuscator injects randomness and redundancies and refines the resulting boolean operations into lookup tables. Instead of executing algorithmic code, the program steps through a chain of precomputed values in lookup tables and retrieves the correct result. Therefore it is difficult to obtain any information about the single rounds by just looking at the source code or binary code, but in our attack we obtain information by observing and changing data during the encryption process.

2.1   Obfuscating an Iterated Block Cipher

The obfuscation process of the cipher implementation is shown in Figure 1. The obfuscator transforms the original source code and the key into a cipher in which the key is embedded and hidden in the rounds. The single rounds of the cipher are unrolled, but the boundaries of each round are clearly recognizable. The cipher contains n rounds π_i^k for each $i = 1, .., n$ with the key k. Including the initial permutation λ the cipher computes the function

$$E^k(M) := \left[\lambda^{-1} \cdot \pi_n^k \cdot \pi_{n-1}^k \cdot ... \cdot \pi_1^k \cdot \lambda\right](M).$$

However, interpretation of any intercepted intermediate results is difficult since the obfuscator maps the original intermediate results after each round to a new representation. This transformation is described in detail in [18].

In the following paragraphs we give an algebraic definition for the transformation into the 96-bit intermediate representation of the obfuscator in [18]. In the first step we define some basic operations. $x|_i^m$ extracts bits i through $i + m$ from a bit string. $EP(x)$ computes the DES expansion permutation.

$$x_1 x_2 ... x_n |_i^m = x_i x_{i+1} ... x_{i+m}$$
$$x_1 x_2 ... x_n |_i = x_i$$

$$EP_i(x) = EP(x)|_{6i}^6$$

$$R_r'^k = EP(R_r^k)$$
$$R_{r,i}'^k = EP_i(R_r^k)$$

The t-box $T_{r,i}^k(L_r, R_r'^k)$ computes the i-th DES s-box in round r for $i = 0..7$ and appends $R(L_r, R_r'^k)$ which takes the first and sixth bit from $R_{r,i}'^k$ and appends two random bits from L_r. The bits from L_r are used to forward the left hand side information in the t-boxes, and the first and sixth bit from $R_{r,i}'^k$ to reconstruct R_r^k from the s-box result in order to forward it to round $r + 1$ as the left hand side input.

$$T_{r,i}^k(L_r, R_r'^k) = S_{r,i}^k(R_{r,i}'^k) \| R(L_r, R_{r,i}'^k)$$

$$T_r^k(L_r, R_r'^k) = T_{r,\gamma_r(0)}^k(L_r, R_r'^k) \| T_{r,\gamma_r(1)}^k(L_r, R_r'^k) \| \cdots \| T_{r,\gamma_r(11)}^k(L_r, R_r'^k)$$

For $i = 8...11$ $T_{r,i}^k(L_r, R_r'^k)$ outputs either random dummy values or bits from L_r.

In order to obfuscate the result γ_r permutes the order of the t-boxes on $T_r = \{T_{r,0}^k....T_{r,11}^k\}$. Additionally, ϕ_r applies a bijective non-linear encoding on 4-bit blocks x_j for $j = 1...24$ where $\phi_r(x) = (\phi_{r,1}(x_1), \phi_{r,2}(x_2), ..., \phi_{r,24}(x_{24}))$ and $x = x_1 x_2...x_{24}$. Since a single t-box consists of 8 bit outputs, two different bijective non-linear encodings belong to one t-box.

In order to do the second step the obfuscated DES implementation needs to be able to recover the original right hand side input to round r, and this gets implemented using function $\alpha_{r,i}^k(y)$ which takes the forwarded bits x_1 and x_2 that describe the row of the s-box.

$$\alpha_{r,i}^k(y, x_1, x_2) = EP_i^{-1}((S_{r,i}^k)^{-1}(y, x_1, x_2))$$

$$L_r = L_r^0 \| L_r^1 \| L_r^2 \| \cdots \| L_r^7$$
$$R_r' = R_r'^0 \| R_r'^1 \| R_r'^2 \| \cdots \| R_r'^7$$

The second step then implements the function $\tau_{r,i}^k$ in which $\mu_r(n)$ describes the corresponding position of the bit in the output of the t-boxes, and PB is the DES p-box operation:

$$\tau_{r,i}^k(x)(L_r^i, R_r'^i) = \underbrace{\alpha_{r,i}^k(x|_{8\gamma_r(i)}^4, x|_{8\gamma_r(i)+4}, x|_{8\gamma_r(i)+5})}_{\text{depends on } R_{r-1} \text{ only}} \|$$
$$EP_i\Big[PB\, \underbrace{(x|_{\gamma_r(0)}^4 \| x|_{\gamma_r(1)}^4 \| \cdots \| x|_{\gamma_r(11)}^4)}_{\text{depends on } R_{r-1} \text{ only}} \oplus$$
$$\underbrace{(x|_{\mu_r(0)} \| \cdots \| x|_{\mu_r(32)})}_{\text{depends on } L_{r-1} \text{ only}} \Big]$$

$$\tau_r^k(x) = \tau_{r,0}^k(x) \| \tau_{r,1}^k(x) \| \cdots \| \tau_{r,11}^k(x)$$

ψ_r and ϕ_r are different non-linear bijective encodings on 4-bit blocks, and δ_r

$$\delta_r(L, R') = \gamma_r(\mu_r((L|0^{24}), R'))$$

$$\mu_r(x_0 x_1 \ldots x_{47}, y_0 \ldots y_{47}) = y_0 \ldots y_5 x_{\mu_r^{-1}(0)} x_{\mu_r^{-1}(1)} y_6 \ldots y_{11} x_{\mu_r^{-1}(2)} x_{\mu_r^{-1}(3)} \ldots y_{42} \ldots y_{47}$$
$$x_{\mu_r^{-1}(22)} x_{\mu_r^{-1}(23)} \ldots x_{\mu_r^{-1}(47)}$$
$$\gamma_r(z_0 z_1 \ldots z_{95}) = z_{\gamma_r^{-1}(0)} \ldots z_{(\gamma_r^{-1}(0)+5)} z_6 z_7 \ldots z_{\gamma_r^{-1}(11)} \ldots z_{(\gamma_r^{-1}(11)+5)} z_{94} z_{95}$$

The obfuscated t-box is

$$T_r'^k(x) = (\phi_r \, T_r^k \, \psi_{r-1}^{-1})(x).$$

Hence the transformed function is:

$$E^k(x) = \left[(\lambda^{-1} \delta_n^{-1} \psi_n^{-1}) \cdot \left((\psi_n \delta_n \tau_n^k \phi_n^{-1}) \cdot (\phi_n T_n^k \psi_{n-1}^{-1}) \right) \cdot \ldots \cdot \right.$$
$$\left. \left((\psi_1 \delta_1 \tau_1^k \phi_1^{-1}) \cdot (\phi_1 T_1^k \psi_0^{-1}) \cdot (\psi_0 \delta_0 \beta \lambda) \right) \right](x)$$

with

$$\beta(L, R) = L \, || \, EP(R)$$

By setting

$$\tau_r'^k = \begin{cases} \psi_0 \, \delta_0 \, \beta \, \lambda & r = 0 \\ \psi_r \, \delta_r \, \tau_r^k \, \phi_r^{-1} & r = 1, .., n \\ \lambda^{-1} \, \delta_n^{-1} \, \psi_n^{-1} & r = n+1 \end{cases}$$

the resulting encryption operation is

$$E^k(x) = \left[\tau_{n+1}'^k \cdot \left(\tau_n'^k \cdot T_n'^k \right) \cdot \ldots \cdot \left(\tau_1'^k \cdot T_1'^k \right) \cdot \tau_0'^k \right](x)$$

Every component $\tau_i'^k$ and $T_i'^k$ is implemented within a separate lookup table. For convenience set

$$\tau_r''^k = \begin{cases} \tau_r'^k & r = 0, \, r = n+1 \\ \tau_r'^k \cdot T_r'^k & r = 1, .., n \end{cases}$$

and obtain

$$E^k(x) = \left[\tau_{n+1}''^k \cdot \tau_n''^k \cdot \ldots \cdot \tau_0''^k \right](x)$$

Figure 2 shows the deobfuscation problem. Given one DES round and the obfuscated intermediate representations an attacker wants to find out the intermediate representation which is encoded by the unknown function σ_r. This σ_r is the inverse of the encoded input to the t-box (by ψ), the permutation of the t-boxes γ_r, and the random distribution of the left hand side μ_r:

$$\sigma_r(L_r, R_r) = \psi_r(\delta_r(L_r, EP(R_r)))$$

$E^k(x)$ contains the key k implicitly in $\tau_r''^k$ (in [18] $\tau_0'^k$ corresponds to M_1, $\tau_{n+1}'^k$ to M_3 and all other $\tau_r'^k$ to M_2). In other words, the implementation of $\tau_r''^k$ hides the decomposition into its components σ_{r-1}^{-1}, π_r^k, and σ_r. Hence, recovering the key boils down to the problem of extracting π_r^k out of τ_r''. In any further explanations we remove λ from any computation since it does not play any role in the attack and can be easily inverted. Therefore $\tau_0''^k = \psi_0$ and $\tau_{n+1}''^k = \psi_n$.

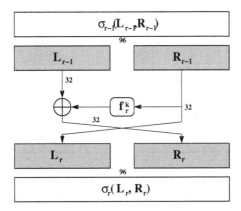

Fig. 2. Round r with the function f_r^k hiding the key k. σ_r is the intermediate representation and L_r and R_r are the left hand and the right hand side of the intermediate result respectively. The rounds π_r^k correspond to $\pi_r^k = f_r^k(R_{r-1} \oplus L_{r-1}, R_{r-1})$ for $r = 1..n$

2.2   Attacking an Obfuscated Iterated Block Cipher

In an example for a naive approach for attacking the obfuscated cipher an adversary encrypts some arbitrary plaintext and intercepts intermediate results to obtain $\sigma_r(L_r, R_r)$. The adversary starts the attack by encrypting plaintexts p that have one single bit set, and afterward examines the obfuscated intermediate results after the first round π_1^k during encryption. By heuristically computing the differences between $(\tau_1'' \tau_0'')(p)$ and $(\tau_1'' \tau_0'')(0)$ for $p \neq 0$ we find that $(\tau_1'' \tau_0'')(p)$ changes deterministically for all p that have one bit set in the left hand side of the plaintext L_0 due to the construction of the t-boxes. However, since the adversary is not able to compute σ_1^{-1} in order to retrieve R_1 any knowledge of R_0 and L_0 is meaningless if she wants to extract the key. An attack that works on the first round by recovering σ_1^{-1} of the cipher is the statistical bucketing attack [18]. This attack exploits some properties of the DES s-boxes and requires about 2^{13} encryptions. In contrast our attack works for any round-based block cipher and requires only dozens of encryptions.

We now describe how we use a simplified differential cryptanalysis called differential fault analysis [19] to recover the key in a few operations. In this attack an adversary flips bits in the input to the last round function f_n^k and computes the different outputs to find out the round function f_n^k of the last round n. When injecting single bit faults into the last round using chosen ciphertexts only dozens of cryptographic operations are necessary in order to find f_n^k. The implementation of this attack requires less information about the intermediate representation than the naive attack since an attacker only needs to flip a single bit in the obfuscated intermediate representation, and it is not necessary to figure out any inverse mappings σ_r^{-1}. Also, this attack is independent from the DES structure and can be applied to any round-based block cipher. We try to apply deterministic changes to $\sigma_{n-1}(L_{n-1}, R_{n-1})$, the state going into the last round, and then run the last round operation.

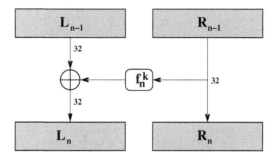

Fig. 3. Last round with the round function f_n^k. In the last round the right hand side and the left hand side of the output are usually not crossed over

Figure 3 shows the last round of the cipher. An attacker knows $R_n = R_{n-1}$ from the ciphertext which is also the input to the round function of the last round. In addition an attacker can modify R_{n-1} even if the mapping of σ_{n-1} is unknown by changing R_n in the ciphertext, decrypting the ciphertext, and encrypting the resulting plaintext afterward. Therefore we have two preconditions for the attack: First, both encryption and decryption operations need to be available, and second, the attacker needs to be able to modify the ciphertext arbitrarily. Using this technique we can find out the positions of $\mu_r(i)$ for $i = 0...32$ which describe the bits for the left-hand side. From the definition of $T_{r,i}^k$ it is clear, that if the attacker keeps the right-hand side input constant, the observed changes in the input to the t-boxes uniquely refer to changes in the left-hand side of the input. The attacker is not able to set L_{n-1} to 0 since she would need to know the round function and hence the key. Therefore, $R_n = 0$ and $L_{n-1} = f_n^k(0) \oplus L_n$.

Now the attacker builds a table of

$$\Delta(c) := \sigma_{n-1}(c, 0) \oplus \sigma_{n-1}(0, 0)$$

for $c = 1...2^{32}$.

Since σ_r contains the unknown non-linear bijection δ_{r-1} it is not possible to build a linear operator in Δ. However, using the table the attacker can always reconstruct the left-hand side of the input in the scenario where the right-hand side is 0. Furthermore, different bits of the left-hand side L_{n-1} can correspond to the same t-box, and in this case the encoding depends on two bits. Therefore, in the first part the attacker tests which bits correspond to the same t-box and then tries all possible bit combinations into this t-box. In this way the attacker gets all possible values for σ_r induced by the left-hand side L_{n-1}. Determining the original value $L_{n-1} \oplus f_n^k(0)$ given the intermediate representation is just a table lookup.

The idea now is to inject faults into the input to the s-box and observe the output. Unfortunately, the attacker does not know how the right-hand side gets encoded in σ_r. In order to get around this problem the attacker feeds a value x into R_{n-1} that is different from 0 and then resets L_{n-1} to 0. Finally, L_n contains $f_n^k(x) \oplus f_n^k(0)$, and the attacker can extract the key for the last round using differential cryptanalysis. Getting the DES key from the round key requires a 2^8 brute-force search.

The problem is that if the right hand side R_{n-1} changes to some value $\neq 0$ the t-box inputs collide with the 16 bits of the left-hand side L_{n-1}. Therefore it is not possible to decode the left-hand side L_{n-1} uniquely since complete new values might show up in the t-boxes that are taking as input bits from the left-hand side.

However, if the attacker sets only one bit in R_{n-1} at most two different t-box outputs are affected, and hence the attacker can simply count the occurrences of the encoded 4-bit values at a certain position in σ_r.

We describe the algorithm for the attack when the specification of the round function is known. We will explain at the end of the algorithm how the algorithm needs to be changed to attack an unknown round function. For convenience we use $D^k(c)$ to describe the decryption of ciphertext c using key k, and $E_i^k(p) = (L_i, R_i)$ to describe iteration of plaintext p for i rounds in the encryption operation using key k. $s^n(k) = s_n^1(k)|...|s_n^8(k)$ is the key schedule for key k in round n, m is the size of the input word, and the sboxes $sb_n(x) = sb_n^1(x_1)|...|sb_n^8(x_8)$:

$$f_n^k(x_1|...|x_8) := sb_n^1(x_1 \oplus s_n^1(k))|...|sb_n^8(x_8 \oplus s_n^8(k))$$

In our simplified model the in- and outputs of the s-box have the same size, and the system computes the xor of the key and the input to the s-box. The algorithm consists of 3 basic operations: A *Set* operation changes any arbitrary variable. When we do a *Compute* we execute an operation in the iterated block cipher. This can be encryption, decryption, or just a single round of the cipher. *Derive* computes values on known variables without executing the cipher. Figure 4 illustrates the single steps of the algorithm.

Our attack algorithm works as follows:

1. **Initialization:** (Figure 4 top left)
   Set $L_n := 0$, $R_n := 0$
   Compute $\sigma_{n-1}(L_{n-1}, R_{n-1}) = E_{n-1}^k(D^k(L_n, R_n))$
   Result: $L_{n-1} = f_n^k(0)$, $R_{n-1} = 0$
   Derive $\Omega = \sigma_{n-1}(L_{n-1}, R_{n-1}) = \sigma_{n-1}(f_n^k(0), 0)$

2. **Reconstruct $\Delta(x)$:** (Figure 4 top right)
   For $j = 0$ to 23:
       Set $m(j) := 0$
   For $i = 0$ to 31:
       Set $L_n := 2^i$, $R_n := 0$
       Compute $\sigma_{n-1}(L_{n-1}, R_{n-1}) = E_{n-1}^k(D^k(L_n, R_n))$
       Set $\Delta(L_n) := \sigma_{n-1}(L_{n-1}, R_{n-1}) \oplus \Omega$
       For $j = 0$ to 23:
           If $\left(\Delta(L_n)|_{4j}^4 \neq 0\right)$
               Set $b[j][m(j)] := i$
               Set $m(j) := m(j) + 1$

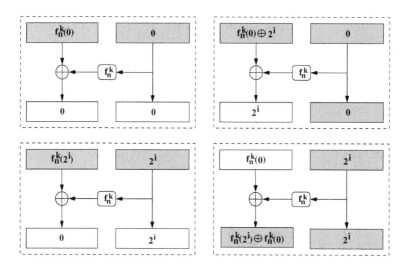

Fig. 4. Attacking the last round of the iterated block cipher. Boxes having a white background indicate that the attacker changed values. The picture on the top left shows the initialization of the algorithm (step 1). Afterward, on the top right we change L_n to 2^i in order to reconstruct $\psi_{n-1}(x)$ (step 2). In the bottom left we set 2^i to be input to the round function. The fault injection takes place on the bottom right (step 3): We reset L_{n-1} to $f_n^k(0)$ and obtain the difference $f_n^k(2^i) \oplus f_n^k(0)$ in L_n

```
For j = 0 to 23:
    For l = 0 to 2^{m(j)} − 1:
        Set e := 0
        For k = 0 to m(j):
            If (((l >> k) & 1) = 1)
                Set e := e + 2^{b[j][k]}
        Set L_n := e, R_n := 0
        Compute σ_{n-1}(L_{n-1}, R_{n-1}) = E^k_{n-1}(D^k(L_n, R_n))
        Set Δ(L_n) := σ_{n-1}(L_{n-1}, R_{n-1}) ⊕ Ω

3. Reset L_{n-1} to f_n^k(0): (Figure 4 bottom left)
    For i = 0 to 31:
        Set L_n := 0, R_n := 2^i
        Compute σ_{n-1}(L_{n-1}, R_{n-1}) = E^k_{n-1}(D^k(L_n, R_n)),
        Result: L_{n-1} = f_n^k(2^i), R_{n-1} = 2^i
        Derive w := σ_{n-1}(L_{n-1}, R_{n-1}) ⊕ Ω = σ_{n-1}(f_n^k(2^i), 2^i) ⊕ σ_{n-1}(0, 0)
        For x in Δ^{-1}
            For j = 0 to 23
                If (Δ(x)|^4_{4j} = w|^4_{4j})
                w|^4_{4j} := 0
        Compute (L'_n, R'_n) = (τ''_n τ''_{n+1})(w) = (σ^{-1}_{n-1} π^k_n)(w)
        Result: L'_n ≈ f_n^k(2^i) ⊕ f_n^k(0), R'_n ≈ 2^i
```

4. **Do differential cryptanalysis to extract the key for the round function f_n^k:**

   $l^s = L_n'|_{4(s-1)}^4$, $r^s = EP(R_n')|_{6(s-1)}^6$

   For $s = 1$ to 8:

   $\quad d^s = 0$

   For $s = 1$ to 8:

   $\quad$ For $i = 0$ to 31:

   $\quad\quad$ Compute $c^s[i]$: $sb_n^s(r^s[i] \oplus c^s[i]) = l^s[i]$

   $\quad\quad$ Compute $d^s[i] = d^s[i] + 1$

   $\quad$ Set $\tilde{c}^s := c^s[\max_{i=1}^m d^s[i]]$

5. **Reconstruct the original key:**

   $k := \tilde{c}^1|\tilde{c}^2|...|\tilde{c}^8$

   Compute $s_n(k)^{-1}$ to retrieve original key

   brute-force search on the remaining bits of the key.

Step 2 of the algorithm reconstructs $\Delta(x)$, in step 3 we inject the fault by resetting L_{n-1} to $f_n^k(0)$ and computing $L_n = f_n^k(R_n) \oplus f_n^k(0)$. In steps 4 and 5 we compute the key given a round function f_n^k by concatenating the components going into the s-boxes, inverting the key schedule, and running a brute-force search on the remaining key bits.

If the key schedule $s_n(k)$ for round n is unknown, we cannot do step 5 to get the key out. In this case we have to compute the key for round n and then use this key to attack round $n - 1$ until we extract all round keys. If the round function f_i^k is unknown, we can first try out different known round functions (e.g. Skipjack, Blowfish, DES etc) for f_i^k. If none of them works, we have to do cryptanalysis to recover the s-boxes from scratch. We make the basic assumption that the round function is based on an s-box with fixed inputs.

This attack is fully automated and can be run without any knowledge of the system. Given the plaintext length as $2n$ and the length of the intermediate representation as $4m$ the attack in steps 1-5 extracts the key in $O(\max(m,n))$ cryptographic operations, and therefore undermines the security of the obfuscation system.

2.3   Summarizing the Attack

We exploit two weaknesses in this attack: First, the boundaries of the rounds are identifiable and protection of intermediate results against tampering is not strong enough. This means that a) hiding the rounds can strengthen the implementation and b) data needs to be safe against leaking of information during execution.

In this attack we show that faults in ciphers are a cheap and efficient technique to extract a secret key from an obfuscated cipher implementation in software. Our attack on obfuscated cipher implementations in software requires only a few cryptographic operations, and therefore an adversary can run the attack on any inexpensive hardware.

We had to modify the original algorithm for differential fault analysis [19] in several steps. The main difference is that it is not possible to inject random faults since the intermediate representation is obfuscated and has multiple points of failure. However, it is still possible to find out a sufficient amount of information about the obfuscated intermediate representation that make it possible for an attacker to inject faults.

In the underlying attack model it is the goal to decrypt some media stream on different machines at the same time. To do this we assume that copy protection of the decryption system is sufficiently strong, and therefore an attacker has to extract the secret key. In the current implementation our attack requires that a decryption system colludes with an encryption system, but actually an attacker only needs to obtain plaintexts for $2m$ chosen plaintexts and the decryption system. Or, since the system is a symmetric block cipher, we run the attack on the encryption system and need $2m$ chosen ciphertexts from the decryption operation. Furthermore, it is an open question how difficult it is to turn an obfuscated decryption system into an encryption system. In this case having the decryption system is sufficient for the attack.

In the recommended variant the system executes the encryption operation $E'(x) = (f^{-1}Eg)(x)$ and the decryption operation $D'(x) = (g^{-1}Df)(x)$ where f and g are non-linear bijective encodings. The current attack is now impossible, but the disadvantage is that given a ciphertext it is only possible to decrypt when f, g, and the key k are known, or the obfuscated decryption program is being used. It is not implementing DES anymore.

It is crucial to fix the weaknesses in the system or implement other techniques to prevent any common attacks that recover the secret key. In the following sections we explore what we can do about the weaknesses and investigate how to strengthen obfuscation techniques against common attacks.

3   Theoretical Considerations

The weaknesses in this attack are specific to the implementation of the obfuscated cipher. We were able to use specific properties of the DES cipher and the obfuscation method in order to extract the secret key. However, theoretical considerations do not necessarily limit any stronger obfuscation techniques. Here we give a simple argument why the general problem of retrieving embedded data from a circuit is NP-hard, and therefore no efficient general deobfuscator exists for this problem.

In MATCH-FIXED-INPUT we are given two circuits, one of which has additional input k. It is the goal to find a k such that the two circuits are equivalent.

Definition: MATCH-FIXED-INPUT: Given circuits two $C(x, k)$ and $C'(x)$ where $x \in \{0, 1\}^n$ and $k \in \{0, 1\}^c$ where $c \in N$ is constant, find $k' \in \{0, 1\}^c$ such that $\forall x : C(x, k') = C(x)$.

Theorem: MATCH-FIXED-INPUT is NP-hard.

Proof: We reduce SAT to MATCH-FIXED-INPUT which is almost trivial. In order to test satisfiability of circuit $D(x)$, set $C(x, k) = D(k)$ and $C'(x) = true$, and run MATCH-FIXED-INPUT. If MATCH-FIXED-INPUT returns a k' such that $C(x, k') = C'(x)$, then according to the definition there exists an x such that $D(x) = true$. If MATCH-FIXED-INPUT does not return a k', then for all x $D(x) = false$. Hence, we reduce SAT to MATCH-FIXED-INPUT. $\square$

For practical purposes, however, this theoretical observation is not much of a relevance since the problem is hard in the worst case but can still be easy for practical purposes. On the average the problem MATCH-FIXED-INPUT is NP-hard, but in several cases heuristic methods can extract the fixed input as in the example of this obfuscated DES cipher.

4   Strengthening Obfuscation

In this section we briefly discuss various mechanisms for defending against our attack using software faults. We first describe some common attacker goals when attacking obfuscated code:

- **Hide data in the program:** The attacker wants to find out certain data values. This case subdivides into the possibility of tracing values during runtime and discovering static values in the code.
- **Protect the program from controlled manipulation:** In this case the attacker wants to force the program to behave in a certain way, e.g. to remove copy protection mechanisms or to cause damage on a system.
- **Hide algorithms of the program:** According to Kerckhoff's principle cryptographic algorithms are usually public, but in some cases it is useful to hide certain properties by which an attacker can recognize the algorithm, i.e. distinguish for example between AES, IDEA or Blowfish [21,22,23].

Often when obfuscating a cipher, commercial tools first encode the plaintext using some hidden encoding function, then run the cipher, and finally decode the ciphertext using some other hidden decoding function. More precisely, the encryption process looks like $E'_k(x) = (F \cdot E_k \cdot G^{-1})(x)$ where E_k is the original DES encryption [18]. Note that F and G must be one-to-one functions so that decryption is possible. The decryption process is similar: $D'_k(x) = (G \cdot D_k \cdot F^{-1})(x)$. This pre- and post-encoding makes chosen ciphertext attacks more difficult since an adversary first needs to recover G. As a result, these encoding makes our fault attack harder to mount. One can still potentially attack the system by using a fault attack against inners levels of the Feistel cipher.

4.1   Defending against a Fault-Based Attack

We mention a few mechanisms for protecting obfuscated systems from a fault attack. One approach is to protect all intermediate results using checksums. These checksums are frequently checked by the obfuscated code. We refer to this approach as *local checking*. Clearly the code for checking these checksums must be hidden in the total program code so that an attacker cannot disable these checkers. One approach for using checksums to ensure code integrity is explained in [24]. In this approach we compute checksums for parts of the program and verify them during program execution. In the extreme we verify a checksum for every single instruction and every data element.

Another approach for checking the computation of obfuscated code is to use *global checking*. The idea is to execute the obfuscated program k times (e.g. $k = 3$) by interleaving the k executions. At the end of the computation the code verifies that all k executions resulted in the same value. As before, the checker must be obfuscated in the code so that it cannot be targeted by the attacker. This global checking approach makes our attack harder since the attacker now has to modify internal data consistently in all k executions of the code.

The problem with the checking approaches is the vulnerability of the checker since it is unprotected against any tampering attack. One approach to make the checker more robust is to obfuscate it and have it verify its own integrity repeatedly while it is checking the program. This variant reduces the maximum time interval an attacker has to run the modified program. In any case the attacker needs to modify to system at more than one place. We note that if the integrity check fails the program should not stop execution immediately since this will tell an attacker where the checker is.

Another approach for making the fault attack more difficult is to diversify the obfuscation mechanism. In other words, each user gets a version of the code that is obfuscated differently (e.g. by using different encoding functions). In diversification we add randomness to the obfuscation methods, and therefore two obfuscated programs are always different after obfuscation. Especially vulnerable places in a program such as the intermediate results of the iterated round-based cipher need to be diversified.

5   Related Work

Informally tamper-resistance of a software implementation measures to what extent the implementation resists arbitrary or deliberate modifications. For example, an implementation can be protected from removing a copy protection mechanism. Thus, obfuscation is a common technique for improving tamper-resistance. Barak et al. [25] give a formal definition of obfuscation using a black-box approach which is the ideal case. They show that in their model, that obfuscation is not possible.

Encrypting the executable binary [26] is the most common approach for hiding code. In binary encryption the program is encrypted and decrypts itself during runtime. The problem is that the program is available in the clear at some point before it gets executed on the processor, and it can be intercepted. Furthermore, the system needs to hide the decryption key, and that reduces recursively to the key obfuscation problem itself.

A common approach for obfuscation is to obstruct common static program analysis [27,28,29]. The main technique for doing this is to insert of additional code that creates pointer aliasing situations. Applying static program analysis to analyze a program containing possible pointer aliasing turns out to be NP-hard [30]. This obfuscation technique only protects against attacks by static program analysis. It is still possible to do dynamic attacks with a debugger or any type of tampering.

The goal of obfuscation is to hide as many program properties as possible. The principle of improving tamper-resistance by obfuscation is that if an attacker cannot find the location for manipulating a value, it is impossible to change this value. In addition an obfuscator can eliminate single points of failure. On the other hand obfuscation never protects against existential modification.

Collberg et al define some metrics for obfuscation in [28]. They classify obfuscation schemes by the confusion of a human reader ("potency"), the successfulness of automatic deobfuscation ("resilience"), the time/space overhead ("cost"), and the blending of obfuscated code with original code ("stealth"). But obfuscation of a secret key requires stronger properties of obfuscation, since any definition of tamper-resistance is missing. A program that is a good obfuscator in these metrics can still have a single point of failure, and therefore it does not protect the program against fault attacks.

Tamper-resistance can also be improved by techniques other than obfuscation. We already mentioned self-checking of code as one possibility [24,31,16]. Protection by software guards is another technique to prevent tampering [32]. Software guards are security modules that implement different tasks of a program and thus eliminate single points of failure. In addition a program can implement anti-debugging techniques in order to prevent tampering with a debugger [33]. Anti-debugging inserts instructions into a program or changes properties in order to confuse a debugger. For example a program can arbitrarily set break points or misalign code. Furthermore, virtual software processors are are a technique for making tampering difficult [13]. Virtual software processors run the original program on a software processor, and in order to reverse engineer the original program, an attacker needs to compromise any protection mechanism of the virtual software processor as well.

Goldreich and Ostrovsky show in [34] that software protection against eavesdropping can be reduced to *oblivious simulation of RAMs*. In their definition a RAM is oblivious if two different inputs with the same running time create equivalent sequences of memory accesses. Oblivious RAM protects against any passive attack and therefore strengthens an obfuscator because it is impossible to find out the memory locations a program accesses. However, it does not protect against the fault injection attack.

Current hardware dongles are based on the idea of oblivious RAM, since the code implementing the license check sits on the dongle.

6   Open Problems

In other areas of information hiding techniques, such as watermarking, benchmark programs are available to measure the strength of a technique to hide information. For example, StirMarks [35] uses a variety of different generic attacks on a watermarked image to make the watermark illegible. It is an open problem to build such a benchmark for code obfuscation and tamper resistance tools. Such a benchmark would take as input some tamper resistant code and attempt to break the tamper resistance. Currently no such benchmark exists and there is no clear model for building such a benchmark.

One of the main open problems in code obfuscation is to come up with a model for obfuscation that can be realized in practice. [25] defines obfuscation using a black-box model that hides all properties of a program. They show that it is not possible to achieve obfuscation in that model. For practical purposes a black box model might not always be necessary. In the example of the obfuscated DES cipher in this paper we only need to make sure that it is impossible to get information about the secret key. The open research problem is to find the most general definition for obfuscation that can be realized in practice.

7   Conclusion

Code obfuscation provides some protection against attackers who want to find out secret data or properties of a program, but it is not sufficient as a stand-alone system. In this study we evaluate the usability of obfuscation when hiding a secret key in an iterated round-based software cipher. We find weaknesses in a commercial state-of-the-art obfuscator. Our attack enables automated extraction of the secret key from the obfuscated program code. We discuss a few methods for defending against these attacks.

References

1. Craver, S.A., Wu, M., Liu, B., Stubblefield, A., Swartzlander, B., Wallach, D.S., Dean, D., Felten, E.W.: Reading between the lines: Lessons from the SDMI challenge. In: Proceedings of the 10th USENIX Security Symposium. (2001)
2. CSS: http://www.dvdcca.org/css (2002)
3. Intertrust: http://www.intertrust.com (2002)
4. Microsoft Windows Media Technologies:
   http://www.microsoft.com/windows/windowsmedia (2002)
5. Adobe EBooks: http://www.adobe.com/epaper/ebooks (2002)
6. Abraham, D.G., Dolan, G.M., Double, G.P., Stevens, J.V.: Transaction Security System. IBM Systems Journal 30 (1991) 206–229
7. Dallas Semiconductor: Soft Microcontroller Data Book. (1993)
8. Trusted Computing Platform Alliance: http://www.trustedpc.org (2002)
9. Anderson, R., Kuhn, M.: Low cost attacks on tamper resistant devices. In: Proceedings of the 5th International Security Protocols Conference. (1997) 125–136
10. Kocher, P., Jaffe, J., Jun, B.: Differential power analysis. Lecture Notes in Computer Science 1666 (1999) 388–397
11. Shamir, A., van Someren, N.: Playing "hide and seek" with stored keys. Lecture Notes in Computer Science 1648 (1999) 118–124
12. Diffie, W., Hellman, M.: New directions in cryptography. IEEE Transactions on Information Theory IT-22 (1976) 644–654

13. Microsoft Corporation: World Intellectual Property Organization, WO 02/01327 A2 (2002)
14. Cloakware Corporation: World Intellectual Property Organization, WO 00/77596 A1 (2000)
15. Intertrust Corporation: US Patent Office, US 6,157,721 (2000)
16. Intel Corporation: US Patent Office, US 6,205,550 (2000)
17. RetroGuard Java Obfuscator: http://www.retrologic.com (2002)
18. Chow, S., Johnson, H., van Oorschot, P.C., Eisen, P.: A White-Box DES Implementation for DRM Applications. In: Proceedings of Workshop on Digital Rights Management 2002. (2002)
19. Biham, E., Shamir, A.: Differential fault analysis of secret key cryptosystems. Lecture Notes in Computer Science **1294** (1997) 513–525
20. Boneh, D., DeMillo, R.A., J.Lipton, R.: On the importance of checking cryptographic protocols for faults. Lecture Notes in Computer Science **1233** (1997) 37–51
21. Schneier, B.: Applied Cryptography. Wiley (1994)
22. Menezes, A.J., Van Oorschot, P.C., Vanstone, S.A.: Handbook of applied cryptography. CRC Press (1997)
23. Daemen, J., Rijmen, V.: Rijndael for AES. In NIST, ed.: The Third Advanced Encryption Standard Candidate Conference, National Institute for Standards and Technology (2000) 343–347
24. Aucsmith, D.: Tamper-resistant software: An implementation. Lecture Notes in Computer Science **1174** (1996) 317–333
25. Barak, B., Goldreich, O., Impagliazzo, R., Rudich, S., Sahai, A., Vadhan, S., Yang, K.: On the (im)possibility of obfuscating programs. Lecture Notes in Computer Science **2139** (2001) 1–18
26. grugq, scut: Armouring the ELF: Binary encryption on the UNIX platform. Phrack Inc. **58** (2001)
27. Wang, C., Davidson, J., Hill, J., Knight, J.: Protection of software-based survivability mechanisms. Proceedings of the 2001 Dependable Systems and Networks (DSN'01) (2001)
28. Collberg, C., Thomborson, C., Low, D.: Manufacturing cheap, resilient, and stealthy opaque constructs. In: The 25th Symposium on Principles of Programming Languages (POPL '98), Association for Computing Machinery (1998) 184–196
29. Steensgaard, B.: Points-to analysis in almost linear time. In: The 23th Symposium on Principles of Programming Languages (POPL '96), Association for Computing Machinery (1996) 32–41
30. Landi, W.: Undecidability of static analysis. ACM Letters on Programming Languages and Systems **1** (1992) 323–337
31. Horne, B., Matheson, L., Sheehan, C., Tarjan, R.E.: Dynamic self-checking techniques for improved tamper-resistance. Lecture Notes in Computer Science **2320** (2001) 141–159
32. Chang, H., Atallah, M.J.: Protecting software code by guards. Lecture Notes in Computer Science **2320** (2001) 160–175
33. Cesare, S.: Linux anti-debugging techniques (fooling the debugger). Security Focus (2000)
34. Goldreich, O., Ostrovsky, R.: Software protection and simulation on oblivious RAMs. Journal of the Association for Computing Machinery **43** (1996) 431–473
35. Petitcolas, F.A.P., Anderson, R.J., Kuhn, M.G.: Attacks on copyright marking systems. Lecture Notes in Computer Science **1525** (1998) 219–239

Breaking and Repairing Asymmetric Public-Key Traitor Tracing

Aggelos Kiayias[1] and Moti Yung[2]

[1] Department of Computer Science and Engineering
University of Connecticut, Storrs, CT, USA
`aggelos@cse.uconn.edu`
[2] Department of Computer Science
Columbia University, New York, NY, USA
`moti@cs.columbia.edu`

Abstract. Traitor tracing schemes are a very useful tool for preventing piracy in digital content distribution systems. A traitor tracing procedure allows the system-manager to reveal the identities of the subscribers that were implicated in the construction of a pirate-device that illegally receives the digital content (called traitors). In an important variant called "asymmetric" traitor tracing, the system-manager is not necessarily trusted, thus the tracing procedure must produce *undeniable* proof of the implication of the traitor subscribers. This *non-repudiation* property of asymmetric schemes has the potential to significantly increase the effectiveness of the tracing procedure against piracy.

In this work, we break the two previous proposals for efficient asymmetric public-key traitor tracing, by showing how traitors can evade the proposed traitor tracing procedures. Then, we present a new efficient Asymmetric Public-Key Traitor Tracing scheme for which we prove its traceability in detail (in the non-black-box model); to the best of our knowledge this is the first such scheme. Our system is capable of proving the implication of *all* traitors that participate in the construction of a pirate-key. We note that even though we break the earlier schemes we employ some of their fundamental techniques and thus consider them important developments towards the solution.

1 Introduction

The secure distribution of a digital content stream to an *exclusive* set of subscribers is an important problem that has many applications in the entertainment industry. The typical setting is that of Pay-TV: the content distributor transmits scrambled streams of video of the channel line-up that are received by the subscribers using a decoder device (e.g. a cable-box). The digital content should be encrypted in such a way so that eavesdroppers are incapable of intercepting the stream. On the other hand, each legitimate subscriber possesses a decryption mechanism (essentially: a cryptographic decryption key) that enables him/her to receive the content.

J. Feigenbaum (Ed.): DRM 2002, LNCS 2696, pp. 32–50, 2003.

One major problem faced by administrators of such systems is "piracy": the illegal reception of the scrambled content that is made possible by taking advantage of "insider information." Current encryption mechanisms are strong enough to ensure that an eavesdropper is incapable of inverting the scrambling method used in the broadcast to the legitimate subscribers. However, illegal reception of the digital content can still occur if some of the legitimate users of the system leak (some of) their key information to a third party. Such users are called *traitors* and a third party that uses subscriber-key information for illegal data reception is called a *pirate*.

The traditional approach to tackle the problem of piracy is to hide the decryption-key information from the legitimate subscribers of the system. This can be a quite tricky problem, since every legitimate user should possess enough key-information to enable the reception of the scrambled digital content. Hiding the key from the user can be achieved by employing tamper resistant hardware (so that the key-information is concealed, but still can be used in a black-box fashion), or, in the software-based setting, program obfuscation can be employed instead. Hardware tamper resistance can provide satisfactory solutions in terms of security. However the cost of constructing and distributing tamper resistant decoders to each subscriber of the system is prohibitive for many digital content providers. Especially in an Internet-based setting it would be extremely desirable that no system-specific physical device should be required and that the decoder software should be downloadable from the distributor's web-site. This suggests that a software obfuscation technique would be more appropriate, however there are no cryptographically strong methods to achieve general software obfuscation and, further, there are indications that it might be actually impossible (see [28,2]), so one has to rely in ad-hoc methods. As a result, no key-concealment method is a complete panacea: there will always be at least one savvy malicious subscriber that will compromise the resistance (hardware tamper-resistance or software obfuscation) of the decoder. Even worse, once the the decoder is broken once, the information on how to repeat this can be distributed to thousands of users using the Internet, thus dramatically scaling up the damages to the content-distributors[1].

Traitor Tracing Schemes: An alternative approach to piracy prevention in digital content distribution systems was proposed by Chor, Fiat and Naor under the framework of Traitor Tracing Schemes (TTS) [8] (see also [9]). In a TTS, each subscriber has a decryption key that is associated with his identity (it can be thought of as a fingerprinted decryption key). Malicious subscribers (traitors) might again try to leak their personal key information to a pirate. However, in

---

[1]   Industry assessment of the risk involved in such exposures was demonstrated recently by the \$ 1 billion lawsuit filed (and currently kept on hold) by Canal Plus (owned by Media giant Vivendi Universal) against the NDS Group (controlled by News Corp. of Rupert Murdoch), alleging that top engineers hired by NDS broke into the security system of Canal Plus Pay-TV service and exposed sensitive user-key information to thousands of potential malicious users by publishing this information on the web [1].

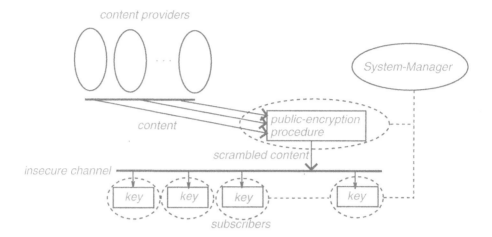

Fig. 1. The Setup of a Public-key Traitor Tracing Scheme

a traitor-tracing scheme the distributor (or the authorities) possess a "traitor tracing" procedure that, given the pirate decoder, is capable of recovering the identities of at least one of the traitors. Even though the existence of such a mechanism cannot eliminate piracy, it can effectively deter users from leaking their personalized keys to a pirate. The probabilistic constructions of [8] were followed by explicit combinatorial designs [30], and later by [13,22], who also considered the combination of traitor tracing schemes with efficient revocation methods (cf. broadcast encryption, [12]).

Public Key Traitor Tracing: Traitor Tracing Schemes have been introduced in the symmetric encryption setting, under the basic assumption that the content distributors essentially coincide with the administrators of the secure broadcasting infrastructure. However it is highly desirable to divide these roles. In public-key traitor tracing, there is one authority that is responsible for the broadcasting infrastructure (which we call the system-manager) and several, non-trusted, content-distributors that may take advantage of the public-key encryption procedure (published by the system-manager) to distribute content to the subscribers of the system. This setting is illustrated in figure 1. Public-key TTSs were presented in [20,4,16].

Asymmetric Traitor Tracing: A shortcoming of the traitor tracing procedure, as it is achieved in all the schemes mentioned above, is the fact that the system-manager does not obtain undeniable *proof* for the implication of a certain set of subscribers in the construction of a pirate device. In these schemes, the system-manager knows all the key information distributed to the users and as a result, if it is malicious, it can implicate an innocent user in the construction of a pirate device. As a result, these schemes do not support *non-repudiation*: subscribers can always deny their implication in the construction of a pirate-device and claim that it was the malicious system-manager that implicated them instead (e.g. some malicious employee of the system-manager) . Of course this does not prohibit the system-manager from taking uni-lateral measures against such users (e.g. disconnect them from the service); however if non-repudiation was possible, this would drastically increase the effectiveness of the traitor tracing scenario against piracy: in a traitor-tracing scheme with non-repudiation, where the tracing procedure produces solid proof for the implication of the traitors, the system-manager might press criminal charges against subscribers that leak their key-information, thus significantly lowering the commercial viability of piracy. Note that in such a scheme tracing becomes a much more challenging task: on the one hand the system-manager should know enough information about the subscriber keys to execute the tracing algorithm; on the other hand the system-manager should be oblivious to a significant portion of a subscriber's personalized-key (otherwise the system-manager would be capable of implicating innocent users in the construction of a pirate-device). This asymmetry of knowledge assuring non-repudiation, gave these schemes the name "asymmetric traitor tracing."

The existence of asymmetric traitor tracing schemes was shown by Pfitzmann [25], who also introduced the setting of *asymmetric traitor tracing*. Nevertheless, this first scheme, was merely a plausibility result that employed generic secure function evaluation techniques (that are completely impractical). Later, the problem was also studied in the context of fingerprinting [26,27]. A "somewhat asymmetric" public-key traitor tracing scheme was presented in [20], using a threshold mechanism to ensure the non-repudiation property (i.e. the capability to implicate innocent users was divided to a number of authorities, who had to collude in order to break the asymmetry of the scheme). This is not a real solution to asymmetry (since it was not as originally defined in the harder model of a *single* authority which performs the management functions). Further, the underlying traitor tracing mechanism of the scheme of [20] was later [29,4] shown to fail against collusions of traitors which include more than a single user. Thus, the problem of efficient (single-authority) public-key traitor tracing remained open, until the recent introduction of two proposals by Watanabe et al. [31] and Komaki et al. [19].

Our Results: In the present work we show the following:

- First, we break the two previous proposals of [31] and [19] for efficient asymmetric public-key traitor tracing: we show that for both schemes it is possible for the traitors to evade tracing.
- Second, we present an efficient Asymmetric Public-Key Traitor Tracing scheme of which we prove its traceability in detail (in the "non-black box" traitor tracing model). Our scheme is capable of proving the implication of *all* traitors that participate in the construction of a pirate-key. As a result our proposal is the first efficient Asymmetric Public-Key Traitor Tracing Scheme. In fact our scheme is comparable in efficiency to previous non-asymmetric traitor tracing schemes as illustrated in figure 2.

Remark: We would like to note that even though we actually break the schemes of [31] and [19] (demonstrating the high level of care which is needed to design

	Ciphertext Size	User-Key Size	Encryption-Key Size	System Type	Asymmetry
[8] scheme 1	$\mathcal{O}(v^4 \log n)$	$\mathcal{O}(v^2 \log n)$	$\mathcal{O}(v^2 \log n)$	generic	NO
[4]	$2v + 1$	$\mathcal{O}(1)$	$2v + 1$	public-key	NO
Our Scheme	$2v + 2$	$\mathcal{O}(1)$	$2v + 2$	public-key	YES

Fig. 2. Comparison of our public-key traitor-tracing scheme with previous work. Note that n is the number of users and v is a parameter of the system, that denotes the maximum size of a traitor collusion that the system can withstand

such subtle systems), their contributions are nevertheless significant, since we have learned a lot from their underlying mechanisms. In particular they introduced the idea of using Oblivious Polynomial Evaluation [23], as the basic building block to achieve asymmetry in public-key traitor tracing schemes; something that we also take advantage in our scheme. Thus, the earlier works represent important steps towards the development of the efficient asymmetric scheme.

2   Preliminaries

We work in a multiplicative cyclic group $\mathcal{G}$ of large prime order over which solving the Decisional Diffie Hellman (DDH) Problem is hard:

Definition 1. DDH. *Let $g \in \mathcal{G}$ be a generator. Consider triples of the form* R, $\langle g^a, g^b, g^c \rangle$ *with $a, b, c < \text{order}(g)$ and triples of the form* D, $\langle g^a, g^b, g^{ab} \rangle$ *with $a, b < \text{order}(g)$. A predicate solves the DDH problem if it can distinguish the collection* D *from the collection* R.

The DDH-Assumption *for $\mathcal{G}$ suggests that any predicate that solves the DDH problem has distinguishing probability negligible in $\log(\text{order}(g))$.*

For example $\mathcal{G}$ can be the subgroup of order q of $\mathbf{Z}_p^*$, where $q \mid p - 1$ and p, q are large primes. In the following g will denote a generator of $\mathcal{G}$. Note that arithmetic in the exponents is performed in the finite field $\mathbf{Z}_q$.

Let $h_0, h_1, \ldots, h_v$ be random elements of $\mathcal{G}$ so that $h_j := g^{r_j}$ for $j = 0, \ldots, v$. For a certain element $y := g^b$ of $\mathcal{G}$ a representation of y with respect to the base $h_0, \ldots, h_v$ is a $(v + 1)$-vector $\boldsymbol{\delta} := \langle \delta_0, \ldots, \delta_v \rangle$ such that $y = h_0^{\delta_0} \ldots h_v^{\delta_v}$, or equivalently $\boldsymbol{\delta} \cdot \boldsymbol{r} = b$ where $\cdot$ denotes the inner product between two vectors. It is well known (see e.g. [6]) that obtaining representations of a given y w.r.t. some given base $h_0, \ldots, h_v$ is as hard as the discrete-log problem over $\mathcal{G}$.

2.1   Oblivious Polynomial Evaluation

A tool that is instrumental in obtaining the non-repudiation property of our scheme is Oblivious Polynomial Evaluation (OPE). An OPE protocol involves two parties, the sender S, who possesses a secret polynomial $P \in \mathbf{Z}_q[x]$, and the receiver R who possesses a secret value $\alpha \in \mathbf{Z}_q$. An OPE protocol allows the receiver to compute the evaluation of the sender's polynomial P over its secret value α (i.e. compute $P(\alpha)$) in such a way so that:

- The sender S cannot extract any non-trivial information about the value α.
- The receiver R cannot extract any information about the polynomial P, other than what can be trivially extracted from the value $P(\alpha)$.

Oblivious Polynomial Evaluation was introduced by Naor and Pinkas in [23], where an efficient construction with two communication flows was presented. The security of the scheme was based on Oblivious Transfer and an intractability assumption related to the Polynomial Reconstruction Problem (see e.g. [14,18]). Later, in [7], it was shown that efficient OPE protocols can be based on the generic assumption of Oblivious Transfer.

Here, we will assume a two communication flow protocol (such as those of [23,7]) where $\{OPE\}(\alpha)$ denotes the data transmitted by the receiver R to the sender S in the first flow, and $\{OPE\}(P(\alpha))$ denotes the data transmitted by the sender to the receiver in the second communication flow. According to the properties of Oblivious Polynomial Evaluation as described above, $\{OPE\}(\alpha)$ does not yield any non-trivial information about the value α, and $\{OPE\}(P(\alpha))$ contains enough information for the receiver to compute $P(\alpha)$ but not any further non-trivial information about the secret polynomial P.

The variant of Oblivious Polynomial Evaluation that we will use has two additional properties. (1) it is malleable: i.e. given $\{OPE\}(\alpha)$ the sender can easily compute $\{OPE\}(\alpha + \alpha')$, for a given (e.g., random) α' and $+$ an operation in the underlying finite field; and (2) it is performed over a publicly committed value, namely α can be thought of as a private key whose public key is publicly known. Indeed, protocols such as [23] can be shown to satisfy these properties due to their structure and using generic techniques. In addition, an OPE protocol can be designed directly to achieve these properties very efficiently [17]. This scheme is robust and exploits zero-knowledge proofs to assure that the receiver is acting on the committed value. In particular we show how it is possible for the receiver to convince the sender that the submitted string $\{OPE\}(\alpha)$ is (i) properly formed, and (ii) it agrees with the public commitment value. Further, the scheme is simulatable in the sense that one can produce protocol transcripts on any given public commitment value. Our design will exploit the above properties in a crucial way.

2.2   Asymmetric Public-Key Traitor Tracing Schemes

An Asymmetric Public-Key Traitor Tracing scheme involves the following entities: the system-manager, who is responsible for administrating the system, issuing subscriber information, and tracing pirate devices; the subscribers, or users, of the system; the channel-providers who use the system to distribute scrambled data to the set of subscribers; and finally, the "judge" who verifies that certain subscribers have been implicated in the construction of a pirate-device. Note that the judge is not assumed to be a trusted party, in fact any

interested party can play the role of the judge. Nevertheless, we use this terminology to emphasize that the tracing procedure should produce solid evidence
for the implication of the traitor users in the construction of a pirate-device.

The description of an asymmetric public-key traitor-tracing scheme is comprised of the following procedures and requirements:

- Join. A protocol between the system-manager and a new user that introduces the new user as a subscriber to the system. The join procedure will
  result in a personalized key for each new subscriber. The join procedure is a
  critical component in the context of asymmetric schemes: on the one hand
  the subscriber should commit to his/her key in a non-repudiable way; on
  the other hand, the system-manager should be oblivious to a portion of the
  subscriber key (to prevent a malicious system-manager from implicating an
  innocent user).
- Encryption. A probabilistic procedure that can be used by any third party
  to send encrypted messages to the set of users.
- Decryption. An algorithm that can be used by any user, in combination with
  his/her secret-key, to decrypt a message.
- Traitor-Tracing and Trial. An algorithm that given the contents of a pirate-
  decoder can be used by the system-manager to reveal the identities of the
  traitor users that participated in the construction of the decoder by revealing
  their keys. The algorithm generates non-repudiable information which can
  be verified in a trial by a judge; see figure 3.

The security of the asymmetric public-key traitor tracing scheme can be
modeled by employing standard notions of security pertaining to public-key encryption. In particular, we remark that definitions of semantic-security against
passive or chosen-ciphertext adversaries can be employed to model security in
our setting without any major modifications.

Further, the scheme is "asymmetric" if it satisfies the following properties:
(i) *frameproof*: the system-manager is incapable of implicating innocent users in
the construction of a pirate decoder; (ii) *direct non-repudiation*: tracing should
produce indisputable proof for the implication of the traitors in the construction
of the pirate decoder; such proof should be impossible to forge by the system-
manager and any interested third party (the judge) can check its validity *without
the participation of the subscribers of the system* (hence the name *direct* non-
repudiation).

3   Flaws in Proposed Asymmetric Public-Key Schemes

In this section we demonstrate that the two previous proposals of asymmetric
public-key traitor tracing schemes are flawed.

3.1   The Scheme of [31] Is Flawed

Let us briefly describe the scheme; for more details the reader is referred to [31].
Following the join procedure, each legitimate user i of the system possesses a

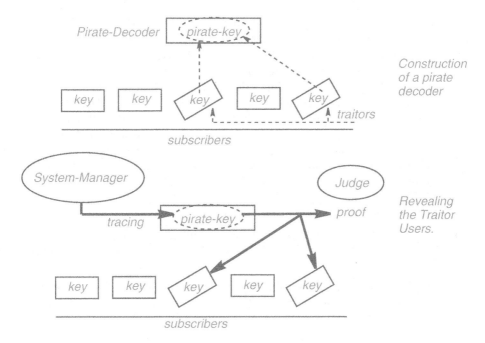

Fig. 3. Traitor Tracing in an Asymmetric Scheme

value $f(z_i, \alpha_i)$ of a bi-variate polynomial $f(x, y) = f_1(x) + y f_2(y)$ where $f_1(x) := a_0 + a_1 x + \ldots + a_k x^k$ and $f_2(x) = b_0 + b_1 x + \ldots + b_k x^k$ are two secret random polynomials of $\mathbf{Z}_q[x]$ (selected by the system-manager during the initialization of the scheme). The join procedure is executed so that the α_i value is not revealed to the authority but nevertheless the authority obtains a commitment of the user to this value (to be used as a proof in case of piracy).

The public-key of the scheme is $\langle g, h_{0,0}, \ldots, h_{0,k}, h_{1,0}, \ldots, h_{1,k} \rangle$ so that $h_{0,i} := g^{a_i}$ and $h_{1,i} := g^{b_i}$ for $i = 1, \ldots, k$. Encryption in this scheme works as follows: given a message $s \in \mathcal{G}$ the sender selects random $r, x_1, \ldots, x_k \in \mathbf{Z}_q$ and computes:

$$\langle g^r, s \cdot h_{1,0}^r, h_{0,0}^r, \ldots, h_{0,k}^r, (x_1, \prod_{j=0}^{k} h_{1,j}^{r x_1^j} = g^{r f_2(x_1)}), \ldots, (x_k, \prod_{j=0}^{k} h_{1,j}^{r x_k^j} = g^{r f_2(x_k)}) \rangle$$

The receiver, a user that possesses $f(z_i, \alpha_i) = f_1(z_i) + \alpha_i f_2(z_i)$, decrypts a ciphertext $\langle G, G', G_0, \ldots, G_k, (x_1, G_1'), \ldots, (x_k, G_k') \rangle$ as follows: first the value $\gamma := (G^{f(z_i, \alpha_i)} / \prod_{j=0}^{k} G_j^{z_i^j})^{\alpha_i^{-1}}$ is computed. Note that the value γ equals $g^{r f_2(z_i)}$. Then the user computes the Lagrange coefficients $\lambda, \lambda_1, \ldots, \lambda_k$ so that $\lambda f(z_i) + \lambda_1 f(x_1) + \ldots + \lambda_k f(x_k) = f(0)$ for any polynomial f of degree at most k (note that this is only possible if $z_i \notin \{x_1, \ldots, x_k\}$ but this can only happen with negligible probability); observe that $\lambda f_2(z_i) + \lambda_1 f_2(x_1) + \ldots + \lambda_k f_2(x_k) = f_2(0)$. Subsequently the user computes the plaintext s by evaluating $G'/(\gamma^\lambda \prod_{j=1}^{k} (G_j')^{\lambda_j})$.

In [31] it is shown that it is computationally hard for a collusion of up to k users to compute another decryption key $\langle z, \alpha, f(z, \alpha)\rangle$. Nevertheless this is not sufficient to ensure tracing. Attacks in previous traitor tracing schemes (in particular against the scheme of [20]) used techniques to combine user-key information in an arbitrary fashion thus disabling "direct" tracing by merely observing the keys found inside the pirate-decoder (see [29,4]). Watanabe et al. [31] claim that such techniques do not seem to apply in their scheme: *"On the other hand, it seems [that such techniques are] not applicable to the threshold-decryption-based scheme such as [Yoshida et al] and ours, since a session key can be computed by combining $k + 1$ shares using the Lagrange interpolation, and simple convex combination of the personal keys of k traitors does not lead to the pirate key."* (page 400, [31]).

Here we show that this assumption is, in fact, false:

Claim 1. Any collusion of traitors of more than a single user, can generate keys that are not traceable in the scheme of [31]. Such keys are random linear combinations of the traitors' keys.

The Break. The break depends on the following fact that we show about the [31] scheme: Given t user-keys $\langle z_i, \alpha_i, f(z_i, \alpha_i)\rangle$ the vector defined below,

$$\langle \delta_0, \ldots, \delta_k, \delta'_0, \ldots, \delta'_k, \Delta \rangle := \langle \sum_{\ell=1}^{t} \mu_\ell, \sum_{\ell=1}^{t} \mu_\ell z_\ell,$$

$$\ldots, \sum_{\ell=1}^{t} \mu_\ell z_\ell^k, \sum_{\ell=1}^{t} \mu_\ell \alpha_\ell, \sum_{\ell=1}^{t} \mu_\ell \alpha_\ell z_\ell, \ldots, \sum_{\ell=1}^{t} \mu_\ell \alpha_\ell z_\ell^k, \sum_{\ell=1}^{t} \mu_\ell f(z_\ell, \alpha_\ell)\rangle$$

can also be used as a key, where $\mu_1, \ldots, \mu_t$ are random elements of $\mathbf{Z}_q$. This can be seen as follows: given the ciphertext

$$\langle G, G', G_0, \ldots, G_k, (x_1, G'_1), \ldots, (x_k, G'_k)\rangle$$

a pirate device employing a key of the above form, computes $\gamma := G^\Delta / \prod_{j=0}^{k} G_j^{\delta_j}$. Observe that $\gamma = g^r \sum_{\ell=1}^{t} \mu_\ell \alpha_\ell f_2(z_\ell)$.

Next the pirate device needs to compute values $\lambda, \lambda_1, \ldots, \lambda_k$ so that

$$\lambda \sum_{\ell=1}^{t} \mu_\ell \alpha_\ell f(z_\ell) + \lambda_1 f(x_1) + \ldots + \lambda_k f(x_k) = f(0)$$

for any polynomial $f \in \mathbf{Z}_q[x]$ of degree at most k. If such values can be computed, then the message can be recovered by the pirate device by computing $G'/(\gamma^\lambda \prod_{j=1}^{k}(G'_j)^{\lambda_j})$.

To complete the description of our break, we show how the values $\lambda, \lambda_1, \ldots, \lambda_k$ can be computed using only the information provided in the pirate-key and the current ciphertext. First observe that if A is a $(k + 1) \times (k + 1)$-matrix so that its i-th row is equal to $\langle 1, x_i, \ldots, x_i^k \rangle$ for $i = 1, \ldots, k$ and its $(k + 1)$-th row equals $\langle \delta'_0, \ldots, \delta'_k \rangle$ it holds that A is non-singular with very high probability provided that $z_1, \ldots, z_t$ do not belong to $\{x_1, \ldots, x_k\}$ (something that can only happen with negligible probability). Then, the system $A \cdot \langle b_0, \ldots, b_k \rangle^T = \langle f(x_1), \ldots, f(x_k), \sum_{\ell=1}^{t} \mu_\ell \alpha_\ell f(z_\ell) \rangle^T$ is solvable for any polynomial $f \in \mathbf{Z}_q[x]$ of degree at most k and defines the coefficients of $f(x)$. It is an immediate conclusion that $b_0 = f(0)$ can be defined as a linear combination of the values $\langle f(x_1), \ldots, f(x_k), \sum_{\ell=1}^{t} \mu_\ell \alpha_\ell f(z_\ell) \rangle$ and the coefficients $\lambda, \lambda_1, \ldots, \lambda_k$ of the linear combination depend only on the matrix A, which is accessible to the pirate device given the pirate-key and the ciphertext.

As a result, a pirate, using keys of the above form, produces pirate-devices that the tracing procedure of the scheme of [31] (which is merely based on checking whether the key(s) found in a pirate-device are equal to some of the subscriber keys) is incapable to trace.

We remark that in [31], a "black-box traitor tracing" algorithm is outlined as well. It is based on "black-box confirmation" (as defined by [4]). Such traitor-tracing methods require *exponential-time* in the number of traitors, and are, therefore, *not* practical for many scenarios.

3.2   The Tracing Scheme of [19] Requires Exponential Time

Let us briefly describe the scheme; for details the reader is referred to [19]. Following the Join procedure, each legitimate user i of the system obtains a point of a random secret polynomial $f(x) := a_0 + a_1 x + \ldots + a_{2k-1} x^{2k-1}$ (this polynomial is privately selected by the system-manager during the initialization of the scheme). As a result, each subscriber will obtain a point $\langle d_i, f(d_i) \rangle$. Note that this point is not known to the system-manager; in fact this is the crucial point that is used by [19] to show the asymmetry property of their scheme. The public-key of the system is set to $\langle g, g^{a_0}, \ldots, g^{a_{2k-1}} \rangle$ and the encryption is defined as follows: a sender encrypts a message s by $\langle g^r, s \cdot (g^{a_0})^r, (g^{a_1})^r, \ldots, (g^{a_{2k-1}})^r \rangle$. A ciphertext $\langle G, G', G_1, \ldots, G_{2k-1} \rangle$ can be decrypted by any subscriber of the system (that possesses a point $\langle d_i, f(d_i) \rangle$ of f) as follows:

$$s = G' \prod_{j=1}^{2k-1} G_j^{d_i^j} / G^{f(d_i)}$$

It is proven in [19] that a coalition of less than $2k$ traitors is incapable of constructing another subscriber key $\langle d, f(d) \rangle$. However it is possible to construct vectors that can be used as keys by taking linear combinations of the form

$$\langle \sum_{\ell=1}^{t} \mu_\ell, \sum_{\ell=1}^{t} \mu_\ell d_\ell, \ldots, \sum_{\ell=1}^{t} \mu_\ell d_\ell^{2k-1}, \sum_{\ell=1}^{t} \mu_\ell f(d_\ell) \rangle$$

Such vectors can be constructed by a traitor collusion of t subscribers and it is not apparent how tracing can be achieved in this case. This fact is mentioned in the paper and it is claimed it is possible to trace those combinations to the users that created them by using coding-theoretic techniques.

Claim 2. Tracing in the scheme of [19] requires exponential time.

Justification. The coding theoretic methods that Komaki et al. ([19]) claim they can use for tracing in their scheme, (note that they do not present a concrete tracing algorithm), require the tracer to *know* the points $\langle d_i, f(d_i)\rangle$ assigned to the users during the Join protocol. However, these same values are also required to be unknown in order to achieve the claimed asymmetry/non-repudiation. This fact went unnoticed in [19], and renders the proposed traceability procedure exponential time, as the tracer will have to use in the decoding algorithm *all* possible values of the underlying finite field $\mathbf{Z}_q$ which is exponentially large (the size of an element in the underlying finite field coincides with the security parameter of the system).

4   The New Scheme

In this section we present our public-key asymmetric traitor tracing scheme. In order to achieve the asymmetry property it is necessary to use a basic underlying mechanism that can provide non-repudiation. To this effect, we assume that every user u possesses a digital signature mechanism sign_u that allows him/her to sign messages. The signature of user u on a message M will be denoted by $\mathsf{sign}_u(M)$. Any interested party can verify the signature of user u on a message M by running the publicly available verification algorithm verify_u.

Initialization. The system-manager selects one random polynomial $Q_1(x) = a_0 + a_1 x + \ldots a_{2v} x^{2v}$ over $\mathbf{Z}_q$ and a random $b \in \mathbf{Z}_q$ and sets $y = g^{a_0}$ and $h_0 = g, h_1 = g^{-a_1}, \ldots, h_{2v} = g^{-a_{2v}}, h' = g^{-b}$. The tuple $\langle y, h_0, \ldots, h_{2v}, h'\rangle$ is published as the public-key of the system. Let $Q(x, y) := Q_1(x) + by$.

Join. The join procedure is a protocol executed by the system-manager and a new user u that wants to obtain the subscription service. The goal of the Join protocol is to allow the user u to compute a point $\langle z_u, \alpha_u, Q(z_u, \alpha_u)\rangle$ of the bi-variate polynomial Q so that: z_u is randomly selected by the system manager, and $\alpha_u = \alpha_u^C + \alpha_c^R$ where α_u^C is a value selected and committed by the user, and the value α_u^R is randomly selected by the system manager. The commitment of the user u to the value α_u^C will be of the form $\langle C_u = g^{\alpha_u^C}, \mathsf{sign}_u(C_u)\rangle$.

The join protocol can be implemented by employing an instantiation of a Malleable OPE over a committed value as specified in subsection 2.1.

After the completion of the Join procedure, the user's secret personal key will be set to the vector $\kappa_u := \langle Q(z_u, \alpha_u), z_u, z_u^2, \ldots, z_u^{2v}, \alpha_u\rangle$ (note that the user u does not need to store the whole κ_u as this can be recovered from the values $z_u, \alpha_u, Q(z_u, \alpha_u)$ as needed; as a result the storage space needed for the secret-key is not proportional to v — however the working space in the receiver should be proportional to v).

The following proposition asserts that the join procedure allows the user to compute a valid secret-key of the system, that is not known (in its entirety) by the system-manager; instead, the system-manager holds a non-repudiable commitment of the user to the secret portion of the user's secret-key.

Proposition 1. *The key κ_u computed by user u is a representation of y w.r.t. the base $h_0, \ldots, h_{2v}, h'$.*

Proof. If $\kappa_u = \langle Q(z_u, \alpha_u), z_u, z_u^2, \ldots, z_u^{2v}, \alpha_u \rangle$, observe that

$$(h_0)^{Q(z_u, \alpha_u)} (h_1)^{z_u} \ldots (h_{2v})^{z_u^{2v}} (h')^{\alpha_u} = g^{Q(z_u, \alpha_u) - a_1 z_u - \ldots - a_{2v} z_u^{2v} - b\alpha_u} = g^{a_0} = y$$

$\square$

Next note that due to the properties of the OPE we are assured that if the join protocol terminates successfully, user u is committed to the secret-key κ_u with overwhelming probability; if the protocol is aborted by the system-manager then the user u cannot compute any representation of y w.r.t the base $h_0, \ldots, h_{2v}, h'$. Further, note that due to the malleability and security of the OPE variant, it follows that an oracle to an invocation of the registration procedure can be simulated by giving a truly random point of the bivariate polynomial Q. This suggests that a malicious adversary cannot create subscribers for which he controls the point over which the system's polynomial Q is evaluated.

The next proposition, assures us that based on the hardness of the discrete logarithm problem, certain limitations on the structure of the pirate keys are imposed. This approach follows the one of Boneh and Franklin [4].

Proposition 2. *Suppose there exists an adversary, that given the public-key $\langle y, h_0, \ldots, h_{2v}, h' \rangle$ of the system and $t < 2v + 2$ random values $\langle z_i, \alpha_i, Q(z_i, \alpha_i) \rangle$ of the bivariate polynomial Q, it outputs a representation of y w.r.t. the base $h_0, \ldots, h_{2v}, h'$ denoted by $\boldsymbol{K} = \langle \delta_0, \ldots, \delta_{2v}, \delta' \rangle$ that is not a linear combination of the vectors $\langle Q(z_i, \alpha_i), z_i, \ldots, z_i^{2v}, \alpha_i \rangle$. Then the discrete-log problem over $\mathcal{G}$ is solvable.*

Proof. Let $\langle g, G \rangle$ be an instance of the discrete-log problem over the group $\mathcal{G}$. Consider the following algorithm that uses the adversary as follows: first we select $z_1, \ldots, z_t, \alpha_1, \ldots, \alpha_t, a_0, a_1, \ldots, a_{2v}, b$ at random from $\mathbf{Z}_q$. We set $Q_1(x) = a_0 + a_1 x + \ldots a_{2v} x^{2v}$, and $Q(x, y) = Q_1(x) + by$. Then we select a $(2v + 2)$-tuple $\langle b_0, b_1, \ldots, b_{2v}, b' \rangle$ at random, from the (right-)kernel of the matrix

$$\begin{pmatrix} Q(z_1, \alpha_1) & z_1 & \ldots & z_1^{2v} & \alpha_1 \\ Q(z_2, \alpha_2) & z_2 & \ldots & z_2^{2v} & \alpha_2 \\ \vdots & \vdots & \ldots & \vdots & \vdots \\ Q(z_t, \alpha_t) & z_t & \ldots & z_t^{2v} & \alpha_t \end{pmatrix}$$

Observe that since $t < 2v + 2$ and the above matrix is of full rank with very high probability (as the z_i's are assumed distinct, and the α_i's are random). Thus, it follows that its right-kernel contains q^{2v+2-t} vectors. The system-manager gives to the adversary the public-key

$$\langle y, h_0, h_1, \ldots, h_{2v}, h' \rangle = \langle g^{a_0}, gG^{b_0}, g^{-a_1}G^{b_1}, \ldots, g^{-a_{2v}}G^{b_{2v}}, g^{-b}G^{b'} \rangle$$

Then, we give to the adversary the values $\langle Q(z_i, \alpha_i), z_i, \alpha_i \rangle$. Finally the adversary outputs a representation $\langle \delta_0, \ldots, \delta_{2v}, \delta' \rangle$ such that it is not a linear combination of the vectors $\langle Q(z_i, \alpha_i), z_i, \ldots, z_i^{2v}, \alpha_i \rangle_{i=1}^t$. Now observe that the matrix below is also of full rank, and that its right-kernel contains $q^{2v+2-t-1}$ vectors.

$$\begin{pmatrix} Q(z_1, \alpha_1) & z_1 & \ldots & z_1^{2v} & \alpha_1 \\ Q(z_2, \alpha_2) & z_2 & \ldots & z_2^{2v} & \alpha_2 \\ \vdots & \vdots & \ldots & \vdots & \vdots \\ Q(z_t, \alpha_t) & z_t & \ldots & z_t^{2v} & \alpha_t \\ \delta_0 & \delta_1 & \ldots & \delta_{2v} & \delta' \end{pmatrix}$$

It follows that the probability that $\langle \delta_0, \delta_1, \ldots, \delta_{2v}, \delta' \rangle \cdot \langle b_0, b_1, \ldots, b_{2v}, b' \rangle$ equals to 0 is at most $1/q$. Finally observe that: $y = h_0^{\delta_0} \ldots h_{2v}^{\delta_{2v}} (h')^{\delta'}$ and as a result

$$\log_g G = (b_0 \delta_0 + \ldots b_v \delta_v + b' \delta')^{-1} (a_0 + a_1 \delta_1 + \ldots + a_{2v} \delta_{2v} + b \delta' - \delta_0)$$

This completes the proof.   □

Encryption. Any (non-trusted) channel provider can use the encryption function to distribute content to the set of subscribers. The encryption operation is defined as follows: the channel provider obtains the public-key of the system, $\mathsf{pk} := \langle y, h_0, \ldots, h_{2v}, h' \rangle$. A plaintext M is encrypted as follows: $\langle y^r \cdot M, h_0^r, \ldots, h_{2v}^r, (h')^r \rangle$, where r is a random integer less than q. So the (probabilistic) encryption function is defined as follows:

$$\mathcal{E}(\mathsf{pk}, M) = \langle y^r \cdot M, h_0^r, \ldots, h_{2v}^r, (h')^r \rangle$$

As a result, $\mathcal{E}$, is an extended ElGamal encryption, for which one can easily show:

Proposition 3. *The encryption function of the system is semantically secure under the Decisional Diffie Hellman Assumption over the group $\mathcal{G}$.*

The proof extends the standard semantic security of ElGamal encryption to discrete-log representations of arbitrary length, see e.g. [4]. We remark that semantic security against a chosen ciphertext security can be achieved also, following the techniques of [10], as it was demonstrated in [4].

Decryption. Any ciphertext can be decrypted using a representation of y w.r.t. the base $h_0, \ldots, h_{2v}, h'$. Given a ciphertext $\tilde{G} := \langle G, G_0, G_1, \ldots, G_{2v}, G' \rangle$ and a representation $\kappa := \langle \delta_0, \ldots, \delta_{2v}, \delta' \rangle$ the decryption function is defined as follows:

$$\mathcal{D}(\tilde{G}, \kappa) := G / ((G')^{\delta'} \prod_{j=0}^{2v} (G_j)^{\delta_j})$$

It is easy to verify that the decryption operation inverts the encryption function. Indeed, for a ciphertext $\tilde{G} = \langle y^r \cdot M, h_0^r, \ldots, h_{2v}^r, (h')^r \rangle$ and a representation $\kappa = \langle \delta_0, \ldots, \delta_{2v}, \delta' \rangle$ of y w.r.t. $\langle h_0, \ldots, h_{2v}, h' \rangle$, it holds that,

$$\mathcal{D}(\tilde{G}, \kappa) = \frac{y^r \cdot M}{((h')^r)^{\delta'} \prod_{j=0}^{2v} (h_j^r)^{\delta_j}} = \frac{y^r M}{y^r} = M$$

> *Input.* A vector $\mathbf{K}$ of the form $\sum_{\ell=1}^{t} \mu_\ell \kappa_{u_\ell}$, where $\{u_1, \ldots, u_t\} \subseteq \{1, \ldots, n\}$ is the set of traitor users and n is the number of all users in the system. Recall that $\kappa_u = \langle Q(z_u, \alpha_u), z_u, \ldots, z_u^{2v}, \alpha_u \rangle$.
> Also part of the input are integers $z_1, \ldots, z_n$, that define a portion of the secret-key κ_u of every user (recall that during the Join protocol these values are selected by the system-manager).
>
> *Output.* The indices $\{u_1, \ldots, u_t\}$ and the values $\{\mu_1, \ldots, \mu_t\}$.

Fig. 4. The Traitor Tracing Problem

Traitor Tracing. It is clear from the definition of the decryption function that any representation of y w.r.t. the base $h_0, \ldots, h_{2v}, h'$ can be used as a decryption-key. Under the security of the encryption function, the set of all possible decryption keys is identified with the set of all representations of y. A malicious coalition of users (traitors) is capable of producing arbitrary representations but, under the hardness of the discrete-logarithm problem, proposition 2 suggests that these representations can only be linear combinations of the secret-keys the malicious coalition possesses. In particular if $u_1, \ldots, u_t$ constitute a malicious collusion of users then they can compute representations of y of the form $\sum_{\ell=1}^{t} \mu_\ell \kappa_{u_\ell}$ where $\mu_1, \ldots, \mu_t$ are random elements of $\mathbf{Z}_q$.

In order to achieve asymmetric traitor tracing, the problem that needs to be resolved is defined in figure 4.

Below we present an efficient algorithmic construction for the Traitor Tracing problem based on Decoding of Algebraic Codes. We are motivated by the work of [4] and [24], that presented similar techniques for traitor tracing based on linear codes decoding. For an introduction to Coding Theory the reader is referred to [21]. First, the tracer, defines the following $(n \times 2v)$-matrix:

$$H := \begin{pmatrix} z_1 & \ldots & z_1^{2v} \\ z_2 & \ldots & z_2^{2v} \\ \vdots & \ldots & \vdots \\ z_n & \ldots & z_n^{2v} \end{pmatrix}$$

Note that the number of users of the system is typically much larger than the parameter v, and as a result we assume that $n > 2v$. Let $\mathcal{C}$ define the code over $\mathbf{Z}_q^n$ that has H as a parity-check matrix (i.e. for all $\mathbf{c} \in \mathcal{C}$ it holds that $\mathbf{c} \cdot H = \mathbf{0}$).

Now let $\lambda_1, \ldots, \lambda_n$ be the Lagrange coefficients so that $\lambda_1 g(z_1) + \ldots + \lambda_n g(z_n) = g(0)$, for all $g \in \mathbf{Z}_q[x]$ with degree$(g) < n$.

Lemma 1. *It holds that*
1. $\mathcal{C} = \{\langle \lambda_1 M(z_1), \ldots, \lambda_n M(z_n) \rangle \mid M \in \mathbf{Z}_q[x], \text{degree}(M) < n - 2v\}$.
2. $\mathcal{C}$ *is a linear code with message-rate* $(n - 2v)/n$ *and distance* $2v + 1$.

Proof. 1. Let $\mathcal{C}'$ denote the linear space in the right-hand-side of the equality above. If $\langle c_1, \ldots, c_n \rangle \in \mathcal{C}'$, it is of the form $\langle \lambda_1 M(z_1), \ldots, \lambda_n M(z_n) \rangle$. Then it is easy to verify that $\langle c_1, \ldots, c_n \rangle$ belongs to $\mathcal{C}$: indeed it holds that $\langle c_1, \ldots, c_n \rangle \cdot \langle z_1^\ell, \ldots, z_n^\ell \rangle = \sum_{i=1}^{n} \lambda_i M(z_i) z_i^\ell$, for any $\ell = 1, \ldots, 2v$. Now observe that

$$\sum_{i=1}^{n} \lambda_i M(z_i) z_i^{\ell} = 0$$

by the choice of $\lambda_1, \ldots, \lambda_n$ (and the fact that degree$(M) < n - 2v$). Since $\langle z_1^{\ell}, \ldots, z_n^{\ell} \rangle$ is the ℓ-th column of H, it follows that $\langle c_1, \ldots, c_n \rangle \cdot H = \mathbf{0}$. This shows that $\mathcal{C}' \subseteq \mathcal{C}$. On the other hand observe that $\dim(\mathcal{C}) = n - 2v = \dim(\mathcal{C}')$. Since $\mathcal{C}'$ is a linear sub-space of $\mathcal{C}$ and it has the same dimension, it follows that $\mathcal{C} = \mathcal{C}'$.

Item 2, is straightforward from item 1: in particular a vector of $\mathbf{Z}_q^{n-2v}$ can be encoded as the coefficients of a polynomial $M \in \mathbf{Z}_q[x]$ of degree less than $n - 2v$. The corresponding codeword of $\mathcal{C}$ will be the vector $\langle \lambda_1 M(z_1), \ldots, \lambda_n M(z_n) \rangle$. To see that the distance of the linear code is $2v+1$ observe that any two different codewords of $\mathcal{C}$ can agree on at most $n - 2v - 1$ positions, or equivalently any two distinct codewords differ on at least $2v + 1$ positions. $\square$

Next we show that $\mathcal{C}$ is a linear code that allows efficient error-correction. In particular it is clear from lemma 1 that $\mathcal{C}$ is a Generalized Reed-Solomon Code (for the definition of Generalized Reed-Solomon Codes, see [21]). Generalized Reed-Solomon Codes can be decoded efficiently by the algorithm of Berlekamp and Welch [3]. This means that for any vector $\boldsymbol{x} \in \mathbf{Z}_q^n$ for which there exists a vector $\boldsymbol{w} \in \mathcal{C}$ that disagrees with $\boldsymbol{x}$ in at most e positions with $e \leq \frac{n-(n-2v)}{2} = v$, it holds that $\boldsymbol{w}$ is unique with this property ($\mathcal{C}$ is a maximum-distance-separable code) and the vector $\boldsymbol{w}$ can be recovered in deterministic polynomial-time.

Let us now proceed to describe the tracing procedure. Given a vector $\boldsymbol{K} = \sum_{\ell=1}^{t} \mu_\ell \boldsymbol{\kappa}_{u_\ell}$, denote $\boldsymbol{K} = \langle K_0, K_1, \ldots, K_{2v}, K' \rangle$; recall that $\{u_1, \ldots, u_t\}$ is the set of traitor users. The tracer concentrates on the $(2v)$-vector $\boldsymbol{\eta} = \langle K_1, \ldots, K_{2v} \rangle$. By the definition of $\boldsymbol{\eta}$ it holds that there exists a vector $\boldsymbol{\nu} = \langle \nu_1, \ldots, \nu_n \rangle$ with $\nu_{u_\ell} = \mu_\ell$ for all $\ell = 1, \ldots, t$ and $\nu_i = 0$ for $i \notin \{u_1, \ldots, u_t\}$, with the property $\langle \nu_1, \ldots, \nu_n \rangle \cdot H = \boldsymbol{\eta}$. It is immediate that the recovery of $\boldsymbol{\nu}$ yields the solution to the traitor tracing problem as defined in figure 4.

The tracer computes an arbitrary vector $\boldsymbol{\delta}$ that satisfies the system of equations $\boldsymbol{\delta} \cdot H = \boldsymbol{\eta}$. Note that such $\boldsymbol{\delta}$ can be found by standard linear algebra since $\boldsymbol{\delta} \cdot H = \boldsymbol{\eta}$ is a system of $2v$ equations with n unknowns, $n > 2v$, and H contains a non-singular minor of size $2v$. It is easy to verify that the vector $\boldsymbol{w} := \boldsymbol{\delta} - \boldsymbol{\nu}$ belongs to the linear code $\mathcal{C}$: indeed, $\boldsymbol{w} \cdot H = \boldsymbol{\delta} \cdot H - \boldsymbol{\nu} \cdot H = \boldsymbol{\eta} - \boldsymbol{\eta} = \mathbf{0}$. As a result the vector $\boldsymbol{\delta}$ can be expressed as $\boldsymbol{\delta} = \boldsymbol{w} + \boldsymbol{\nu}$.

Provided that $t \leq v$ it holds that the Hamming weight of $\boldsymbol{\nu}$ is less or equal to v and as a result $\boldsymbol{\delta}$ is a n-vector that differs in at most v positions from the vector $\boldsymbol{w}$ that belongs in $\mathcal{C}$. Due to the properties of the linear code $\mathcal{C}$ it holds that $\boldsymbol{w}$ will be the unique vector of $\mathcal{C}$ with this property, and furthermore $\boldsymbol{w}$ can be recovered in deterministic polynomial-time if we feed $\boldsymbol{\delta}$ to the decoding procedure for $\mathcal{C}$ (which is essentially the Berlekamp-Welch algorithm, [3]). The recovery of $\boldsymbol{w}$, immediately will result in the recovery of $\boldsymbol{\nu} = \boldsymbol{\delta} - \boldsymbol{w}$. As mentioned above the recovery of $\boldsymbol{\nu}$ solves the traitor tracing problem.

Efficiency. Our tracing algorithm has time complexity $\mathcal{O}(n^2)$, if the Berlekamp-Welch algorithm is implemented in the straightforward manner; more efficient implementations are possible that reduce the time-complexity to $\mathcal{O}(n(\log n)^2)$. We remark that it is possible to trace even if the number of traitors exceeds the bound v; this can be done by employing the decoding algorithm of Guruswami and Sudan [14] that will produce a *list* of possible sets of traitor users, provided that the size of the traitor collusion is less or equal to $n - \sqrt{n(n-2v)}$.

The Trial. The system-manager obtains the output of the tracing procedure on the pirate key $\boldsymbol{K} = \langle K_0, K_1, \ldots, K_{2v}, K' \rangle$ with $\boldsymbol{K} = \sum_{\ell=1}^{t} \mu_\ell \boldsymbol{\kappa}_{u_\ell}$ where $\{u_1, \ldots, u_t\} \subseteq \{1, \ldots, n\}$ is the set of traitor users (note that due to proposition 2 the pirate-key is ensured to be of this form). The output of the tracing is the vector $\boldsymbol{\nu} = \langle \nu_1, \ldots, \nu_n \rangle$ where $\nu_{u_\ell} = \mu_\ell$ for $\ell = 1, \ldots, t$ and $\nu_i = 0$ for all $i \in \{1, \ldots, n\} - \{u_1, \ldots, u_t\}$. The system-manager has to prove to the judge that the users $\{u_1, \ldots, u_t\}$ were implicated in the construction of the pirate key $\boldsymbol{K}$. This can be done as follows: the system-manager transmits to the judge the vector $\boldsymbol{\nu}$, the pirate key $\boldsymbol{K}$, the values $\alpha_{u_1}^R, \ldots, \alpha_{u_t}^R$ and the commitments of the implicated subscribers $C_{u_1}; \text{sign}_{u_1}(C_{u_1}), \ldots C_{u_t}; \text{sign}_{u_t}(C_{u_t})$ that were generated when the traitors joined the system as subscribers. The judge verifies all signatures using the publicly known verification algorithms $\text{verify}_{u_1}, \ldots, \text{verify}_{u_t}$.

Then, the judge examines whether the claim of the system-manager regarding the implication of the users $\{u_1, \ldots, u_t\}$ is correct; this is done as follows: the judge tests whether

$$\prod_{\ell=1}^{t}(C_{u_\ell} g^{\alpha_{u_\ell}^R})^{\nu_{u_\ell}} \stackrel{?}{=} g^{K'}$$

if the test passes, then the judge concludes that indeed the users $\{u_1, \ldots, u_t\}$ were implicated in the construction of the pirate key $\boldsymbol{K}$.

Theorem 1. *1. If $\{u_1, \ldots, u_t\}$ are the traitor users whose keys have been used in the construction of the pirate-key $\boldsymbol{K}$, the judge will verify this fact using the information provided by the tracer.*
2. Under the security of the underlying malleable OPE, if the system-manager can implicate an innocent user in the construction of a pirate-key $\boldsymbol{K}$ it follows that the discrete-log problem over $\mathcal{G}$ is solvable with overwhelming probability.

Proof. 1. First, observe that $K' = \sum_{\ell=1}^{t} \mu_\ell \alpha_{u_\ell}$. Because of the properties of the tracing procedure it holds that $\nu_{u_\ell} = \mu_\ell$ for $\ell = 1, \ldots, t$. Since $C_u = g^{\alpha_u^C}$ for all $u \in \{1, \ldots, n\}$, it holds that $\prod_{\ell=1}^{t}(C_{u_\ell} g^{\alpha_{u_\ell}^R})^{\nu_\ell} = g^{K'}$ (recall that $\alpha_{u_\ell} = \alpha_{u_\ell}^C + \alpha_{u_\ell}^R$).
2. Suppose that the system-manager convinces the judge that users $u_0, u_1, \ldots, u_t$ are implicated in the pirate-key $\boldsymbol{K}$ but $\boldsymbol{K} = \sum_{\ell=1}^{t} \mu_\ell \boldsymbol{\kappa}_{u_\ell}$ (i.e. the key of user u_0 is not among the ones that are used in the definition of $\boldsymbol{K}$). Since the judge agrees to the implication of the users $u_0, u_1, \ldots, u_t$ it holds that $\prod_{\ell=0}^{t}(C_{u_\ell} g^{y_\ell})^{\nu_{u_\ell}} = g^{K'}$, where $K', \boldsymbol{\nu}, y_0, \ldots, y_t$ are supplied by the system-manager. Below we show how to use such a cheating system manager to solve the discrete log problem over $\mathcal{G}$.

Given a challenge for the discrete-logarithm problem $\langle g, G \rangle$ over $\mathcal{G}$, we simulate the Join protocol for the users $u_0, \ldots, u_t$. On the one hand, we execute the

Join protocol exactly as defined for users $u_1, \ldots, u_t$; on the other hand, we simulate the join protocol so that the public commitment value of user u_0, denoted by C_{u_0} equals G. (recall that the Join protocol — based on the underlying OPE — is "simulatable", namely, we can run simulations of the Join protocol on a given public commitment $C_u = g^x$ for which we do not know the discrete log base g, with overwhelming probability of success). Subsequently, we construct a pirate-key $\boldsymbol{K}$ based on the values $z_{u_1}, \alpha_{u_1}, Q(z_{u_1}, \alpha_{u_1}), \ldots, z_{u_t}, \alpha_{u_t}, Q(z_{u_t}, \alpha_{u_t})$ (which we know, from the output of the Join protocol for the users $u_1, \ldots, u_t$), and we give this value to the system-manager. Then, we obtain the values $x_0, x_1, \ldots, x_t, y_0, \ldots, y_t$ and K' by simulating the system-manager; it follows that the discrete-logarithm of G can be computed as

$$\log_g(G) = (x_0)^{-1}(K' - x_1\alpha_{u_1} - \ldots - x_t\alpha_{u_t} - y_0 x_0 - \ldots y_t x_t)(\bmod q)$$

This completes the proof. $\qquad\qquad\qquad\qquad\qquad\qquad\qquad\qquad\qquad\square$

Black-Box Traitor Tracing. Black-box traceability is an important enhancement of the traitor tracing procedure, where the tracer is capable of recovering the identities of the traitor users using merely black-box access to the pirate-decoder. Not surprisingly our scheme is not likely to satisfy this property (in an efficient way) as it belongs in the family of public-key traitor tracing schemes that includes the schemes of [20,4] that cannot support this desirable enhanced traceability property in an efficient way as shown in [15]. A weaker form of black-box traitor tracing, called black-box confirmation, that can be potentially applied in this family of schemes was presented in [5]; this technique can give a black-box traitor tracing algorithm that has exponential running-time in the number of traitors and is applicable to our scheme as well.

Practical Considerations. Broadcasting streams of digital content using solely the encryption function of a traitor tracing scheme can be quite expensive. A content distributor takes the most out of such a scheme, if it broadcasts short-lived session keys (suitable for a block-cipher such as the AES [11]) to all subscribers using the encryption function of the TTS, and then in each session uses the block-cipher to scramble the digital content stream. Sessions should be *short* so that users are discouraged from distributing the (not fingerprinted) session-keys. There is an evident trade-off between the degree of protection against piracy and the efficiency of the digital content distribution scheme with respect to the session-length parameter. Finding an optimal value for this parameter is important for a practical implementation of a traitor tracing scheme in a certain context; it involves risk assessment, weighing damages against the cost of repetitive distribution.

Note that we assumed a system-manager which performs honestly in subscribing users (during the Join protocol). In case this is not sufficient, we can require the system-manager to sign the Join protocol transcript and keep the corresponding private record. This will enable complaints against the system-manager to be solved in court as well.

References

1. *Canal Plus files $ 1 billion lawsuit on News Corp arm*, Reuters, 03.12.02, 7:46 PM ET. (Also http://www.wired.com/news/politics/0,1283,51005,00.html).
2. Boaz Barak, Oded Goldreich, Russell Impagliazzo, Steven Rudich, Amit Sahai, Salil P. Vadhan and Ke Yang, *On the (Im)possibility of Obfuscating Programs*, CRYPTO 2001.
3. Elwyn R. Berlekamp and L. Welch, *Error Correction of Algebraic Block Codes*. U.S. Patent, Number 4,633,470 1986.
4. Dan Boneh and Matthew Franklin, *An Efficient Public Key Traitor Tracing Scheme*, CRYPTO 1999.
5. Dan Boneh and Matthew Franklin, *An Efficient Public Key Traitor Tracing Scheme*, manuscript, full-version of [4], 2001.
6. Stefan Brands, *Rethinking Public Key Infrastructures and Digital Certificates – Building in Privacy*, Ph.D. thesis, Technical University of Eindhoven, 1999.
7. Yan-Cheng Chang and Chi-Jen Lu, *Oblivious Polynomial Evaluation and Oblivious Neural Learning*, Asiacrypt 2001.
8. Benny Chor, Amos Fiat, and Moni Naor, *Tracing Traitors*, CRYPTO 1994.
9. Benny Chor, Amos Fiat, Moni Naor, and Benny Pinkas, *Tracing Traitors*, IEEE Transactions on Information Theory, Vol. 46, no. 3, pp. 893-910, 2000.
10. Ronald Cramer and Victor Shoup, *A Practical Public Key Cryptosystem Provably Secure Against Adaptive Chosen Ciphertext Attack*, CRYPTO 1998.
11. J. Daemen and V. Rijmen, *The design of Rijndael- AES the advanced encryption standard*, Springer Verlag, 2002.
12. Amos Fiat and Moni Naor, *Broadcast Encryption* CRYPTO 1993.
13. Eli Gafni, Jessica Staddon and Yiqun Lisa Yin, *Efficient Methods for Integrating Traceability and Broadcast Encryption*, CRYPTO 1999.
14. Venkatesan Guruswami and Madhu Sudan, *Improved Decoding of Reed-Solomon and Algebraic-Geometric Codes*. In the Proceedings of the 39th Annual Symposium on Foundations of Computer Science, IEEE Computer Society, pp. 28–39, 1998.
15. Aggelos Kiayias and Moti Yung, *Self Protecting Pirates and Black-Box Traitor Tracing*, CRYPTO 2001.
16. Aggelos Kiayias and Moti Yung, *Traitor Tracing with Constant Transmission Rate*, Eurocrypt 2002.
17. Aggelos Kiayias and Moti Yung, *Robust Malleable Oblivious Polynomial Evaluation*, manuscript.
18. Aggelos Kiayias and Moti Yung, *Cryptographic Hardness Based on the Decoding of Reed-Solomon Codes*, ICALP 2002.
19. Hirotaka Komaki, Yuji Watanabe, Goichiro Hanaoka, and Hideki Imai, *Efficient Asymmetric Self-Enforcement Scheme with Public Traceability*, Public Key Cryptography 2001.
20. K. Kurosawa and Y. Desmedt, *Optimum Traitor Tracing and Asymmetric Schemes*, Eurocrypt 1998.
21. F. J. MacWilliams and N. Sloane, *The Theory of Error Correcting Codes*. North Holland, Amsterdam, 1977.
22. Dalit Naor, Moni Naor and Jeffrey B. Lotspiech *Revocation and Tracing Schemes for Stateless Receivers*, CRYPTO 2001.
23. Moni Naor and Benny Pinkas, *Oblivious Transfer and Polynomial Evaluation*. In the Proceedings of the 31th ACM Symposium on the Theory of Computing, 1999. (Full version available from authors).

24. Moni Naor and Benny Pinkas, *Efficient Trace and Revoke Schemes* , In the Proceedings of Financial Crypto '2000, Anguilla, February 2000.
25. Birgit Pfitzmann, *Trials of Traced Traitors*, Information Hiding Workshop, Spring LNCS 1174, pp. 49-63, 1996.
26. Birgit Pfitzmann and Matthias Schunter, *Asymmetric Fingerprinting*, Eurocrypt 1996.
27. Brigitt Pfitzmann and M. Waidner, *Asymmetric fingerprinting for larger collusions*, in proc. ACM Conference on Computer and Communication Security, pp. 151–160, 1997.
28. Tomas Sander and Christian F. Tschudin, *On Software Protection via Function Hiding*, Information Hiding 1998.
29. Douglas Stinson and Ruizhong Wei, *Key preassigned traceability schemes for broadcast encryption*, In the Proceedings of SAC'98, Lecture Notes in Computer Science 1556, Springer Verlag, pp.144–156, 1998.
30. Douglas R. Stinson and Ruizhong Wei, *Combinatorial Properties and Constructions of Traceability Schemes and Frameproof Codes*, SIAM J. on Discrete Math, Vol. 11, no. 1, 1998.
31. Yuji Watanabe, Goichiro Hanaoka and Hideki Imai *Efficient Asymmetric Public-Key Traitor Tracing without Trusted Agents*, CT-RSA 2001.

Key Challenges in DRM: An Industry Perspective

Brian A. LaMacchia*

Microsoft Corporation
One Microsoft Way
Redmond, WA 98052-6399 USA
`bal@microsoft.com`

Abstract. The desires for robust digital rights management (DRM) systems are not new to the commercial world. Indeed, industrial research, development and deployment of systems with DRM aspects (most notably crude copy-control schemes) have a long history. Yet to date the industry has not seen much commercial success from shipping these systems on top of platforms that support general-purpose computing. There are many factors contributing to this lack of acceptance of current DRM systems, but I see three specific areas of work that are key adoption blockers today and ripe for further academic and commercial research. The lack of a general-purpose rights expression/authorization language, robust trust management engines and attestable trusted computing bases (TCBs) all hamper industrial development and deployment of DRM systems for digital content. In this paper I briefly describe each of these challenges, provide examples of how the industry is approaching each problem, and discuss how the solutions to each one of them are dependent on the others.

1 Introduction

When we think about digital rights management (DRM) systems, we tend to focus on the content that is to be managed by the system and the infrastructure needed to protect the content while it is in the system. Questions about content protections quickly turn into questions about content encryption, which generally yields questions about management of various types of cryptographic keys. This is comforting for us because the cryptography of DRM is familiar, and as a community we have developed (and continue to improve) a vast body of knowledge in cryptography and related spaces. If the design and construction of DRM systems was solely a matter of choosing the right cryptographic techniques to apply we would be in great shape: simply choose the algorithms we want to use for encryption, key management, secret sharing, traitor tracing, etc., and we could go build the systems.

---

* The views expressed in this paper are those of its author and are not necessarily those of Microsoft Corporation.

J. Feigenbaum (Ed.): DRM 2002, LNCS 2696, pp. 51–60, 2003.

Of course, DRM systems are not solely a collection and application of crypto-graphic techniques to content. In addition to the managed content there are also policies describing the access rules for that content, and a DRM system must manage these policies in addition to the content controlled by the policies. Unlike content management, policy management is not just a matter of encrypting some bits and distributing the decryption keys in the proper manner. A DRM system must perform all of the policy-related tasks necessary to "project policy, with confidence that the policy will be respected, from the content owner to the remote environment where the content will be used." Thus, policy management also includes tasks such as authoring, distributing, and evaluating policy expressions, for we must be able to create and reason about policy statements first before we can address the problem of projecting those statements into remote execution environments.

Collectively we have given significantly more attention in our research and development to content management rather than policy management, yet the key technical challenges we face today relate to the latter. In this paper I outline three of these challenges: authoring policy expressions, evaluating policy expressions, and projecting policy expressions with confidence into remote environments. Work is required in all three areas in order to make interoperable DRM systems built on top of general-purpose computing platforms viable.

2   Authoring Policy Expressions

A DRM policy management system has two core components: a language for expressing policy statements and an evaluator that can make decisions on the basis of such expressions. Both components are critical to acceptance of the DRM system. If the language is not sufficiently expressive to allow users (content owners, distributors and consumers) to write the types of policies they wish, then they will not be willing to use the system and the system will not attract content. Similarly, if the language is not easy enough for users to reason about and clearly communicate managed content policies (either directly or with support from appropriate tools) then user acceptance of the system will be low. Interoperability of statements written in the language is also a requirement as the policy evaluator must consider statements from many different sources (policy specifications, authentication credentials, authorization credentials) when making content access decisions.

When taken together, these requirements indicate that the success of DRM systems will depend in part on a "general-purpose" rights expression language (REL)–an extensible syntax and semantics for expressing grants of authorizations[1]. An REL is a type of policy authorization language where the focus of the

---

[1] The need for industry-standard authorization languages is much broader than just the DRM space; as we continue to build larger and larger distributed systems we need a *lingua franca* for communicating authorizations among all networked nodes. The need is especially apparent in the "web services" model of distributed programming as it is expected that any networked node can dynamically discover, learn how to communicate with and access any available service (with proper authorization).

language is on expressing and transferring rights (capabilities) from one party to another in an interoperable format. Issuance rights (the right to issue grants of other rights) and delegation rights (the right to delegate a grant to another party) are core concepts in an REL. A "general-purpose" REL must also allow flexibility and extensibility in the types of rights and resources that it references. There are a number of efforts within various standards bodies working on general authorization languages [1,7,8,9], but the most advanced work to date on a rights expression language is that based on the XML Rights Management Language (XrML 2.X) [5], including the REL and RDD groups within MPEG-21 [11] and the RLTC group within OASIS [14].

XrML 2.X is a direct descendant of Stefik's Digital Property Rights Language (DPRL) [15]. The first version of DPRL (version 1.0) focused on specifying machine-enforceable rights; a subsequent update (version 2.0) enabled the specification of more complex rights (potentially including fees, terms and conditions) for digital works. In 2000 the data model in DPRL was converted to XML and the resulting language, together with some additional language extensions, was named XrML 1.0. Version 2.0 of XrML, released by ContentGuard in November 2001, restructured the syntax and added a number of features that significantly increased the expressive power of the language.

XrML 2.X was designed to make it easy to create policy statements–called *licenses*–that represent arbitrary authorization grants from one party to another. A single authorization statement in XrML is always of the form, "*Issuer* authorizes *principal* to exercise a *right* with respect to a *resource* subject to (zero or more) *conditions*." Multiple authorizations from the same issuer may be grouped together into a single license. For example, "John says 'Bill has the right to print the book'" is an example of the form of authorization statements expressible in XrML–John is the issuer, Bill is the principal, and printing (with respect to the book resource) is the right being granted. Grants may be chained together either through direct trust of the issuer or transitively through licenses that grant rights to issue other licenses. As an example of the latter situation consider the following two licenses:

1. Alice says, "Bob has the right to issue a license to anyone to print the book."
2. Bob says, "Carol has the right to print the book."

If only Alice is implicitly trusted by the DRM system, then license #2 alone is insufficient to prove that Carol has the right to print the book. However, if both licenses #1 and #2 are present then the XrML evaluator can determine that Alice granted Bob the right to issue licenses such as license #2, and therefore the presence of both licenses proves Carol has the right to print the book.

Two other features of XrML 2.X are particularly important in the DRM space. First, XrML 2.X licenses may include patterns, variables and quantifiers anywhere within a grant. This allows us to write licenses such as "Alice says, 'Anyone who can read the book has the right to print the book,' " where one or more clauses of the licenses are instantiated at evaluation time. Without such expressions it is difficult to write licenses that refer to groups of principals or resources (especially resources that may not yet exist at the time the license is granted). Second, XrML 2.X licenses may also contain *prerequisite rights* that condition the grant contained within the license. If the grant in a license contains one or more prerequisite rights, then the grant is valid only in the presence of other licenses that prove that the prerequisites are also satisfied. For example, suppose Alice issues a license that says, "Bob has the right to read the book if Bob is a member of the book club." In this license the phrase "if Bob is a member of the book club" is a prerequisite right; the license is only valid in the presence of other licenses that prove Bob's membership in the club.

The prerequisite rights feature implies that the "compliance checking" algorithm for XrML 2.X is more complicated than simple "chain walking," such as that used by X.509/PKIX certificates [13]. When evaluating an X.509/PKIX certificate, the job of the compliance checker is to construct a valid chain of related certificates (a path through the certificate graph) from a trusted root certificate to the end-entity certificate that needs to be validated. In contrast, evaluating an XrML 2.X license may require constructing a valid directed acyclic graph (DAG) that proves multiple conditions in parallel in order to prove the validity of a single license. Each additional prerequisite right in an encountered license creates an additional branch to be satisfied. (In the degenerate case where no prerequisite rights are present the DAG collapses down to a single chain of licenses.) Thus, the complexity of a general-purpose rights expression language like XrML 2.X necessitates a similarly advanced license compliance checker (policy evaluator).

Perhaps the most challenging issue yet to resolve in the field of policy expression languages is the tension that arises naturally when attempting to represent liability-based systems such as copyright law through explicit expressions of rights or permissions. Policy evaluators want expressions and credentials that can be evaluated and determined to be true facts or false statements. Evaluating laws, however, often calls for a fact-finder to balance competing interests and make judgment calls[2]. It is possible that short-term progress can be made by establishing safe harbors for system behaviors that approximate the balance of interests [6], but long-term solutions remain hidden.

3   Evaluating Policy Expressions

When we think about policy management systems we tend to focus first on the types of statements we want to make and how parties will author them. Once a set of semantics for policy statements has been agreed to our attention turns to designing algorithm to evaluate such statements. The policy evaluator has to be able to reason correctly about all the types of policy statements and credentials it

---

[2] The canonical example of the potential fuzziness of copyright law in the U.S. is the process of determining whether a particular use of a copyrighted work is fair or infringing. The fact-finder is directed (17 USC 107) to consider and weigh at least four different factors in each case. Under the U.S. copyright regime it is impossible to know whether a particular use is a fair use without an inquiry and determination by a court of law.

may encounter when making a trust decision, thus the design of the evaluator is going to be influenced by the design of the language. This is especially true in the DRM case, as the DRM policy evaluator may need to inspect and verify many different credentials in order to make its decision[3]. A DRM policy evaluator has to decide for each requested access whether the policy (or policies) relevant to the request allows it to occur, given the credentials. This formulation of DRM policy evaluation is the "compliance checking" decision problem in trust management [3], and since the policies and credentials governing access to a resource managed by the DRM system may be arbitrarily complex, it is clear that our DRM policy evaluator is just an instance of a robust, general-purpose trust management engine.

Starting with the development of PolicyMaker [3] we have seen a succession of active research [2,4] and commercial deployment [10] of general-purpose trust management engines. The attractiveness of this approach has grown with the increased complexity of distributed systems as well as the types of resources that need to be protected. In the .NET Framework's Common Language Runtime, for example, the trust management engine at the core of the policy system is responsible for dynamically associating authorizations with every piece of executable code loaded into a process. Content distribution adds another dimension (or two) to the problem, because the set of resources to be protected is in fact the entire set of content potentially available to the client over the network, and the types of activities authorized with respect to any particular piece of content may be arbitrarily precise. That is, the set of objects to be managed by a DRM system is unbounded (all potentially-available content), and even if the set of subjects granted access to that content is limited to a small number of users, the number of credentials granting access rights to those users is also likely to be unbounded. Paradoxically, the fact that these sets are unbounded makes general-purpose trust management engines *more* attractive as policy evaluators as it is the programmatic nature of a trust management engine that allows it to efficiently deal with instances drawn from arbitrarily large sets of subjects, objects and credentials.

While trust management algorithms may work well in policy environments with potentially unbounded input sets, human reasoning suffers. One of the primary lessons learned from real-world implementations of trust management engines is that they are often too general (and thus too complex) for most users to be able to reason about effectively. DRM systems will need complex policy evaluators in order to perform the reasoning and decision-making tasks we desire, but system builders will also need to make engineering tradeoffs to simplify the model wherever possible for users. By way of example, the .NET Framework initially exposes a "simplified" policy model and administration tools that were designed to be much easier to understand than a general-purpose trust management engine yet still meet the needs of most customer scenarios. For users and administrators who require more functionality than that exposed

---

[3] As DRM systems provide conditional access to content they manage, at a minimum access decisions are always based on at least two sets of statements: content-specific policies and credentials that relate to the party requesting access to the content.

in the simplified model it is possible to "dive beneath the surface" and access the full power of the underlying trust management engine. Such tradeoffs and multi-tiered policy authoring and administration systems will almost certainly be necessary if generalized DRM systems are to be successful.

The need for good user interfaces for describing and configuring trust management policies is an open work area for DRM system policy evaluators. One of the major challenges of any security system is creating a management interface that is comprehensible to its users. Lack of an easy-to-understand interface can significantly slow or completely inhibit acceptance of a new technology[4]. The move from trust management models based solely on programming languages [2,3,4] to hybrid models that include more familiar management structures [10] is indicative of the types of improvements that need to be made in tools for creating and inspecting content policies and credentials. Such improvements will be especially important given the complexity of general-purpose rights expressions languages.

4   Projecting Policy Expressions with Confidence into Remote Environments

In addition to authoring and evaluating policy expressions, a DRM system operating across multiple nodes in a network must be able to accomplish a third important task: projecting policy to remote nodes with confidence that the policy will be respected. Fear about platform behavior is anathema to the distribution of information, and such fear is rampant today across all segments of potential DRM users. Owners of digital content will not distribute their works to platforms they consider "hostile" (or potentially so) and the same is true of individual users requested to reveal private information to remote systems. Every content owner needs some way to be convinced that the remote system receiving his or her valuable information will behave as the owner expects, which ultimately means that the remote system will implement the policy that the content owner has defined and associated with his content.

In computer systems security research, we routinely design security protocols that are grounded in trusted computing bases (TCBs). Policy authors must implicitly trust TCBs to operate correctly and behave in accordance with their design parameters, for any TCB is ultimately capable of violating the policy it is supposed to enforce. For local policy enforcement we care about the local TCB that is interpreting the policy, but in DRM systems is it not sufficient for the content owner to trust the TCB for the system on which he creates (authors) the policy for his content[5]. Additionally, the content owner must also

---

[4] As an example, consider the poor performance to date of authentication protocols based on X.509/PKIX client certificates. Cumbersome user enrollment protocols and procedures, coupled with inadequate user interfaces for communicating key- and certificate-related information to users, has blocked significant use of the technology.

[5] Without loss of generality we assume here that the content owner is also the author of the content access policy in a DRM system. Of course the content owner may have delegated that authority to another party (e.g. the operator of a digital library).

have confidence that remote nodes receiving the policy will behave as the author expects and faithfully implement the defined policies. That is, in DRM systems we need the ability to be able to prove to the local node (and, ultimately, the content owner) that a remote node is operating with and relying on a TCB with known properties. (Depending on the scenario we may also need to prove to the remote node that the local node is running a TCB with certain properties.) Only after all parties to the transaction are convinced that the relevant network nodes are operating with behaviors that are defined, understood and acceptable can the content transaction occur.

In order to prove their existence and operation to a remote entity, DRM system node TCBs need an additional property: *attestability*. An *attestable TCB* is a TCB that is able to convince a remote party that it is running and behaving according to some specification[6]. Specifically, an attestable TCB must have four key properties: it must be open, auditable, comprehensible and provable to a remote party. The need for openness is obvious: parties depending on the behavior of a TCB must be able to inspect the construction of the TCB in order to convince themselves that the TCB implements its specification correctly. Once the TCB is running, it must be possible to audit its behavior and check for deviations from the specification, thus the need for the second property. Comprehensibility is an aspect of openness but deserves to be called out explicitly: it is important that the operation of the TCB not only be observable (open) but also understandable by those observing it[7]. (There is an obvious tension here between the need to make the policy evaluator more complex–to handle the various types of authorizations and resources–and the need to make it "attestable.") Finally, the TCB must support one or more mechanisms to prove to remote parties that it is operating.

There are two separate industry initiatives underway currently that are attempting to build attestable TCBs on top of personal computer hardware and software: the Trusted Computing Platform Alliance (TCPA) [12,16,17] and Microsoft's "Palladium" initiative[8]. TCPA is specifying changes to the PC hardware platform to allow the platform to make attestations about the entire software stack running on the computer (starting with the BIOS boot block). In contrast, the goal of "Palladium" is to create a separate, parallel execution en-

---

[6] It is important to note that a TCB is attestable relative to some threat model that is part of the behavior specification. For example, an attestable TCB that depends on a hardware-based cryptographic key for the attestability property only has that property so long as the hardware containing the key material has not been compromised. There are thus many flavors of attestability depending on the mechanism used to make and convey the proof of correct operation.

[7] One fact implied by the need for comprehensibility is that it is not sufficient to simply publish the source code for a software-based TCB. Additionally, the algorithms used in the source code must be understandable to all observers. This means, for example, that we may need to use simpler, less-efficient algorithms inside a TCB than we would otherwise. The most likely place such a need will arise initially is in number-theoretic algorithms (e.g. bignum multiplication).

[8] Microsoft is also a member of the TCPA.

vironment inside the computer that is rigidly controlled by the user, and make attestations only about code loaded and executing in that parallel environment.

Both TCPA and "Palladium" leverage hardware-based public-key cryptography to generate attestations about software. A hardware component[9] is added to the PC motherboard that can perform RSA digital signatures and compute SHA1 cryptographic hash values (along with other cryptographic operations). The component is similar to a smartcard core–it includes a small amount of physical storage and one or more RSA key pairs. The hardware component computes the SHA1 hash value of the software stack of interest[10]. A digital signature over the hash value is then created by an RSA key that was certified by some third party as being associated with the cryptographic hardware component. The digital signature together with whatever certifications the third party provided for the signing key forms the attestation. Whether the attestation will convince a remote party is thus an instance of the typical scenario for using some form of public key infrastructure: the remote party must be convinced to his satisfaction that the RSA signing key belongs to a TCPA- (respectively, "Palladium"-) enabled platform. Assuming that the certifications are sufficient to accomplish this, the remote party can further deduce that a particular set of software is executing on the machine.

The attestations produced in TCPA- or "Palladium"-based systems are necessarily conditioned on maintaining the integrity of the cryptographic hardware. If the hardware is compromised then it is no longer possible to prove that the TCB is actually running, since the hash value computed by the hardware could be incorrect or the private key could be extracted from the chip and made to sign non-corresponding hash values. When evaluating an attestation produced on one of these systems the remote/relying party must evaluate the risk that the generating node's hardware has been compromised. Hardware significantly improves the security of the attesting keys over what is possible to do with software alone and addresses the vast majority of scenarios that require shared attestations, but relying parties must still understand the risk profiles and weigh them against their particular scenario.

We began this section by describing policy projection in DRM systems; it should now be clear that attestable TCBs are one mechanism for doing so. A content owner distributing his content can ask a remote node to prove it is running a TCB that can understand the owner's policy (and will enforce it) before sending content to the node. In fact, once we have an attestable TCB, the TCB itself can make attestations recursively about the code running on top of it, so a stack of related attestations could be required. Ultimately, though, everything depends on the attestable TCB and the fact that all parties understand the TCB and believe that it operates properly.

---

[9] In TCPA the hardware component is called the "Trusted Platform Module" (TPM). In "Palladium" it is called the "security support component" (SSC).

[10] In TCPA everything from the boot block forward can be hashed; in "Palladium" the software of interest is a security kernel that runs in a special CPU mode. How the two types of systems guarantee that the software of interest is hashed is beyond the scope of this paper.

The attempts to build attestable TCBs described above depend on hardware cryptographic components for some core key storage and cryptographic computation. Assuming that the hardware components have not been tampered with it is possible to use the hardware to attest to the operation of a software component; the software component can then recursively attest to the operation of other pieces of software "higher up the stack." Software components within the TCB can be inspected and audited for proper operation, but the same is not easily true for hardware components. We need to figure out how to build the hardware components of an attestable TCB so that they too are open, auditable and comprehensible to all parties. Today we implicitly trust the manufacturer of the hardware that the parts behave as specified[11], and it is unclear what we can do to improve the accessibility of any hardware component.

5   Summary

In this paper I have summarized three policy-related technical challenges and some approaches to solving them currently being pursued by DRM system builders. From a policy perspective, the ultimate goal of a distributed DRM system is for content authors to be able to project policies governing their content into remote environments with confidence that those policies will be respected by the remote nodes. The first policy-related challenge is to define an interoperable rights expression language that is sufficiently expressive that it can encode the types of content policies desired while still being comprehensible to content users. Finding the right balance between usability and complexity when designing DRM policy evaluators is the second challenge and in many ways progress in this area is co-dependent on advancements in policy languages. Finally, once we have a widely-accepted, interoperable rights expression language and policy evaluators that can interpret policies and credentials authored in the language, we will also need to create attestable TCBs to serve as the foundations of DRM system nodes. Content owners, distributors and consumers must mutually have confidence that all nodes participating in a DRM system will behave as expected in order for content and their corresponding policies to be introduced into and flow through the system.

References

1. J. Ayars, *XMCL–the eXtensible Media Commerce Language*, draft as of June 2001. Available at http://xmcl.org/specification.html.
2. M. Blaze, J. Feigenbaum, and A. D. Keromytis, "KeyNote: Trust Management for Public Key Infrastructures," *Proceedings of the Sixth International Workshop on Security Protocols*, B. Christianson, B. Crispo, W. Harbinson and M. Roe, eds., Lecture Notes in Computer Science **1550**, Springer-Verlag, NY (1999), 59–63.

---

[11] To be precise, while it is possible today to inspect a hardware component and deduce its operation, the process can be quite time-consuming and may require specialized instruments. (Not many people have the skills and equipment to "shave the top off a chip" and probe its inner workings to confirm behavior.)

3. M. Blaze, J. Feigenbaum, and J. Lacy, "Decentralized Trust Management," *Proceedings 1996 IEEE Symposium on Security and Privacy*, 164–173, May 1996.

4. Y.-H. Chu, J. Feigenbaum, B. LaMacchia, P. Resnick and M. Strauss, "REFEREE: Trust Management for Web Applications," *Proceedings of the Sixth International World Wide Web Conference*, Santa Clara, CA, April 1997. Reprinted in Computer Networks and ISDN Systems 29 (1997), 953-964.

5. "eXtensible Rights Markup Language (XrML) 2.1," submission by ContentGuard to the OASIS Rights Language Technical Committee, May 2002. Available at `http://www.oasis-open.org/committees/rights/documents/xrml200205.zip`.

6. B. Fox and B. LaMacchia, "A Safe Harbor for Designers of DRM Systems," *Communications of the ACM*, to appear.

7. S. Godik and T. Moses, eds., "OASIS eXtensible Access Control Markup Language (XACML)," OASIS eXtensible Access Control Markup Language Technical Committee, Working Draft, September 2002.

8. P. Hallam-Baker and E. Maler, eds., "Assertions and Protocol for the OASIS Security Assertion Markup Language (SAML)," OASIS XML-Based Security Services Technical Committee, May 2002.

9. R. Iannella, ed., "Open Digital Rights Language (ODRL), Version 1.1." Available at `http://odrl.net/1.1/ODRL-11.pdf`.

10. B. LaMacchia, S. Lange, M. Lyons, R. Martin and K. Price, *.NET Framework Security*, Addison-Wesley, April 2002.

11. Moving Picture Experts Group (MPEG), ISO/IEC JTC1/SC29/WG11. Working documents available at
`http://mpeg.telecomitalialab.com/working_documents.htm`.

12. S. Pearson, ed., *Trusted Computing Platforms, TCPA Technology in Context*, Prentice Hall PTR, July 2002.

13. PKIX Working Group, Internet Engineering Task Force. RFC 3280, "Internet X.509 Public Key Infrastructure: Certificate and Certificate Revocation List (CRL) Profile," R. Housley, W. Ford, W. Polk, D. Solo, eds., April 2002. Available at `http://www.ietf.org/rfc/rfc3280.txt`.

14. H. Reddy, Chairperson, OASIS Rights Language Technical Committee. Charter and documents availabe at `http://www.oasis-open.org/committees/rights/`.

15. M. Stefik, *The Digital Property Rights Language, Manual and Tutorial, Version 1.02*, September 18th, 1996. Xerox Palo Alto Research Center, Palo Alto, CA.

16. Trusted Computing Platform Alliance, *TCPA Main Specification, Version 1.1b*. Available at `http://www.trustedcomputing.org/docs/main%20v1_1b.pdf`.

17. Trusted Computing Platform Alliance, *TCPA PC Specific Implementation Specification, Version 1.00*. Available at `http://www.trustedcomputing.org/docs/TCPA_PCSpecificSpecification_v100.pdf`.

Public Key Broadcast Encryption
for Stateless Receivers

Yevgeniy Dodis and Nelly Fazio

Courant Institute of Mathematical Sciences
New York University
New York, NY 10012, USA
{dodis,fazio}@cs.nyu.edu

Abstract. A *broadcast encryption* scheme allows the sender to securely distribute data to a dynamically changing set of users over an insecure channel. One of the most challenging settings for this problem is that of *stateless receivers*, where each user is given a fixed set of keys which cannot be updated through the lifetime of the system. This setting was considered by Naor, Naor and Lotspiech [17], who also present a very efficient "Subset Difference" (SD) method for solving this problem. The efficiency of this method (which also enjoys efficient traitor tracing mechanism and several other useful features) was recently improved by Halevi and Shamir [12], who called their refinement the "Layered SD" (LSD) method. Both of the above methods were originally designed to work in the centralized symmetric key setting, where only the trusted designer of the system can encrypt messages to users. On the other hand, in many applications it is desirable not to store the secret keys "on-line", or to allow untrusted users to broadcast information. This leads to the question of building a *public key* broadcast encryption scheme for stateless receivers; in particular, of extending the elegant SD/LSD methods to the public key setting. Naor et al. [17] notice that the natural technique for doing so will result in an enormous public key and very large storage for every user. In fact, [17] pose this question of reducing the public key size and user's storage as the first open problem of their paper. We resolve this question in the affirmative, by demonstrating that an $O(1)$ size public key can be achieved for both of SD/LSD methods, in addition to the same (small) user's storage and ciphertext size as in the symmetric key setting.

1 Introduction

BROADCAST ENCRYPTION. Broadcast encryption provides a convenient way to distribute digital content to subscribers over an insecure broadcast channel. Namely, it allows the sender to deliver information to a dynamically changing sets of users in such a way that only the "qualified" users can recover the data. Not surprisingly, it has found many applications including pay-TV systems, distribution of copyrighted material, streaming audio/video and many others.

J. Feigenbaum (Ed.): DRM 2002, LNCS 2696, pp. 61–80, 2003.

Since its introduction by Fiat and Naor [8], the problem received significant attention, and many of its variants have been studied. To name just a few, the set of receivers can be fixed, slowly changing or rapidly changing; the scheme can support a single, bounded or unbounded number of broadcasts; it might or might not be possible to periodically refresh users' secret keys; the scheme might support bounded or unbounded number of "revoked" users; it might be possible to trace "pirates" who gave away an illegal decryption device (this is called *traitor tracing*); the scheme could be private or public key based; etc. We mention just several of the relevant works [23,15,16,24,4,5,9,14,10,18,22].

We study one of the most difficult variants of the problem when the receivers are *stateless*. Namely, each user is given a fixed set of keys which cannot be updated through the lifetime of the system. In particular, they do not change when other users join or leave the system, or evolve based on the history of past transmissions. Instead, each transmission must be decrypted solely on the base of the fixed initial configuration of each user's decryption device. As argued by Naor, Naor and Lotspiech [17] (who were the first to explicitly concentrate on this scenario), the stateless receivers case is quite common. For example, the receivers might not be constantly on-line to view past history or update their secret keys, or the keys might be put "once-and-for-all" into a tamper-resistant device. Additionally, the scheme should support an unbounded number of broadcasts, and be capable — at least in principle — to revoke an a-priori unbounded number of users (possibly at the cost of reduced efficiency). In particular, even the coalition of *all* the "non-privileged" users should not be able to decrypt a given transmission, even if this set is adaptively chosen by a central adversary. Finally, the above features also imply that consecutive broadcasts can revoke arbitrary and potentially unrelated subsets of users, without the need of any "key maintenance".

Up to date, the only type of scheme enjoying all these properties was designed by Naor et al. [17] (and was recently improved by Halevi and Shamir [12]). We will describe these schemes in more detail shortly.

PUBLIC VS. SYMMETRIC KEY. As we mentioned, one important distinction between various broadcast encryption schemes is whether they are public key or symmetric key based. In the latter variant, only the trusted designer of the system can broadcast data to the receivers. In other words, in order to encrypt the content, one needs to know some sensitive information (typically, the secret keys of all the users of the system) whose disclosure will compromise the security of the system. Even though symmetric key broadcast encryption is sufficient for many applications, it has a few shortcomings. For example, it requires the sender to store all the secret keys of the system, making it a single point of failure. Additionally, in certain situations we would like to allow possibly untrusted users to broadcast information, which is not possible in the symmetric setting.

In contrast, in the public key setting the trusted designer of the system publishes a short public key which enables anybody to broadcast data, thus overcoming the above mentioned deficiencies of the symmetric setting.

The original schemes of [17] were primarily designed for the symmetric key setting. Briefly, the so called *Subset-Cover* methodology of [17] (described in detail later) has the system designer (called the *Center*) generate many "computationally unrelated" secret keys $k_1, \ldots, k_w$ (where w is "large") and distribute various subsets of these keys to different users. To encrypt the message to a specified subset of privileged users, a certain small, carefully chosen subset of these keys is used. Even though this suggests that the Center must store all w keys, this typically does not have to be the case. Indeed, standard symmetric key tools like pseudorandom functions can be used to significantly compress the storage requirement of the Center (typically, to a single random seed). This is indeed the case for the two specific instantiations of the Subset-Cover framework proposed by [17] — the *Complete Subtree* (CS) method and a more efficient *Subset Difference* (SD) method — as well as for the further improved *Layered Subset Difference* (LSD) method of [12]. Similarly, even though each user might need to have too many of the secret keys $k_1, \ldots, k_w$ (which is really the case in the more efficient SD/LSD methods), it is possible — albeit somewhat more difficult — to compress the user's storage using similar tools, as was indeed done by [17].

As already noted by Naor et al. [17], the general Subset-Cover framework can in principle be adapted to the public key setting, by having each key k_j replaced by some pair of public/secret keys (PK_j, SK_j). Unfortunately, the simple compression methods of the symmetric key setting are much harder to come by in the public key setting. Even ignoring the problem with the user's storage, the natural implementation will have to publish all the local public keys $PK_1, \ldots, PK_w$, yielding a huge public key for the system. Naor et al. [17] briefly mention that the tools from *Identity-Based Cryptography* [20] seem to overcome this problem (we explain this below). In particular, they seem to resolve it completely at least for the (less efficient) CS method, where each user needs to know very few secret keys anyway. However, the Identity-Based Encryption (IBE) scheme alone does not seem to be sufficient for the more efficient SD/LSD methods, since it does not resolve the problem of compressing large storage requirement of each user. In fact, the question of efficiently extending the SD (and similar LSD) method(s) to the public key setting was given as the first open problem in [17].

OUR MAIN RESULT. We resolve this problem in the affirmative, by non-trivially utilizing the concept of *Hierarchical Identity-Based Encryption* (HIBE) [11,13]. In particular, we show that one can get essentially all the benefits of the symmetric key versions of the SD/LSD methods (including the same small storage per user) in the public key setting, while having a fixed *constant size* public key. As an intermediate step toward this goal, we indicate which changes should be made to the general Subset-Cover framework of [17] in order to translate it to the public key setting, and also formally verify that "plain" IBE is indeed sufficient to translate the (less efficient) CS method to the public key setting. The particular parameters we get can be summarized as follows when revoking r out of N total users (in all cases, the public key size and the storage of the Center are $O(1)$):

- **CS method**. The ciphertext consists of $r \log(N/r)$ identity based encryptions, each users stores $O(\log N)$ keys and needs to perform a single identity based decryption.
- **SD method**. The ciphertext consists of $(2r - 1)$ hierarchical identity based encryptions (of "depth" at most $\log N$ each), each users stores $O(\log^2 N)$ keys and needs to perform a single hierarchical identity based decryption.
- **LSD method**. For any $\epsilon > 0$, the ciphertext consists of $O(r/\epsilon)$ hierarchical identity based encryptions (of "depth" at most $\log N$ each), each users stores $O(\log^{1+\epsilon} N)$ keys and needs to perform a single hierarchical identity based decryption.

Interestingly, when instantiated with the best currently known IBE [3] and HIBE [11] schemes, the CS method actually becomes slightly preferable to the "in principle" more efficient SD/LSD methods. This is due to the fact that the length of the encryption of the specific HIBE [11] is proportional to the "depth" in the hierarchy (see Appendix A). Thus, the actual transmission rate in SD/LSD methods deteriorates to $O(r \log N)$, as in the CS method (while the latter still having a smaller storage requirement per user and a slightly cheaper decryption time). Still, if a more efficient HIBE is found, the original "transmission rate" advantages of the SD/LSD methods will again kick into effect.

COMPARISON TO EXISTING PUBLIC KEY SCHEMES. There already exist several (quite similar to each other) public key broadcast encryption schemes [18,22,6] in the stateless receivers scenario, all based on the decisional Diffie-Hellman assumption. However, all these schemes can revoke up to at most an a-priori fixed number of users, $r_{\max}$. Moreover, the size of the transmission is $O(r_{\max})$ even if no users are revoked. In contrast, the SD/LSD methods allow to revoke a dynamically changing (and potentially unbounded) number of users r, at the cost of having $O(r)$-size ciphertext transmission. More importantly, the reason the schemes of [18,22,6] support only a bounded number of revoked users, is that the public key (as well as encryption/decryption times) are proportional to $r_{\max}$. In contrast, the analogs of CS/SD/LSD schemes we construct all have a constant size public key, and the decryption time is at most logarithmic in the total number of users N. Finally, the schemes of [18,22,6] support only a limited form of traitor tracing (either "non-black-box" or "black-box confirmation"), while (as was shown in [17]) the CS/SD/LSD methods enjoy a significantly more powerful kind of "black-box" traitor tracing.

On a technical note, the Subset-Cover framework of [17] supports only the so called CCA1-security [2,19] (chosen ciphertext security in the pre-processing mode [7]), since the message is encrypted independently with several "computationally unrelated" keys. On the other hand, the recently proposed scheme of [6] supports full chosen ciphertext security (so called CCA2 [2,7]). Even though it seems hard to extend the Subset-Cover framework to achieve CCA2-security, it is possible to achieve a slightly relaxed (but essentially as useful) notion of gCCA2-security recently proposed by [21,1], as we will discuss later.

2   Definitions

2.1   Broadcast Encryption

Definition 1 (BROADCAST ENCRYPTION SCHEME).
A Broadcast Encryption Scheme is a quadruple of poly-*time algorithms* (KeyGen, Reg, Enc, Dec), *where:*

- KeyGen, *the* key generation algorithm, *is a probabilistic algorithm used by the Center to set up all the parameters of the scheme.* KeyGen *takes as input a security parameter* 1^λ *and possibly a revocation threshold* r_{max} *(i.e. the maximum number of users that can be revoked) and generate the public key* PK *and the master secret key* SK.
- Reg, *the* registration algorithm, *is a probabilistic algorithm used by the Center to compute the secret initialization data to be delivered to a new user when he/she subscribes to the system.*
- Enc, *the* encryption algorithm, *is a probabilistic algorithm used to encapsulate a given session key* k *in such a way that the revoked users cannot recover it.* Enc *takes as input the public key* PK, *the session key* k *and a set* $\mathcal{R}$ *of revoked users (with* $|\mathcal{R}| \leq r_{max}$, *if a threshold has been specified to the* KeyGen *algorithm) and returns the ciphertext to be broadcast.*
- Dec, *the* decryption algorithm, *is a deterministic algorithm that takes as input the secret data of a user* u *and the ciphertext broadcast by the Center and returns the session key* k *that was sent if* u *was not in the set* $\mathcal{R}$ *when the ciphertext was constructed, or the special symbol* $\perp$ *otherwise.*

All the schemes that we will discuss are completely flexible in terms of the revocation threshold r_{max}, i.e. they can tolerate an unbounded number of revoked users, at the only cost of increasing the length of the ciphertext.

Following [17], we briefly define the CCA1-security of broadcast encryption (as stated earlier, one can define CCA2-security as well). Upon seeing the public key PK, the adversary repeatedly perform (in any adaptively-chosen order) the following two steps: (1) corrupt any user u, thus obtaining the secret information u got when joining the system (let us denote by $\mathcal{R}$ the final set of corrupted users; in case r_{max} is specified, we require $|\mathcal{R}| \leq r_{max}$); (2) ask any user to decrypt a ciphertext of her choice. Then the adversary selects some session key k and gets back the value $\mathsf{Enc}(PK, k', \mathcal{R})$, where k' is either equal to k, or equal to a totally random session key. The scheme is CCA1-secure if no polynomial adversary can distinguish these two cases with non-negligible advantage.

2.2   Identity-Based Encryption

An *Identity-Based Encryption* (IBE) scheme is a Public Key Cryptosystem where public keys can be arbitrary bitstrings, from which a trusted entity known as *Private Key Generator* (PKG) can extract the corresponding private keys.

The main advantage of such Cryptosystems is that each user can have as public key some identifier ID that everybody knows (e.g. his/her e-mail address), so that there is no need any more for the use of certificates binding a given public key to its legitimate holder.

Although a formal definition of IBE cryptosystems have been known for a while [20], the first fully functional proposal fitting all the requirements appeared only quite recently in [3] (see Appendix A).

Definition 2 (IDENTITY-BASED ENCRYPTION SCHEME).
An Identity-Based Encryption scheme is a quadruple of poly-*time algorithms* (Setup, Extract, Encrypt, Decrypt), *where:*

- Setup *is a probabilistic algorithm used by the PKG to initialize the global parameters of the system. Given a security parameter* 1^λ*,* Setup *generates the system parameters* params *and a secret key* master-key*. Then, the PKG publishes* params *as the global public key and keeps* master-key *secret.*
- Extract *is a (possibly) probabilistic algorithm used by the PKG to derive private keys from arbitrary identifiers.* Extract *takes as input* params*, an identifier* ID $\in \{0,1\}^*$ *and* master-key*, and returns the private key d capable of decrypting ciphertexts intended for the holder of the given identifier* ID*.*
- Encrypt *is a probabilistic algorithm used to securely send a message M to the user with identifier* ID *within the* IBE *system with global public key* params*.* Encrypt *takes as input* params*,* ID *and M and returns a ciphertext C.*
- Decrypt *is a deterministic algorithm used to recover the message M from a ciphertext C intended for a user with identifier* ID*.* Decrypt *takes as input* params*,* ID*, C and the private key d (corresponding to* ID*) and returns M.*

Clearly, these four algorithms should satisfy the standard consistency constraint: for all possible values of the global parameters params output by Setup, and for all identifiers ID $\in \{0,1\}^*$, if d is the private key extracted from ID using master-key then for all message M it must be that:

$$\mathsf{Decrypt}(\texttt{params}, \mathrm{ID}, \mathsf{Encrypt}(\texttt{params}, \mathrm{ID}, M), d) = M.$$

As before, we briefly define the CCA1-security of IBE's, even though the currently known IBE's support a stronger kind of CCA2-security[1]. Upon seeing the public params, the adversary repeatedly perform (in any adaptively-chosen order) the following two steps: (1) execute an extraction query for any identifier ID that she chooses, thus learning the corresponding private key d of this user (let us denote by $\mathcal{R}$ the final set of corrupted users); (2) ask any user with identifier ID to decrypt a given ciphertext C of her choice. Then the adversary selects some message M and some identifier ID $\notin \mathcal{R}$, and gets back the value Encrypt(params, ID, M'), where M' is either equal to M, or is equal to a totally random message. The scheme is CCA1-secure if no polynomial adversary can distinguish these two cases with non-negligible advantage.

2.3   Hierarchical Identity-Based Encryption

An Hierarchical Identity-Based Encryption (HIBE) scheme is a natural and very powerful extension of a regular Identity-Based Encryption scheme. Intuitively,

---

[1] See [3] for the definition of CCA2-security for IBE.

HIBE allows to organize the users into a tree hierarchy. Each user gets the secret key from its parent in the hierarchy (and all the users share a few global parameters). Now, anybody can encrypt message to any given user by only knowing *its position in the hierarchy*, specified as an *ID-tuple* (or *hierarchical* identifier), $HID \equiv (ID_1, \ldots, ID_t)$. This means that the user is located at level t and its ancestors, starting from the parent up to the root, have hierarchical identifiers $(ID_1, \ldots, ID_{t-1})$, $(ID_1, \ldots, ID_{t-2})$, ..., (ID_1), root.

Definition 3 (HIERARCHICAL IDENTITY-BASED ENCRYPTION SCHEME).
A Hierarchical Identity-Based Encryption scheme is a five-tuple of probabilistic polynomial-time algorithms (Root Setup, Lower-level Setup, Extract, Encrypt, Decrypt), *where:*

- Root Setup *is run by* root *to start-up an instance of* HIBE. Root Setup *takes as input a security parameter* 1^λ, *and returns the global public key* params *to be made available to everybody, and the master secret key* master-key *to be known only by the* root.
- Lower-level Setup *takes as input an ID-tuple* $(ID_1, \ldots, ID_t)$ *(t > 0) and the corresponding secret key, and returns some local secret information which can be used in the* Extract *procedure below. Notice that the output cannot contain any parameter that needs to be made public, but only private information to be stored at the local node.*
- Extract *is run by a user with ID-tuple* $(ID_1, \ldots, ID_t)$ *(t = 0 corresponds to* root*) to compute, using* params, *its secret key, and maybe other local secret data output by* Lower-level Setup *when t > 0, the secret key for an immediate lower level child with ID-tuple of the form* $(ID_1, \ldots, ID_t, ID_{t+1})$.
- Encrypt *takes as input* params, *the recipient's ID-tuple* $(ID_1, \ldots, ID_t)$ *and a message M, and returns the ciphertext C intended for user* $(ID_1, \ldots, ID_t)$.
- Decrypt *is run by the user* $(ID_1, \ldots, ID_t)$ *to recover the plaintext M from the ciphertext C, given as input* params, $(ID_1, \ldots, ID_t)$, *C and the user's private key.*

As expected, the correctness property states that the user with hierarchical identifier $HID \equiv (ID_1, \ldots, ID_t)$ should always correctly recover messages encrypted for him/her. We notice that in the case of HIBE, all the ancestors of the given user can understand the messages encrypted for this user. For example, one way to do it would be to first derive the corresponding secret key for the descendant by running a series of Extract operations, and then to decrypt the ciphertext. In specific schemes, however, there might be a more efficient/direct way to perform such decryption. For example, the HIBE of [11] enjoys a more efficient decryption by any ancestor of the given node than by the node itself (see Appendix A).

Finally, we briefly define the CCA1-security of HIBE's[2]. Intuitively, it more or less states that only the designated user $(ID_1, \ldots, ID_t)$ *and its ancestors* can decrypt messages sent to this user, while no other user of the system can. Upon see-

---

[2] See [11] for the definition of CCA2-security for HIBE.

ing the public key `params`, the adversary repeatedly perform (in any adaptively-chosen order) the following two steps: (1) learn the private key d corresponding to any ID-tuple $(\mathrm{ID}_1, \ldots, \mathrm{ID}_t)$ that she chooses, by means of an *extraction query* (let us denote by $\mathcal{R}$ the final set of corrupted users); (2) ask any user with any ID-tuple $(\mathrm{ID}_1, \ldots, \mathrm{ID}_t)$ to decrypt a given ciphertext C of her choice. Then the adversary selects some message M and some ID-tuple $(\mathrm{ID}_1, \ldots, \mathrm{ID}_t)$ such that $(\mathrm{ID}_1, \ldots, \mathrm{ID}_i) \notin \mathcal{R}$ for $0 \leq i \leq t$ (so that no ancestor of this user is corrupted), and gets back the value $\mathsf{Encrypt}(\mathtt{params}, (\mathrm{ID}_1, \ldots, \mathrm{ID}_t), M')$, where M' is either equal to M, or is equal to a totally random message. The scheme is CCA1-secure if no polynomial adversary can distinguish these two cases with non-negligible advantage.

3   The Subset-Cover Framework

In [17], the authors presented the *Subset-Cover Framework* as a formal environment within which one can define and analyze the security of revocation schemes. Briefly, the main idea of the framework is to define a family $\mathcal{S}$ of subsets of the universe $\mathcal{N}$ of users in the system, and to associate each subset with a key, which is made available exactly to all the users belonging to the given subset. When the Center wants to broadcast a message to all the subscribers but those in some set $\mathcal{R}$, it "covers" the set $\mathcal{N} \setminus \mathcal{R}$ of "privileged" users using subsets from the family $\mathcal{S}$ (i.e. the Center determines a partition of $\mathcal{N} \setminus \mathcal{R}$, where all the subsets are elements of $\mathcal{S}$), and then encrypts the session key used to masquerade the message with all the keys associated to the subsets in the found partition.

A revocation scheme within the Subset-Cover framework is fully specified by defining the particular Subset-Cover family $\mathcal{S}$ used, the cover-finding algorithm and the key assignment employed to deliver to each user the keys corresponding to all the sets the user belongs to. We remark that the key assignment method does not necessarily give each user all the needed keys *explicitly*, but may provide some succinct representation sufficient to efficiently derive all the needed keys.

As specific examples, the *Complete Subtree* (CS) method and the *Subset Difference* (SD) method were formalized and proven secure within the Subset-Cover framework; recently, in [12] the *Layered Subset Difference* (LSD) method was introduced as an improvement on the SD method, that achieves a lower per user storage requirement at the cost of a small increase in the length of each broadcast.

Although all the above methods were proposed for the symmetric setting, in some applications it might be desirable to have revocation schemes within the Subset-Cover framework in the public key scenario. To this aim, in [17] the authors presented a general technique to transpose any Subset-Cover revocation scheme to the asymmetric setting. The basic idea of this method is to make the public keys associated to each subset in the family $\mathcal{S}$ available to all the (not necessarily trusted) parties interested in broadcasting information, in the form of a *Public Key File* (PKF).

The price paid for the full generality of this technique is a high inefficiency in term of storage required to maintain and distribute the PKF. However, for specific schemes, it might be possible to come up with public key cryptosystems that allows to compress the PKF to a reasonable size. For instance, it was already observed in [17] that the use of an Identity-Based Encryption (IBE) scheme (such as the one proposed in [3]) would be helpful for the CS method. A solution for the more interesting case of the SD method (or equivalently for the LSD scheme) was left as an open problem.

We answer the question in the affirmative, by showing that any Hierarchical Identity-Based Encryption (HIBE) scheme can be used to reduce the PKF to $O(1)$ size, while maintaining the same small storage for every user. As a warm-up, we first briefly describe the CS method (referring the interested reader to [17] for more details) and then we show how to take advantage of the properties of an IBE scheme to extend the CS method. Afterwards, we describe the SD method and its extension to the public key setting by means of any HIBE scheme. We also show that the same technique can be used for the LSD variant as well.

For each method, our emphasis will be on developing its characteristic key assignment to the users, since this is the main difficulty we will face. In other words, we will not discuss in any detail the algorithmic technicalities needed to find the subset cover for the set of privileged users, since these methods remain identical to the symmetric key setting.

A NOTE ON KEY INDISTINGUISHABILITY. To prove the generic security of the Subset-Cover framework for a given key assignment in the symmetric setting, [17] introduced an intermediate notion of *key indistinguishability*. Intuitively, it stated that any secret key k_j corresponding to the subset S_j remains pseudorandom to the adversary, even if she learns all the secret information belonging to all the users outside of S_j. Obviously, such intermediate notion does not make sense in the public key setting, since secret keys are never pseudorandom in public key cryptography. Instead, we notice that the argument of [17] easily extends to the public key setting, provided the public key encryption corresponding to the set S_j remains "secure" (in this case, CCA1-secure) even when the adversary learns all the secret information belonging to all the users outside of S_j. We omit the obvious formalization of this claim.

4 Public Key Extension of the CS Method

THE ORIGINAL SCHEME. In the CS scheme, the users are organized in a tree structure: for the sake of simplicity, let us assume that the total number N of users in the system is a power of 2 (i.e. $N = 2^t$, for some integer t), and let us associate each user to a leaf of the complete binary tree $\mathcal{T}$ of height t. The Subset-Cover family $\mathcal{S}$ is then set to be the collection of all the complete subtrees of $\mathcal{T}$. More precisely, if v_j is a node in $\mathcal{T}$, the generic $S_j \in \mathcal{S}$ is the set of all the leaves of the complete subtree of $\mathcal{T}$ rooted at v_j (thus, in this case $|\mathcal{S}| = 2N - 1$).

To associate a key to each element of $\mathcal{S}$, the Center simply assigns, during an initialization step, a random number $\mathcal{L}_j$ to each node v_j in $\mathcal{T}$, and then $\mathcal{L}_j$ is used to perform all the encryption/decryption operations relative to the subset S_j. Furthermore, since each user needs to know the keys corresponding to all the subsets he/she belongs to, during the subscription step the Center gives the subscriber all the keys $\mathcal{L}_j$ relative to each node v_j in the path from the root down to the leaf representing the subscriber.

Notice that also the Center needs to keep track of all these keys: to limit the memory usage, a solution could be to use a pseudo-random function to derive all the $2N - 1$ keys from some fixed, short seed.

As for the efficiency of the scheme, we notice that the storage requirement on each subscriber is just $O(\log N)$, with a transmission rate (i.e. the length of the broadcast message) of $r \log \frac{N}{r}$, due to the fact that the cover algorithm needs a logarithmic number of subtrees to exclude each of the r revoked users in $\mathcal{R}$ (see [17] for more details).

EXTENSION TO THE PUBLIC KEY SETTING. As mentioned above, a naive approach to the problem of transposing the CS method to the asymmetric setting yields a total number of $2N - 1$ public keys. The cause of the inefficiency of such solution is that all the public keys are stored explicitly in the PKF; to overcome this problem we have to employ a scheme that allows an implicit and compact representation of the PKF from which to easily extract the needed information: the functionalities of any Identity-Based Encryption scheme come handy in this situation, yielding the efficient solution described below.

As a preliminary step, a fixed mapping is introduced to assign an identifier $\mathrm{ID}(S_j)$ to each subset S_j of the family $\mathcal{S}$. For example, a simple mapping could be to label each edge in the complete binary tree $\mathcal{T}$ with 0 or 1 (depending on whether the edge connects the node with its right or left child), and then assign to the subset S_j rooted at v_j the bitstring obtained reading off all the labels in the path from the root down to v_j.

Afterwards, the Center runs the Setup algorithm of an IBE scheme to create an instance of the system in which it will play the role of the *Private Key Generator* (PKG). Then, the Center publishes the parameters of the system params and the description of the mapping used to assign an identifier to each subset: these two pieces of data constitute the PKF, and requires $O(1)$ space.

To generate the private key $\mathcal{L}_j^{\mathrm{PRI}}$ corresponding to each subset $S_j \in \mathcal{S}$, the Center sets:

$$\mathcal{L}_j^{\mathrm{PRI}} \leftarrow \mathsf{Extract}(\mathtt{params}, \mathrm{ID}(S_j), \mathtt{master\text{-}key}).$$

At this point, the Center can distribute to each subscriber the private data necessary to decrypt the broadcast, as in the original, symmetric scheme. Moreover, whenever a (not necessarily trusted) party wants to broadcast a message, it can encrypt the session key k used to protect the broadcast under the public keys $\mathcal{L}_{i_j}^{\mathrm{PUB}} = \mathrm{ID}(S_{i_j})$ relative to all the subsets that make up the cover of the chosen set of privileged users. To this aim, this party only needs to know the parameters of the IBE system params and the description of the mapping $\mathrm{ID}(\cdot)$, and then it can compute:

$$\mathcal{C}_j \leftarrow \mathsf{Encrypt}(\mathtt{params}, \mathrm{ID}(S_{i_j}), k)$$

for all the subset S_{i_j} in the cover.

SECURITY. The formal CCA1-security of the scheme follows almost immediately from the powerful security definition of IBE. Indeed, when revoking some set $\mathcal{R}$ of users, the adversary does not learn any of the secret keys used for transmitting the message to the remaining users $\mathcal{N} \backslash \mathcal{R}$ (since only sets disjoint from $\mathcal{R}$ are used in the cover), so the CCA1-security of broadcast encryption immediately follows by a simple hybrid argument over the sets covering $\mathcal{N} \backslash \mathcal{R}$.

A CONCRETE INSTANTIATION. Finally, if we apply the above idea in conjunction with the specific IBE scheme proposed in [3] (see Appendix A), the public key extension matches the original variant in all the efficiency parameters; more precisely, the storage requirement on each user is still $O(\log N)$ and the transmission rate is $r \log \frac{N}{r}$, where $r = |\mathcal{R}|$.

5 Public Key Extension of the SD Method

To improve the transmission rate, the SD scheme uses a more sophisticated Subset-Cover family $\mathcal{S}$: each user will belong to more subsets, thus allowing for greater freedom (and hence higher efficiency) in the choice of the cover. On the flip side, this will create a problem of compressing the user's storage which will need to be addressed.

As before, the users are associated to the leaves of the complete binary tree $\mathcal{T}$, but the generic subset S_{ij} is now defined in term of two nodes $v_i, v_j \in \mathcal{T}$ (with v_i ancestor of v_j), which we will call respectively *primary root* and *secondary root* of S_{ij}. Specifically, each subset S_{ij} consists of all the leaves of the subtree rooted at v_i except those in the subtree rooted at v_j [3].

Due to the large number of subsets that contain a given user, it is no longer possible to employ an information-theoretic key assignment, directly associating a random key to each element in the family $\mathcal{S}$ (as it was done in the CS method), because this would require each subscriber to store a huge amount of secret data: to overcome this problem, a more involved, computational technique is required.

The idea behind the solution proposed in [17] is to derive the set of actual keys $\{\mathcal{L}_{ij}\}$ from some (much smaller) set of "proto-keys" $\{\mathcal{P}_{ij}\}$ satisfying the following properties:

1. given the proto-key $\mathcal{P}_{ij}$ it is easy to derive the key $\mathcal{L}_{ij}$;
2. given the proto-key $\mathcal{P}_{il}$ it is easy to derive the proto-key $\mathcal{P}_{ij}$, for any node v_j descendent of node v_l;
3. it is computationally difficult to obtain any information about a proto-key $\mathcal{P}_{ij}$ without knowing the proto-key $\mathcal{P}_{il}$ for some ancestor v_l of v_j (and descendent of v_i).

In particular, the last property implies that given the knowledge of the key $\mathcal{L}_{ij}$ it is computationally difficult to recover the proto-key $\mathcal{P}_{ij}$.

---

[3] The denomination of the SD method is due to the fact that each subset S_{ij} can be expressed as the set-difference of the two subsets S_i and S_j as defined in the CS method: $S_{ij} = S_i \setminus S_j$.

Once we have defined a way to generate a family of proto-keys featuring the above properties (which we will call a "proto-key assignment"), it is possible to make available to each subscriber the $O(N)$ secret keys corresponding to all the subsets he/she belongs to, by giving him/her only $O(\log^2 N)$ proto-keys, as described below.

Let u be the leaf representing the user within the tree $\mathcal{T}$ and let $r_{\mathcal{T}}$ be the root of $\mathcal{T}$. Furthermore, let $r_{\mathcal{T}} \equiv u_0, u_1, \ldots, u_t \equiv u$ be all the ancestors of u on the path from $r_{\mathcal{T}}$ down to u, and denote by s_h the sibling of u_h, $h = 1, \ldots, t$.

By definition, the subtree difference sets S_{ij} containing u are precisely those whose primary root v_i is one of the u_h's and whose secondary root v_j is a descendent[4] of $s_{h'}$ for some $h' > h$.

For instance, among the subsets whose primary root is $r_{\mathcal{T}}$, the ones containing u are those whose secondary root v_j is a descendent of some s_h. Notice that, by the first property of the proto-keys assignment described above, to compute the key $\mathcal{L}_{r_{\mathcal{T}}v_j}$ corresponding to such subset, it is enough to know the proto-key $\mathcal{P}_{r_{\mathcal{T}}v_j}$, which in turn (for the second property) can be obtained from the proto-key $\mathcal{P}_{r_{\mathcal{T}}s_h}$; thus, by giving the user the $t = \log N$ proto-keys $\mathcal{P}_{r_{\mathcal{T}}s_1}, \ldots, \mathcal{P}_{r_{\mathcal{T}}s_t}$, he/she will be able to efficiently compute the keys relative to all the subsets $S_{r_{\mathcal{T}}v_j}$ he/she belongs to.

Repeating the same reasoning for all the $\log N$ ancestor u_h of u, we can conclude that $O(\log^2 N)$ proto-keys suffice to allow the user u to recover all the $O(N)$ relevant keys.

THE ORIGINAL SCHEME. We now describe the key assignment for the SD method of [17] as a particular instance of the proto-key assignment described above.

In the initialization phase, the Center associates to each internal node v_i in $\mathcal{T}$ a random number LABEL$_i$, which can be thought as the proto-key $\mathcal{P}_{ii}$ for the improper subtree difference set S_{ii}. Then, to generate the proto-keys for all the subsets S_{ij}, a pseudo random generator $\mathcal{G} : \{0,1\}^n \longrightarrow \{0,1\}^{3n}$ is used, where n is the desired length of the keys $\mathcal{L}_{ij}$. For notational convenience, given an input x, we will denote with $\mathcal{G}_L(x)$ the n leftmost bits of $\mathcal{G}(x)$, with $\mathcal{G}_R(x)$ the n rightmost bits of $\mathcal{G}(x)$, and with $\mathcal{G}_M(x)$ the remaining n central bits of $\mathcal{G}(x)$.

Using the generator $\mathcal{G}$, we can express the relationship between a proto-key $\mathcal{P}_{ij}$ and the proto-key $\mathcal{P}_{il}$ (with v_l parent of v_j) as follows[5]:

$$
\mathcal{P}_{ij} = \begin{cases} \mathcal{G}_L(\mathcal{P}_{il}) & \text{if } v_j \text{ is the left child of } v_l \\ \mathcal{G}_R(\mathcal{P}_{il}) & \text{if } v_j \text{ is the right child of } v_l \end{cases}
$$

Furthermore, the key $\mathcal{L}_{ij}$ associated to the subset S_{ij} can be derived from the proto-key $\mathcal{P}_{ij}$ as $\mathcal{L}_{ij} = \mathcal{G}_M(\mathcal{P}_{ij})$.

By construction, the first two properties of the proto-key assignment are satisfied; as for the third one, the use of a pseudorandom generator guarantees the computational hardness of obtaining any information about a proto-key $\mathcal{P}_{ij}$ or a key $\mathcal{L}_{ij}$, without knowledge of any proto-key $\mathcal{P}_{il}$, for some v_l ancestor of v_j.

---

[4] For our purposes, a node v will be considered among its own descendents.

[5] In [17], the authors refer to what we call here the "proto-key" $\mathcal{P}_{ij}$ as LABEL$_i$.

Notice that the Center can avoid to store all the $N - 1$ labels LABEL_i by reusing the technique of the generator $\mathcal{G}$. Namely, the Center associates to the root $r_{\mathcal{T}}$ of the tree $\mathcal{T}$ a random seed s of length n; to generate each LABEL_i, it repeatedly applies the generator $\mathcal{G}$ taking, at each edge on the path going from the root down to the node v_i, the left part $\mathcal{G}_L$ or right part $\mathcal{G}_R$ depending on the direction of the edge, and finally applying $\mathcal{G}_M$ once it gets to the node v_i.

As already observed, the use of a proto-key assignment allows to cut the storage requirement on the subscribers down to $O(\log^2 N)$. More interestingly, since in [17] the authors showed how to cover any privileged set excluding r revoked users using only $2r - 1$ subsets, the SD scheme enjoys an $O(r)$ transmission rate, thus being the only known broadcast encryption scheme supporting any number of revocations at the cost of a proportional increase in the length of the ciphertext (and independent of the total number of users).

EXTENSION TO THE PUBLIC KEY SETTING. To extend the SD scheme to the asymmetric scenario, one would like to generalize the basic idea used for the case of the CS method: namely, define an ID mapping for all the subsets $S_{ij} \in \mathcal{S}$ and then employ an IBE scheme to extract all the relevant private keys. However, as already observed, to avoid an explosion of the user's storage, it is necessary to use a scheme satisfying the characteristic properties of a "proto-key assignment", whereas ordinary IBE schemes do not seem to support the crucial property, since this requires the capability of deriving "children" proto-keys from a given proto-key. Luckily, the more powerful notion of general Hierarchical Identity-Based Encryption (such as the one recently proposed in [11]), offers all the functionalities needed, leading to the solution described below.

First, to define a mapping $\text{HID}(\cdot)$ assigning a hierarchical identifier to each set S_{ij} of the family $\mathcal{S}$, we will reuse the $\text{ID}(\cdot)$ mapping introduced in the public key extension of the CS method, which associates to each node in the tree $\mathcal{T}$ a bitstring of 0's and 1's, depending on its position within $\mathcal{T}$.

Preliminarily, we extend the $\text{ID}(\cdot)$ mapping to the improper subsets of the form S_{ii}, letting $\text{ID}(S_{ii}) = \text{ID}(v_i)$. Next, we notice that if v_i is an ancestor of v_j and we think of $\text{ID}(v_i)$ and $\text{ID}(v_j)$ as hierarchical sequences of one-digit identifiers (rather than as unique, monolithic IDs), then $\text{ID}(v_i)$ will be a prefix of $\text{ID}(v_j)$. So let us denote with $\text{ID}(v_j) \backslash \text{ID}(v_i)$ the *hierarchical* identifier made up by the sequence of single-bit identifiers in the suffix of $\text{ID}(v_j)$ coming right after the prefix $\text{ID}(v_i)$.

Now we can define the $\text{HID}(\cdot)$ mapping on all the elements of $\mathcal{S}$ as follows:

$$\text{HID}(S_{ij}) = (\text{ID}(S_{ii}), [\text{ID}(v_j) \backslash \text{ID}(v_i)], 2)$$

where the operator "," is used to highlight the juxtaposition of hierarchical identifiers. Notice, the depth of this identifier is two plus the depth of v_i relative to v_j in our tree, and the symbol 2 is used as terminator (we will see why soon).

Once the $\text{HID}(\cdot)$ mapping has been specified, to complete the initialization phase, the Center runs the Setup algorithm of a HIBE scheme and publishes params and a description of the mapping $\text{HID}(\cdot)$ as the Public Key File. Besides, the distribution of the secret decryption data to the subscribers will be carried out as another instantiation of the proto-keys assignment, as described below.

The key $\mathcal{L}_{ij}^{\mathrm{PRI}}$ relative to a given subset S_{ij} will be the private key extracted from the public key $\mathcal{L}_{ij}^{\mathrm{PUB}} = \mathrm{HID}(S_{ij})$. As described in Section 2.3, to extract the private key $\mathcal{L}_{ij}^{\mathrm{PRI}}$ from the hierarchical identifier $\mathrm{HID}(S_{ij}) = (\mathrm{ID}(S_{ii}), [\mathrm{ID}(v_j)\backslash\mathrm{ID}(v_i)], 2)$, it is necessary to know the private key $\mathcal{P}_{ij}$ of the local PKG corresponding to its parent $(\mathrm{ID}(S_{ii}), [\mathrm{ID}(v_j)\backslash\mathrm{ID}(v_i)])$, or of any ancestor of $\mathrm{HID}(S_{ij})$ lying higher in the tree hierarchy. Such key $\mathcal{P}_{ij}$ is defined to be the proto-key associated to S_{ij}; formally[6]:

$$\mathcal{L}_{ij}^{\mathrm{PRI}} \leftarrow \mathsf{Extract}(\mathbf{params}, (\mathrm{ID}(S_{ii}), [\mathrm{ID}(v_j)\backslash\mathrm{ID}(v_i)], 2), \mathcal{P}_{ij})$$
$$\mathcal{P}_{ij} \leftarrow \mathsf{Extract}(\mathbf{params}, (\mathrm{ID}(S_{ii}), [\mathrm{ID}(v_j)\backslash\mathrm{ID}(v_i)]), \mathcal{P}_{il})$$
$$\mathcal{P}_{ii} \leftarrow \mathsf{Extract}(\mathbf{params}, (\mathrm{ID}(S_{ii})), \mathbf{master\text{-}key})$$

where v_l is the parent of v_j, and $\mathbf{master\text{-}key}$ is the master key output by the Setup algorithm and known only to the root PKG, role that in our setting is played by the Center.

From the above definitions, it is clear that the first two properties of a proto-key assignment are fulfilled; on the other hand, the validity of the third one hinges upon the security of the HIBE scheme, that ensures the computational difficulty of obtaining a private key for any identifier without knowing the private key of a local PKG lying higher in the hierarchy of the system.

Direct consequence of the application of the proto-key assignment to the public key extension, is that the storage requirement on each subscriber is still $O(\log^2 N)$. On the other hand, the cover finding algorithm characteristic of the SD method ensures that $2r - 1$ ciphertexts will suffice in the worst case to broadcast the session key to all the privileged users in the system.

SECURITY. The formal CCA1-security of the scheme again follows almost immediately from the powerful security definition of HIBE. Indeed, when revoking some set $\mathcal{R}$ of users, none of the proto-keys the adversary learns is an ancestor of any of the hierarchical identifies corresponding to the sets covering $\mathcal{N}\backslash\mathcal{R}$. This property is fairly easy to verify, and a simple hybrid argument will again complete the security proof. We remark that only CCA1-security is achieved by the SD (as well as the CS) scheme(s), since the adversary is disallowed to ask the decryption oracle after the challenge is obtained.

A NOTE ON gCCA2-SECURITY. As mentioned earlier, it seems hard to achieve CCA2-security within the Subset-Cover framework. Intuitively, this is because each ciphertext ψ consists of an implicit representation of $\mathcal{N}\setminus\mathcal{R}$, along with as many encrypted copies of the message as there are subsets in the cover. Besides, each user can decrypt only one of such independent encryptions of the

---

[6] We remark that the values of keys and proto-keys are not uniquely defined by these probabilistic assignments. In particular, deriving the value of the "same" key twice from some of its ancestors will likely result in different keys. However, any value we get is equally functional by the definition of HIBE.

message. Hence, by arbitrarily modifying any one of such independent encryption components (say, corresponding to some subset S), the adversary can construct a "new" ciphertext which will be correctly decrypted by any user $u \in \mathcal{N} \setminus (\mathcal{R} \cup S)$.

On the other hand, the proposed scheme turns out to be gCCA2-secure if we assume that the underlying HIBE is CCA2-secure. Recall [1] that in order to assess gCCA2-security, we need to introduce a family of efficient equivalence relations $\{\mathcal{R}_u\}$, one for each user u [7]. While in a CCA2 attack the adversary cannot ask to see the decryption of just one ciphertext (i.e. the challenge), in the gCCA2 attack the adversary is forbidden to ask the decryption (according to user u) of all ciphertexts $\mathcal{R}_u$-equivalent to the challenge. For our purpose, we will use the following definition of $\mathcal{R}_u$-equivalence:

> Consider a user u and two ciphertexts ψ_1 and ψ_2, both covering u with the same subset S_u. We say that ψ_1 and ψ_2 are $\mathcal{R}_u$-equivalent if their ciphertext components relative to subset S_u are the same.

A standard argument suffices to show that any adversary that breaks our public key extension of the SD scheme via a gCCA2 attack (according to the family of equivalence relations defined above) can be used to construct an adversary that breaks the CCA2-security of the underlying HIBE.

Similarly, the public key CS method described in Section 4 can be proven gCCA2-secure (according to the same family $\{\mathcal{R}_u\}$ of equivalence relations), assuming the CCA2-security of the underlying regular IBE.

A CONCRETE INSTANTIATION. We now consider how an actual implementation of our public key extension would perform in the practice. Since the only known implementation of a fully functional HIBE is the one recently proposed in [11], we discuss its efficiency below (see Appendix A).

One interesting characteristic of the HIBE of [11] is that a ciphertext encrypted for a given user in the system can be easily recovered by any of its ancestor — actually, the decryption process gets more and more efficient as we go higher in the hierarchy. As a consequence, instead of deriving the private key $\mathcal{L}_{ij}^{\mathrm{PRI}}$ required to decrypt the ciphertext from its "ancestor" proto-key $\mathcal{P}_{il}$, the user can directly obtain the message broadcast using $\mathcal{P}_{il}$ itself, thus saving up to $O(\log N)$ factor in the decryption time.

On the flip side, the specific HIBE of [11] yields ciphertexts whose length is proportional to the nesting depth of the hierarchical identifier to which the encrypted message is being sent: it follows that the transmission rate of such a concrete instantiation of our public key extension would be $O(r \log N)$, due to the fact that the hierarchical identifier $\mathrm{HID}(S_{ij})$ can have nesting depth proportional to the height $t = \log N$ of the tree $\mathcal{T}$.

Therefore, when used in conjunction with the HIBE of [11], the asymmetric variation of the SD scheme proposed above leads to the same decryption time and transmission rate of the public key extension of the CS method, while imposing a greater storage requirement on each single user. Nevertheless, we feel that

---

[7] See [6] for a formal definition of gCCA2-security in the Broadcast Encryption setting.

our technique gives an interesting solution to the problem of obtaining a fixed Public Key File size, when generalizing the SD method to the asymmetric setting: besides, if a more efficient implementation of HIBE should become available, the parameters of our scheme would automatically improve, possibly reaching the efficiency of the SD method for the symmetric scenario.

6   Public Key Extension of the LSD Method

THE ORIGINAL SCHEME. Recently, an improvement to the SD method, known as the *Layered Subset Difference* (LSD) method, was proposed in [12]. In its basic form, this method reduces the amount of secret data that each subscriber needs to store, from $O(\log^2 N)$ to $O(\log^{3/2} N)$, at the cost of doubling the maximum size of the cover. The authors also presented a generalization of the basic scheme that achieves a storage requirement of $O(\log^{1+\epsilon} N)$, for any $\epsilon > 0$, while increasing the length of the broadcast by a factor of $1/\epsilon$, which still yields a transmission rate of $O(r)$, for fixed values of ϵ.

The main idea behind the LSD scheme is to reduce the size of the family $\mathcal{S}$ by only considering a subcollection $\mathcal{S}'$ of *useful* subsets. The key observation to reach this goal is that any subtree difference set S_{ij} can be rewritten as the disjoint union $S_{ik} \cup S_{kj}$, for any node v_k lying in the path from v_i to v_j.

To define the sub-collection $\mathcal{S}'$, consecutive levels of the tree $\mathcal{T}$ are grouped into *layers*, and certain subsets of $\mathcal{S}$ are called *local* or *special*. In particular, local subsets are those whose primary and secondary roots both lie within the same layer, while *special* subset are those having as their primary root a node lying exactly on the boundary between two adjacent layers. The sub-collection $\mathcal{S}'$ consists exactly of all the local and special subsets of $\mathcal{S}$. In this way, the number of proto-keys that each user needs in order to decrypt each broadcast can be reduced, while the Center can preserve the functionalities of the system by at most doubling the size of the cover. This is because any subset $S_{ij} \in \mathcal{S}$ can be obtained as the union of a local subset and a special subset in $\mathcal{S}'$.

EXTENSION TO THE PUBLIC KEY SETTING. Since the LSD scheme only differs from the SD method of [17] for the use of a smaller subcollection $\mathcal{S}'$ of the Subset-Cover family $\mathcal{S}$, we can extend it to the asymmetric setting applying exactly the same idea used to generalize the SD method to the public key scenario: indeed, any HIBE scheme can be employed to distribute the necessary proto-keys to the users of the system, according to the same label-distribution strategy defined for the original LSD scheme in its conventional symmetric mode.

A CONCRETE INSTANTIATION. As for the efficiency parameters of such public key extension, we can repeat the same discussion outlined for the SD scheme: namely, if we use the HIBE proposed in [11] (which is currently the only known implementation of a fully functional HIBE scheme), the public key extension maintains the same storage requirement as the original, symmetric LSD scheme, whereas the transmission rate deteriorates by a factor of $\log N$. Again, should a more efficient HIBE scheme be proposed, our solution would consequently improve, approaching the performance of the conventional LSD scheme.

6.1 Inclusion-Exclusion Trees

In [12], the authors also considered an alternative approach to the problem of specifying the set of revoked users $\mathcal{R}$ that shouldn't be a able to recover the broadcasted message. Such technique is based on the use of *Inclusion-Exclusion Trees* (IE-Trees), which offer a convenient way of describing a large set of privileged users with relative few nested inclusion and exclusion conditions on the nodes of the tree $\mathcal{T}$.

The advantage of such technique is that from an IE-Tree it is possible to derive a cover whose size is proportional to the number of conditions specified by the IE-Tree itself.

Without going in the details of this approach (for which we refer the reader to [12]), we notice here that our extension to the Public Key setting can be coupled with the use of IE-Trees in the case of both the SD scheme and the LSD scheme, since once a cover of the set of privileged users has been obtained, both the encryption and the decryption steps can be performed making use of our HIBE-based technique presented above.

References

1. J.H. An, Y. Dodis, and T. Rabin. On the Security of Joint Signature and Encryption. In *Advances in Cryptology - EuroCrypt '02*, pages 83–107, Berlin, 2002. Springer-Verlag. LNCS 2332.
2. M. Bellare, A. Desai, E. Jokipii, and P. Rogaway. A Concrete Security Treatment of Symmetric Encryption: Analysis of the DES Modes of Operation. In *Proceedings of the 38th Annual Symposium on Foundations of Computer Science - FOCS '97*, pages 394–403, 1997.
3. D. Boneh and M. Frankling. Identity-Based Encryption from the Weil Pairing. In *Advances in Cryptology - Crypto '01*, pages 213–229, Berlin, 2001. Springer-Verlag. LNCS 2139.
4. R. Canetti, J. Garay, G. Itkis, D. Micciancio, M. Naor, and B. Pinkas. Multicast Security: A Taxonomy and some Efficient Constructions. In *Proceedings of IEEE INFOCOM '99*, volume 2, pages 708–716, 1999.
5. R. Canetti, T. Malkin, and K. Nissim. Efficient Communication-Storage Tradeoffs for Multicast Encryption. In *Theory and Application of Cryptographic Techniques*, pages 459–474, 1999.
6. Y. Dodis and N. Fazio. Public Key Trace and Revoke Scheme Secure against Adaptive Chosen Ciphertext Attack. In *Public Key cryptography - PKC '03*, pages 100–115, Berlin, 2003. Springer-Verlag. LNCS 2567.
7. D. Dolev, C. Dwork, and M. Naor. Nonmalleable Criptography. *SIAM Journal on Discrete Mathematics*, 30(2):391–437, 2000.
8. A. Fiat and M. Naor. Broadcast Encryption. In *Advances in Cryptology - Crypto '93*, pages 480–491, Berlin, 1993. Springer-Verlag. LNCS 773.
9. E. Gafni, J. Staddon, and Y. L. Yin. Efficient Methods for Integrating Traceability and Broadcast Encryption. In *Advances in Cryptology - Crypto '99*, pages 372–387, Berlin, 1999. Springer-Verlag. LNCS 1666.
10. A Garay, J. Staddon, and A. Wool. Long-Lived Broadcast Encryption. In *Advances in Cryptology - Crypto 2000*, pages 333–352, Berlin, 2000. Springer-Verlag. LNCS 1880.

11. C. Gentry and A. Silverberg. Hierarchical ID-Based Cryptography. In *Advances in Cryptology - AsiaCrypt '02*, pages 548–566, Berlin, 2002. Springer-Verlag. LNCS 2501.
12. D. Halevy and A. Shamir. The LSD Broadcast Encryption Scheme. In *Advances in Cryptology - Crypto '02*, pages 47–60, Berlin, 2002. Springer-Verlag. LNCS 2442.
13. J. Horwitz and B. Lynn. Toward Hierarchical Identity-Based Encryption. In *Advances in Cryptology - EuroCrypt '02*, pages 466–481, Berlin, 2002. Springer-Verlag. LNCS 2332.
14. R. Kumar, S. Rajagopalan, and A. Sahai. Coding Constructions for Blacklisting Problems without Computational Assumptions. In *Advances in Cryptology - Crypto '99*, pages 609–623, Berlin, 1999. Springer-Verlag. LNCS 1666.
15. M. Luby and J. Staddon. Combinatorial Bounds for Broadcast Encryption. In *Advances in Cryptology - EuroCrypt '98*, pages 512–526, Berlin, 1998. Springer-Verlag. LNCS 1403.
16. D.A. McGrew and A.T. Sherman. Key Establishment in Large Dynamic Groups Using One-Way Function Trees. Manuscript, 1998.
17. D. Naor, M. Naor, and J. Lotspiech. Revocation and Tracing Schemes for Stateless Receivers. In *Advances in Cryptology - Crypto '01*, pages 41–62, Berlin, 2001. Springer-Verlag. LNCS 2139.
18. M. Naor and B. Pinkas. Efficient Trace and Revoke Schemes. In *Financial Cryptography - FC 2000*, pages 1–20, Berlin, 2000. Springer-Verlag. LNCS 1962.
19. M. Naor and M. Yung. Public-key Cryptosystems Provably Secure against Chosen Ciphertext Attacks. In *22nd Annual ACM Symposium on Theory of Computing*, pages 427–437, Berlin, 1990. Springer-Verlag. LNCS 547.
20. A. Shamir. Identity Based Cryptosystems and Signatures Schemes. In *Advances in Cryptology - Crypto '84*, pages 47–53, Berlin, 1984. Springer-Verlag. LNCS 196.
21. V. Shoup. A Proposal for an ISO Standard for Public-Key Encryption. Manuscript, 2001.
22. W.G. Tzeng and Z.J. Tzeng. A Public-Key Traitor Tracing Scheme with Revocation Using Dynamics Shares. In *Public Key Cryptography - PKC '01*, pages 207–224, Berlin, 2001. Springer-Verlag. LNCS 1992.
23. D. Wallner, E. Harder, and R. Agee. Key Management for Multicast: Issues and Architectures. Available at `ftp://ftp.ietf.org/rfc/rfc2627.txt`, 1997.
24. C.K. Wong, M. Gouda, and S. Lam. Secure Group Communications Using Key Graphs. In *Proceedings of the ACM SIGCOMM '98*, 1998.

A   Currently Best IBE/HIBE Schemes

We briefly describe the currently best IBE scheme of [3] and the HIBE [11]. We will only describe the "basic" chosen plaintext (CPA) secure versions of these schemes, since both schemes utilize random oracles, and amplifying the security from CPA to CCA1/CCA2 can be done by a variety of standard means in the random oracle model (see [3,11] for the details). Also, since the HIBE of [11] is a generalization of the IBE of [3], we first describe their common features.

COMMON FEATURES.. Let $\mathbb{G}_1, \mathbb{G}_2$ be two cyclic groups of a large prime order q, where $\mathbb{G}_1$ is represented additively, and $\mathbb{G}_2$ multiplicatively. We assume the existence of a symmetric *bilinear mapping* $\hat{e} : \mathbb{G}_1 \times \mathbb{G}_1 \to \mathbb{G}_2$. Namely, for any $P, Q \in \mathbb{G}_1$, $a, b \in \mathbb{Z}_q$, we have:

$$\hat{e}(aP, bQ) = \hat{e}(bP, aQ) = \hat{e}(P, Q)^{ab} = \hat{e}(Q, P)^{ab} \qquad (1)$$

We assume also the existence of the parameter generation algorithm $\mathcal{I}$ which, on input 1^λ, outputs a prime q, the description of $\mathbb{G}_1, \mathbb{G}_2$ of order q and a bilinear map $\hat{e}$, so that $\hat{e}$ is polynomial-time computable in λ. We mention that the security of both schemes below is based on the *Bilinear Diffie-Hellman* (BDH) *assumption*: for random $P \in \mathbb{G}_1$, $a, b, c \in \mathbb{Z}_q$, it is computationally hard to compute $\hat{e}(P, P)^{abc} \in \mathbb{G}_2$ when given only P, aP, bP, cP.

IBE OF [3]. We follow the same notation as the the one we will later use for the HIBE of [11].

- Setup. Run $\mathcal{I}(1^\lambda)$ to get $\mathbb{G}_1, \mathbb{G}_2, \hat{e}$, pick a random $s_0 \in \mathbb{Z}_q$, $P_0 \in \mathbb{G}_1$, set $Q_0 = s_0 P_0$, and output params $= (\mathbb{G}_1, \mathbb{G}_2, \hat{e}, P_0, Q_0, H_1, H_2)$, master-key $= s_0$. Here $H_1 : \{0, 1\}^* \to \mathbb{G}_1$, $H_2 : \mathbb{G}_2 \to \{0, 1\}^n$ are cryptographic hash functions, modeled as random oracles (i.e., they output a truly random string on every input), and n is the length of the messages encrypted.
- Extract. Set the secret key of user ID to $S_1 = s_0 P_1$, where $P_1 = H_1(\text{ID})$ is a random point in $\mathbb{G}_1$ derived from ID by means of a random oracle.
- Encrypt. To encrypt a message $M \in \{0, 1\}^n$ for user ID using public value Q_0, compute $P_1 = H_1(\text{ID}) \in \mathbb{G}_1$, choose a random $r \in \mathbb{Z}_q$, set $g = \hat{e}(Q_0, rP_1) \in \mathbb{G}_2$ and return $C = [rP_0, M \oplus H_2(g)]$.
- Decrypt. To decrypt $C = [U_0, V]$ using S_1 and Q_0, set $f_0 = \hat{e}(U_0, S_1)$ and output $V \oplus H_2(f_0)$.

To see the correctness of the decryption, notice that:

$$f_0 = \hat{e}(U_0, S_1) = \hat{e}(rP_0, s_0 P_1) \overset{(1)}{=} \hat{e}(s_0 P_0, rP_1) = \hat{e}(Q_0, rP_1) = g.$$

HIBE OF [11]. We will see that the IBE scheme above is the special case of the scheme below when depth $t = 1$.

- Root Setup. Same as Setup for IBE. Namely, run $\mathcal{I}(1^\lambda)$ to get $\mathbb{G}_1, \mathbb{G}_2, \hat{e}$, pick a random $s_0 \in \mathbb{Z}_q$, $P_0 \in \mathbb{G}_1$, set $Q_0 = s_0 P_0$, and output params $= (\mathbb{G}_1, \mathbb{G}_2, \hat{e}, P_0, Q_0, H_1, H_2)$, master-key $= s_0$.
- Lower-level Setup. Each user at level $t \geq 1$ picks a random local secret $s_t \in \mathbb{Z}_q$ (recall, root has s_0) and keeps it secret.
- Extract. Every user $(\text{ID}_1, \ldots, \text{ID}_t)$ at level $t \geq 0$ will have a secret point $S_t \in \mathbb{G}_1$ (see below; we assume that the root has $S_0 = 0_{\mathbb{G}_1}$), and $(t-1)$ "translation points" $Q_1 \ldots Q_{t-1} \in \mathbb{G}_1$ (notice, Q_0 is in the public key). Recursively, to assign the secret key to its child ID_{t+1}, the parent $(\text{ID}_1, \ldots, \text{ID}_t)$ computes $P_{t+1} = H_1(\text{ID}_1 \ldots \text{ID}_{t+1}) \in \mathbb{G}_1$, picks a random $s_t \in \mathbb{Z}_q$, sets the child's secret point $S_{t+1} = S_t + s_t P_{t+1}$, the child's final translation point $Q_t = s_t P_0$, and sends to the child the values S_{t+1}, Q_t together with its own $t - 1$ translation points $Q_1 \ldots Q_{t-1}$. Unwrapping the notation, the child's secret key is $(S_{t+1} = \sum_{i=1}^{t+1} s_{i-1} P_i, \ Q_1 = s_1 P_0, \ldots, \ Q_t = s_t P_0)$.

- Encrypt. To encrypt a message $M \in \{0,1\}^n$ for $(\mathrm{ID}_1, \ldots, \mathrm{ID}_t)$ using public value Q_0, compute $P_i = H_1(\mathrm{ID}_1 \ldots \mathrm{ID}_i) \in \mathbb{G}_1$ for all $1 \leq i \leq t$, choose a random $r \in \mathbb{Z}_q$, set $g = \hat{e}(Q_0, \ rP_1) \in \mathbb{G}_2$ and return:

$$C = [rP_0, \ M \oplus H_2(g), \ rP_2, \ldots, \ rP_t]$$

Intuitively, the first two components correspond to the IBE encryption we described earlier for the top-level user (ID_1). Unfortunately, user $(\mathrm{ID}_1, \ldots, \mathrm{ID}_t)$ cannot quite decrypt it using its "translated" secret point S_{t+1}, so additional values $rP_2, \ldots, rP_t$ are given. Combining them with secret translation points $Q_1 \ldots Q_{t-1}$, the message M is recovered. This is described below.

- Decrypt. To decrypt $C = [U_0, V, U_2, \ldots, U_t]$ using S_t and $Q_1 \ldots Q_{t-1}$, set $f_0 = \hat{e}(U_0, S_t)$, $f_i = \hat{e}(Q_{i-1}, U_i)$ for $2 \leq i \leq t$ and output $M = V \oplus H_2(f_0/(f_2 \ldots f_t))$.

To see the correctness of the decryption, notice that:

$$f_0 = \hat{e}(U_0, S_t) = \hat{e}\left(rP_0, \ \sum_{i=1}^{t} s_{i-1}P_i\right) = \prod_{i=1}^{t} \hat{e}(rP_0, \ s_{i-1}P_i)$$

$$\overset{(1)}{=} \prod_{i=1}^{t} \hat{e}(s_{i-1}P_0, \ rP_i) = \hat{e}(Q_0, \ rP_1) \cdot \prod_{i=2}^{t} \hat{e}(Q_{i-1}, \ U_i) = g \cdot f_2 \cdots f_t$$

Finally, we remark on the specific feature of the above scheme. The ciphertext for the user at level t literally contains the shorter ciphertext for every ancestor of the user. Thus, it is more efficient to decrypt for the ancestor than for the user itself.

Traitor Tracing for Shortened
and Corrupted Fingerprints

Reihaneh Safavi-Naini and Yejing Wang

School of Information Technology and Computer Science
University of Wollongong, Wollongong 2522, Australia
{rei,yejing}@uow.edu.au

Abstract. We consider tracing fingerprinted media data such as images and video data. We consider pirate objects that are constructed by a group of up to c colluders who have used a range of attacks including 'cut and paste', averaging (to weaken the embedded marks), and cropping (to remove part of the fingerprint). We have two main results: First, we give an efficient algorithm for tracing shortened fingerprints that are obtained from a class of generalized Reed-Solomon codes. Second, we propose combined mark detection and tracing using soft-decision decoding and show that it gives a more powerful tracing algorithm. We conclude the paper by discussing our results and giving possible directions for future research.

1 Introduction

Traitor tracing [3] is studied in two related scenarios: *key fingerprinting* in the context of broadcast encryption [3,26,18] and *data fingerprinting* in the context of copy protection. In broadcast encryption, a decoder box has a unique set of keys and the aim is to trace at least one of the c colluders who have constructed a pirate decoder that can decrypt the broadcast. In data fingerprinting the distributer of a digital object, for example a software, embeds an individual fingerprint which is a q-ary string (also called a *mark sequence*) in each copy of the object, enabling a pirate copy to be traced to a traitor. Collusion secure data fingerprinting is considered in [1,2,19]. A pirate copy is constructed by a set of at most c colluders who compare their objects, find some of the mark positions and construct an object that has one of their marks in the found positions.

c-Traceability codes (c-TA) for data fingerprinting [25] use Hamming distance between a pirate word and codewords to trace one of the at most c possible colluders who have constructed a pirate object. Tracing in this case is the same as the traditional decoding problem in error-correcting codes.

We consider *fingerprinting for media data* such as images or video clips. To protect against illegal copying and to be able to trace pirates, a seller embeds a unique fingerprint which is a q-ary string of length ℓ, in each copy of the protected object. We assume embedding is by dividing the object into blocks (for example 50×50 pixel blocks) and using a robust watermarking algorithm to embed symbols of a fingerprinting sequence one by one in each block [5].

J. Feigenbaum (Ed.): DRM 2002, LNCS 2696, pp. 81–100, 2003.

When a pirate object is found, the embedded fingerprint sequence is recovered and traced to a traitor. The output of the watermarking algorithm is either one of the q-ary symbols of the alphabet, or '?' which means the algorithm cannot decide an embedded mark.

We consider the case that the pirate object is constructed by a collusion of up to c colluders each having a distinct fingerprinted copy of the object. We assume the colluders do not know which blocks are used for embedding marks. However they may compare their objects to find marked blocks. That is although we do not assume that marked blocks in different objects are not exactly the same in different copies (for example different pixel values in different copies of an image) but they are more 'similar' compared to the same block marked with a different symbol.

The pirate object is constructed by (i) cut and paste of parts of different copies, (ii) using averaging attack to weaken the marks and defeat the mark detection algorithm, and (iii) cropping the object and removing some parts of the fingerprint. The pirate fingerprint recovered from a pirate object will be a sequence, possibly of shorter length compared to the original fingerprints, having some erased marks and in each of the non-erased positions, a mark from one of the colluders. The result of cut and paste attack on the object is that each component of the pirate fingerprint is from the fingerprint of one of the colluders or is an *erased mark*. In averaging attack, the pirate object is obtained by finding the average values of object elements, for example pixels in images. This attack reduces the strength of the embedded marks and in watermark recovery phase introduces errors in the recovered fingerprints. If this attack is used on all blocks and if there are enough colluders [12], then majority of the marks will be erased and tracing will fail. In [6] a bound on the size of collusion to make the mark undecidable is derived. Using c-traceability codes for fingerprinting sequences as above, will still have the same upper bound on collusion security. However if large enough portions of the fingerprinting sequence is recovered, the pirate object can be traced to one of the colluders.

Cropping attack will remove parts of the fingerprint and will result in a shorter fingerprint. Collusion secure fingerprinting codes and traceability codes protect against attacks of type (i) and (ii), as long as the number of erased (unrecognisable) marks are not too many. However they fail completely if the pirate fingerprint is shortened even by one component.

Tracing shortened fingerprints was considered in [22] and a tracing algorithm based on Levenshtein distance was proposed. The tracing algorithm, instead of Hamming distance, used the length of the longest substring common between the pirate word and each codeword to measure similarity between the two, and chose the most similar codeword as a colluder. Instead of error-correcting codes deletion correcting codes were used to construct fingerprinting codes. The drawback of this method is that (i) tracing algorithm is computationally expensive and (ii) construction of deletion correcting codes that satisfy the required conditions is an open problem.

In this paper we have two main contributions.

1. We consider the problem of tracing shortened fingerprints and show that using certain generalized Reed-Solomon (GRS) codes for fingerprinting allows shortened fingerprints to be correctly traced. We show that for GRS codes deletion decoding can be formulated as a polynomial interpolation problem and the list decoding algorithm of Gurswami and Sudan [11] can be used to find the closest, in this case 'most similar', code vector to the given shortened pirate word. This removes both shortcomings of the previous method by giving a construction for codes that can protect against deletion of fingerprint components, and also giving an efficient algorithm for tracing. We use this list decoding algorithm to find a bound on the number of deletions that can be tolerated, if the fingerprinting code is from the special class of GRS codes.

   Using list decoding for deletion correction to our knowledge is the first algebraic method for deletion correction and has wider applications such as synchronising signals. Although the tracing algorithms are for GRS codes but the general method of tracing shortened fingerprints and combined watermarking and tracing algorithm is applicable to all c-TA codes that are based on error-correcting codes and have list decoding and (or) soft-decision decoding algorithm including algebraic geometry codes (AG-codes) [16,10].

2. We consider fingerprints in which strength of the marks is weakened and so the mark detection algorithm cannot easily produce a single output for each mark. Attacks such as averaging results in uncertainty in detection of the marks and so the recovered fingerprints will be likely to have errors which would result in incorrect tracing. We propose a *combined mark detection and tracing algorithm* and show that it can be used to construct a more powerful tracing algorithm. We will consider two complementary types of tracing algorithms: 'hard-tracing' algorithms of traceability codes applied to a 'hard-detected' fingerprint (pirate sequence), and 'soft-tracing' algorithms that will be used on 'soft-detected' fingerprints. A 'soft-detected' fingerprint, also called a *pirate matrix*, is a matrix whose columns correspond to the probability distributions on the watermarking symbols. That is column j gives a probability distribution on the symbols of the watermarking code to occur in the jth position of the fingerprint.

   Soft-tracing uses the notion of *generalized distance*. Tracing is by finding the codeword that has the highest 'similarity' or shortest generalized distance, with the pirate matrix. The tracing algorithm in general is computationally expensive but if the fingerprinting code is RS code, then the soft-decision decoding of [16] can be used to efficiently find a colluder.

Pirate sequences can be thought of as special types of pirate matrices where each column has a single one and the rest of the elements are zeros. A tracing algorithm takes a pirate matrix and outputs a colluder and is powerful if it can trace a large set of pirate matrices. We will show that the set of pirate matrices that can be traced by hard-tracing is different from the set that can be traced by soft-tracing and so combining the two will result in a more powerful tracing compared to using only hard-tracing.

An interesting result of soft-tracing is that if the fingerprinting code is obtained from an error-correcting code whose minimum distance satisfies $d > (1 - 1/c) + e$, then pirate matrices that are constructed by colluders of size up to c can be correctly traced. In this bound e is the maximum number of columns that are 'undecidable' and have at least two symbols with the same maximum probability. The marks in such column can not be decided and is effectively an erased marks. Assuming no erasure ($e = 0$) we have $d > \ell(1 - 1/c^2)$. Comparing this bound with the bound $d > (1 - 1/c^2)$ for traceability codes [25] shows that the required minimum distance for soft-tracing is less than that of hard-tracing.

An interesting open problem is to combine the above two results and consider fingerprints that are shortened and weakened.

1.1   Related Works

Fingerprinting Media Data

A traditional method of fingerprinting a media object is by using watermarking to embed a signal in the object such that a detector with a correct key can recover the watermark [4]. A common attack for removing watermark in such objects is 'cropping' where parts of the object are removed. This is a very effective and depending on the size of the cropped part can completely remove (detector cannot recover) the mark or weaken it. An alternative fingerprinting method [5] is to divide the object into blocks and embed a q-ary fingerprint in the object by using a watermarking algorithm to embedded each element of the fingerprint in a separate block. Now if the object is cropped, the recovered pirate fingerprint will be generally shorter than the embedded one. This is the approach considered in this paper.

Collusion attack in the case of media data is similar to collusion attack in data fingerprinting. That is, colluders will compare their objects, detect mark places where the embedded marks (symbols) are different (different versions of the same block) and construct a pirate object such that each block contains one of the versions that they have. We refer to this attack as basic *collusion attack*. Colluders may also try to make the marks unreadable in which case an *erasure* occurs. We note that a 'cut and paste' attack where colluders construct the pirate object by pasting parts obtained from their individual copies can be described as a combination of cropping and basic collusion attack with erasure.

Collusion Secure Fingerprinting

Boneh and Shaw studied collusion security for data fingerprinting and defined and constructed *c-frame-proof codes* [1,2] in which collusions of up to c colluders cannot frame another user, and *c-secure codes* with ε-error, in which given a pirate copy that is constructed by a collusion of up to c colluders, at least one traitor can be traced and the probability of correct tracing is at least $1 - \varepsilon$. To construct a pirate object, colluders may use a basic collusion attack with erasure. This is captured in a 'marking assumption'. In [12] the marking assumption is extended to the case that all positions, including undetected positions, are erasable.

Staddon et al [25] defined q-ary c-*traceability codes* where the construction of pirate word is as above but does not include erasure, and tracing algorithm uses the Hamming distance between the pirate word and the set of codewords. In [24] it was shown that by using list decoding algorithm [28,11] for GRS codes, a set of traitors who are at distance at most $\ell - \ell/c$ from the pirate word can be found.

Traceability systems are also studied in the context of broadcast encryption schemes [3,26,27,18,9,21]. In [15] pirate strategies are discussed and the corresponding decoders are categorized. It has been shown [14] that tracing traitor is impossible for some type of decoders when the number of traitors exceeds a bound.

A related notion is IPP-codes, or codes with *Identifiable Parent Property*. In a c-IPP code the intersection of all collusions that can construct a pirate word is non-empty and so all traitors in the intersection of all such subsets are identifiable traitors. IPP-code are defined in [13] and constructed in [25,23].

Other related works are *dynamic tracing* scheme [7] and *sequential tracing* scheme [20] which require the feedback from the channel.

In [22] q-ary fingerprinting for perceptual content and the question of tracing with shortened fingerprint is considered. As noted earlier the tracing algorithm is computationally expensive and construction of a good deletion correcting code is an open problem.

The rest of the paper is organized as follows. In Section 2 we propose a deletion decoding algorithm for GRS codes and show that GRS codes can be used to trace shortened fingerprints. In Section 3 we introduce combined mark detection and tracing algorithm and in Section 4 show that soft-decision decoding of [17,16] can be used for correctly tracing a colluder. In Section 5 we conclude the paper.

2   An Algebraic Approach to Tracing Shortened Fingerprints

List decoding for an error-correcting code of minimum distance d can correct error patterns with Hamming weight higher than $\frac{d-1}{2}$. List decoding [11] for a GRS code of length ℓ and dimension k, takes a received word and outputs a list of codewords that are at distance up to $\ell - \sqrt{k\ell}$. We model tracing of shortened fingerprint as a list decoding problem and show the correctness of the algorithm. First we show GRS codes that satisfy a certain condition can correct deletions (Section 2.2), and then formulate decoding of shortened words as a conventional decoding problem (Section 2.3) and give an efficient tracing algorithm for shortened fingerprints (Section 2.4) that are constructed by up to c colluders.

2.1   Preliminaries

In this subsection we give definitions and review known results that will be used in the rest of this paper.

Traceability Codes with Shortened Pirate Words

Let Σ be a q-ary alphabet, Σ^* the set of strings over Σ, and Σ^ℓ the set of vectors, also called words, of length ℓ over Σ. Staddon et al [25] defined c-traceability code (c-TA) as follows.

Definition 1. *([25]) Let Γ be code of length ℓ over an alphabet Σ having n codewords. Let $C = \{u^{(1)}, \cdots, u^{(b)}\} \subseteq \Gamma$ be a collusion set where $u^{(i)} = (u_1^{(i)}, u_2^{(i)}, \cdots, u_\ell^{(i)})$, for $1 \le i \le b \le c$. Define*

$$desc(C) = \{(y_1, \cdots, y_\ell) : y_j \in \{u_j^{(i)} : 1 \le i \le b\}, 1 \le j \le \ell\}$$

Γ is called a c-$TA_q(\ell, n)$ code if the following condition is satisfied: for any $C \subseteq \Gamma$, $|C| \le c$, and for any $(y_1, y_2, \cdots, y_\ell) \in desc(C)$, there is a $u^{(i)} \in C$ such that

$$|\{j : y_j = u_j^{(i)}\}| > |\{j : y_j = v_j\}|$$

for any $(v_1, v_2, \cdots, v_\ell) \in \Gamma \setminus C$.

Safavi-Naini et al [22] extended c-TA codes to allow deletions and erasures in the pirate word. A *subword* y of $u = (u_1, \cdots, u_\ell)$ is a vector,

$$y = (u_{i_1}, u_{i_2}, \cdots, u_{i_{\ell'}}), \quad 1 \le i_1 < i_2 < \cdots < i_{\ell'} \le \ell.$$

Let $|y|$ denote the length of y. A *common subword* of two codewords $u^{(1)}$ and $u^{(2)}$ is a subword of both $u^{(1)}$ and $u^{(2)}$. For $u^{(1)}, u^{(2)} \in \Gamma$, define

$$\rho(u^{(1)}, u^{(2)}) = \max\{|y| : y \text{ is a common subword of } u^{(1)} \text{ and } u^{(2)}\}$$

For a code Γ denote by

$$\rho(\Gamma) = \max_{u^{(1)}, u^{(2)} \in \Gamma, \, u^{(1)} \neq u^{(2)}} \rho(u^{(1)}, u^{(2)}).$$

the length of the maximum common substring between two codewords. The value $\rho(u^{(1)}, u^{(2)})$ can be seen as a measure of similarity between two vectors.

The following definition generalizes c-TA codes to allow tracing when the pirate fingerprint is shorter than the embedded one.

Definition 2. *([22]) Let r and c be integers, Γ be a code of length ℓ over Σ with n codewords, and $C \subseteq \Gamma$. Define*

$$desc(C; r) = \{y = (y_1, \cdots, y_{\ell'}) : y \text{ is a subword of some } z \in desc(C),$$
$$\ell - r \le \ell' \le \ell\}$$
$$\Sigma^{\ell, r} = \{y \in \Sigma^* : \ell - r \le |y| \le \ell\}$$

Γ is called a c-$TA_q(\ell, n; r)$ if there is a tracing function $A : \Sigma^{\ell, r} \to \Gamma$ such that $A(y) \in C$ for any $C \subseteq \Gamma$, $|C| \le c$, and any $y \in desc(C; r)$.

Theorem 1 gives a sufficient condition for c-$TA_q(\ell, n; r)$ codes in terms of $\rho(\Gamma)$.

Theorem 1. *(Lemma 1, [22]) Let Γ be a code of length ℓ over Σ, and $r, c > 0$ be integers. If*

$$\rho(\Gamma) < \frac{\ell - r}{c^2}$$

then Γ is a $c\text{-}TA_q(\ell, |\Gamma|; r)$.

For these codes, given a pirate word x, to trace a colluder, the codeword u with $\max_{u \in \Gamma} \rho(u, x)$ must be found. The tracing algorithm in general is an exhaustive search and the cost of search grows exponentially with the code dimension.

GRS Codes and List Decoding

Generalized Reed-Solomon codes (GRS codes) are defined in [29]. Let F_q be a field of q elements, $\ell \leq q$ be an integer, $\alpha_1, \alpha_2, \cdots, \alpha_\ell \in F_q$ be distinct elements, and $v_1, v_2, \cdots, v_\ell \in F_q$ be non-zero elements. Write $\alpha = (\alpha_1, \alpha_2, \cdots, \alpha_\ell)$ and $v = (v_1, v_2, \cdots, v_\ell)$. A $(k+1)$-dimension GRS code is the set of all vectors

$$(v_1 f(\alpha_1), \ v_2 f(\alpha_2), \ \cdots, \ v_\ell f(\alpha_\ell))$$

where f runs over all polynomials with $\deg(f) \leq k$ over F_q. This code is denoted by $\text{GRS}_{k+1}(\alpha, v)$. Sudan and Guruswami [28,11] gave an elegant list decoding algorithm for GRS codes. Let

$$F_q[x]_k = \{f(x) : f(x) \text{ is a polynomial over } F_q \text{ with } \deg(f) \leq k\}.$$

Theorem 2. *([11]) Let Γ be a $\text{GRS}_{k+1}(\alpha, v)$, and k, ℓ, t be integers such that*

$$\ell \geq \log q, \quad t > \sqrt{k\ell}, \tag{1}$$

$(x_1, y_1), \cdots, (x_\ell, y_\ell) \in F_q^2$ *be given. There is an algorithm which outputs all $p(x) \in F_q[x]_k$ satisfying $y_i = p(x_i)$ for at least t values of $i = 1, 2, \cdots, \ell$ and the running time is*

$$O\left(\max\left\{\frac{k^3 \ell^6 t^6}{(t^2 - k\ell)^6}, \frac{t^6}{k^3}\right\}\right).$$

In a $\text{GRS}_{k+1}(\alpha, v)$ code, any $(k+1)$-tuple in $k+1$ chosen positions determines a unique codeword. In the following we show that in a $\text{GRS}_{k+1}(\alpha, v)$ code a substring of length $2k + 2$ determines a unique codeword.

2.2 Deletion Correcting Capability for GRS Codes

Let Γ be a $\text{GRS}_{k+1}(\alpha, v)$ code of length ℓ where $\alpha_1, \alpha_2, \cdots, \alpha_\ell \in F_q$ are ℓ distinct elements, $v_1, v_2, \cdots, v_\ell \in F_q^*$ are ℓ non-zero elements. We will show that Γ, for certain choice of α and v, satisfies the condition of Theorem 1 and hence is a $c\text{-}TA_q(\ell, |\Gamma|; r)$ and determine c and r. The main result of this section is given in Theorem 4 which can be proved using Lemma 1 and Theorem 3 (Proofs of this Lemma and Theorem are omitted due to space limitation).

Suppose $\ell > 2k+2$. Let $I = \{i_1, i_2, \cdots, i_{2k+2}\}$, $I' = \{i'_1, i'_2, \cdots, i'_{2k+2}\}$ be two $(2k+2)$-subsets of $\{1, 2, \cdots, \ell\}$ such that

$$\begin{cases} 1 \le i_1 < i_2 < \cdots < i_{2k+2} \le \ell \\ 1 \le i'_1 < i'_2 < \cdots < i'_{2k+2} \le \ell \\ i_j = i'_j \quad \text{for at most } k \text{ values of } j \in \{1, 2, \cdots, 2k+2\} \end{cases} \tag{2}$$

Consider the following $K \times K$ matrix

$$\begin{pmatrix} v_{i_1} & v_{i_1}\alpha_{i_1} & v_{i_1}\alpha_{i_1}^2 & \cdots & v_{i_1}\alpha_{i_1}^k & v_{i'_1} & v_{i'_1}\alpha_{i'_1} & v_{i'_1}\alpha_{i'_1}^2 & \cdots & v_{i'_1}\alpha_{i'_1}^k \\ v_{i_2} & v_{i_2}\alpha_{i_2} & v_{i_2}\alpha_{i_2}^2 & \cdots & v_{i_2}\alpha_{i_2}^k & v_{i'_2} & v_{i'_2}\alpha_{i'_2} & v_{i'_2}\alpha_{i'_2}^2 & \cdots & v_{i'_2}\alpha_{i'_2}^k \\ v_{i_3} & v_{i_3}\alpha_{i_3} & v_{i_3}\alpha_{i_3}^2 & \cdots & v_{i_3}\alpha_{i_3}^k & v_{i'_3} & v_{i'_3}\alpha_{i'_3} & v_{i'_3}\alpha_{i'_3}^2 & \cdots & v_{i'_3}\alpha_{i'_3}^k \\ \vdots & & & & & \vdots & & & & \\ v_{i_K} & v_{i_K}\alpha_{i_K} & v_{i_K}\alpha_{i_K}^2 & \cdots & v_{i_K}\alpha_{i_K}^k & v_{i'_K} & v_{i'_K}\alpha_{i'_K} & v_{i'_K}\alpha_{i'_K}^2 & \cdots & v_{i'_K}\alpha_{i'_K}^k \end{pmatrix} \tag{3}$$

where $K = 2k+2$.

Lemma 1. *Let I and I' be two $(2k+2)$-sets satisfying (2), and the rank of (3) be $2k+2$. Then there are no non-zero polynomials $f, g \in F_q[x]_k$, $f \ne g$, such that*

$$(v_{i_1}f(\alpha_{i_1}), v_{i_2}f(\alpha_{i_2}), \cdots, v_{i_{2k+2}}f(\alpha_{i_{2k+2}}))$$
$$= (v_{i'_1}g(\alpha_{i'_1}), v_{i'_2}g(\alpha_{i'_2}), \cdots, v_{i'_{2k+2}}g(\alpha_{i'_{2k+2}})) \tag{4}$$

Theorem 3. *Let $GRS_{k+1}(\alpha, v)$ code of length $\ell > 2k+2$ over F_q be given. If α and v satisfy that*

[P] the rank of (3) for any two $(2k+2)$-sets I, I' satisfying (2) is $2k+2$

then $\rho(\Gamma) \le 2k+1$.

Theorem 3 bounds the length of the longest common subwords of any two codewords of Γ and can be used to determine deletion correcting capability of the code.

Theorem 4. *Let a $GRS_{k+1}(\alpha, v)$ code of length $\ell > 2k+2$ be given. If α and v satisfy property [P], then $GRS_{k+1}(\alpha, v)$ is a c-$TA_q(\ell, q^k; r)$ and*

$$r < \ell - (2k+1)c^2.$$

2.3   Decoding a Shortened Word

Theorem 4 shows that using a $GRS_{k+1}(\alpha, v)$ code for fingerprinting allows a pirate word of length at least $(2k+1)c^2+1$ to be traced to one of the c colluders. Using Theorem 1, the tracing algorithm has to find the codeword that has a common substring of length at least equal to $(\ell - r)/c$ with the pirate word. As noted before the cost of an exhaustive search grows exponentially with the code dimension. In this section we formulate deletion decoding problem of a shortened pirate word as an error-correction problem and in Section 2.4, will use the list decoding algorithm of [11] to find at least one of the colluders.

Let Γ be a c-$\text{TA}_q(\ell, n; r)$ code and assume a shortened pirate word,

$$y = (y_1, y_2, \cdots, y_{\ell-r}) \in desc(C; r) \tag{5}$$

is given. Then y is a subword of $z \in desc(C)$ and is obtained by r deletions from z. However, the positions where deletions have occurred are not known. Denote by Y_j the set of possible values of the jth component of z, for $j = 1, 2, \cdots, \ell$. Then we have,

$$\begin{aligned}
Y_j &= \{y_j, y_{j-1}, \cdots, y_1\}, \quad \text{for } j \in \{1, 2, \cdots, r\} \\
Y_j &= \{y_j, y_{j-1}, \cdots, y_{j-r}\}, \quad \text{for } j \in \{r+1, r+2, \cdots, \ell-r\} \\
Y_j &= \{y_{\ell-r}, y_{\ell-r-1}, \cdots, y_{j-r}\}, \quad \text{for } j \in \{\ell-r+1, \ell-r+2, \cdots, \ell\}
\end{aligned} \tag{6}$$

The sets $Y_1, Y_2, \cdots, Y_\ell$ define a set Z of words

$$Z = \{(z_1, z_2, \cdots, z_\ell) \in \Sigma^\ell : z_j \in Y_j, 1 \leq j \leq \ell\}$$

which contains words having y as a subword and could result in y. Not all elements of Z are in $desc(C)$. Tracing problem is to find a codeword u which is close (Hamming distance) to some $z \in Z \cap desc(C)$.

2.4   Tracing Algorithm

We use the list decoding algorithm of GRS codes to give an efficient tracing algorithm. Let Γ be a $\text{GRS}_{k+1}(\alpha, v)$ code of length ℓ over F_q with α, v satisfy property [P]. It is known in [22] that if a collusion $C \subseteq \Gamma$, $|C| \leq c$, produces a sequence $y \in desc(C; r)$, then there exists a codeword $u \in C$ such that

$$\rho(y, u) \geq \frac{\ell - r}{c} \tag{7}$$

and $\rho(y, v) < \rho(y, u)$ for all $v \in \Gamma \setminus C$. That is a vector $u \in \Gamma$ satisfying (7) is a member of C. For a $\text{GRS}_{k+1}(\alpha, v)$, (7) gives the fact that there exist $\alpha_{i_1}, \alpha_{i_2}, \cdots, \alpha_{i_{\ell-r}}$ such that at least $(\ell - r)/c$ of the following equations

$$f(\alpha_{i_1}) = y_1, \ f(\alpha_{i_2}) = y_2, \ \cdots, \ f(\alpha_{i_{\ell-r}}) = y_{\ell-r} \tag{8}$$

are satisfied, where $f \in F_q[x]_k$ is the polynomial corresponding to u. The tracing algorithm for a shortened pirate word $y \in desc(C; r)$ outputs polynomials that satisfy at least $(\ell-r)/c$ equations in (8). We will use the list decoding algorithm in [11] to solve this problem.

For $y \in desc(C; r)$, we define a set

$$\begin{aligned}
S(y) = &\left(\cup_{j=1}^{r} \{(\alpha_j, y_j), (\alpha_j, y_{j-1}), \cdots, (\alpha_j, y_1)\} \right) \\
&\cup \left(\cup_{j=r+1}^{\ell-r} \{(\alpha_j, y_j), (\alpha_j, y_{j-1}), \cdots, (\alpha_j, y_{j-r})\} \right) \\
&\cup \left(\cup_{j=\ell-r+1}^{\ell} \{(\alpha_j, y_{\ell-r}), (\alpha_j, y_{\ell-r-1}), \cdots, (\alpha_j, y_{j-r})\} \right)
\end{aligned} \tag{9}$$

$S(y)$ is the set of all possible points in all polynomials (codewords) that have y as a subword. This is obtained by considering all possible values of such polynomials at point α_j, $j = 1, 2, \cdots, \ell$ as was shown in the set Y_j in (6). It is easy to see that the following holds.

$$|S(y)| \leq \sum_{j=1}^{r} j + (\ell - 2r)(r+1) + \sum_{j=1}^{r} j$$
$$= (\ell - r)(r+1) \tag{10}$$

Now a colluder has a polynomial that passes through at least $(\ell - r)/c$ points of $S(y)$. Note that a polynomial can only go through one of the points of the form $(\alpha_j, y_{j'})$, $y_{j'} \in Y_j$ for every j. We use list decoding algorithm of [11] to find these polynomials.

Theorem 5. *Let a $GRS_{k+1}(\alpha, v)$ code of length $\ell > 2k + 2$ over F_q be given, where α, v satisfy property [P], r and c be integers such that*

$$r < \min \left\{ \frac{\ell - c^2 k}{c^2 k + 1}, \ell - (2k+1)c^2 \right\} \tag{11}$$

There is an algorithm, for which on any input $y = y_1 y_2 \cdots y_{\ell'} \in desc(C; r)$, it outputs the following list: $\{u \in C : \rho(u, y) \geq \ell'/c\}$. The running time is

$$O \left(max \left\{ \frac{k^3 |S(y)|^6 \ell'^6}{(\ell'^2 - k|S(y)|)^6 c^6}, \frac{\ell'^6}{k^3 c^6} \right\} \right).$$

Theorem 5 shows that tracing is a polynomial time algorithm. This is a major improvement compared to the exponential time required by brute force decoding algorithm.

3   Soft-Decision Decoding

In this section we consider corrupted fingerprints. We assume up to c colluders construct a pirate object by first applying cut-and-paste (but not cropping) to their copies, hence resulting in a pirate sequence that is in the feasible set of the colluders, and then trying to weaken the marks using averaging or other attacks that make the mark detection less reliable. We note that if the collusion size is not large and so the marks cannot be completely removed, the above strategy will have a good chance of creating an untraceable object. This is because using the traditional method of mark detection followed by tracing will fail if marks are not correctly detected.

We propose a *combined mark detection and tracing* algorithm that increases the chance of successful tracing by carrying the useful information from the mark detection stage to the tracing stage. Traditional mark detection methods are *hard-detection* and in each position output the symbol with the maximum probability. We consider mark detectors that have a 'soft' output. That is instead of a single mark for each position, they output a *reliability vector* for that position and so the input to the tracing algorithm is a $q \times \ell$ reliability matrix. A reliability matrix, also called a *pirate matrix*, constructed by a group of c colluder will have each of its columns contributed by one colluder. We assume a c-TA code is used for fingerprinting and the tracing algorithm uses minimum Hamming distance for tracing. Replacing 'hard-detected' pirate words with reliability matrices is similar to representing the channel output with a reliability matrix and using a soft-decision decoding algorithm to find the most likely codeword [16]. However, in the case of tracing the aim is to find a *definite* pirate and there is no guarantee that the output of a soft-decision decoder is a colluder. It is worth noting that using minimum Hamming distance for tracing in c-TA codes, guarantees correct tracing of a colluder because the number of symbols contributed by the colluder who is closest to the pirate word is bigger than a certain bound. In another words, success of tracing is not due to the maximum likelihood property of minimum distance decoding.

The remaining question is whether it is possible to use the information in the reliability matrix to have a 'more powerful' tracing algorithm. We answer this question in affirmative by firstly giving a definition of 'more powerful' in terms of the size of the set of pirate matrices that are traceable, and then showing an algorithm that compared to the traditional hard-detection tracing is more powerful.

3.1   Background

Soft-decision decoding was proposed by Forney [8], and later developed by numerous authors. Koetter et al [17,16] extended the list decoding algorithm of Gurswami and Sudan [11] to give an algebraic soft-decoding algorithm for RS codes. In this section we review soft-decision decoding of [16] and characterize a set of reliability matrices that will be decoded to a unique codeword u using the generalized distance measure (or similarity) used in [16].

Let $\Sigma = \{1, 2, \cdots, q\}$ be an alphabet and Γ be a code of length ℓ over Σ. A $q \times \ell$ matrix $\Pi = (\pi_{i,j})_{1 \le i \le q, 1 \le j \le \ell}$ is called a *reliability matrix*, or a *pirate matrix*, if $\sum_{1 \le i \le q} \pi_{i,j} = 1$ for every j, $1 \le j \le \ell$. The inner product of two $q \times \ell$ matrices $A = (a_{i,j})$ and $B = (b_{i,j})$ is defined as

$$\langle A, B \rangle = \sum_{i=1}^{q} \sum_{j=1}^{\ell} a_{i,j} b_{i,j} \qquad (12)$$

A vector $x = (x_1, x_2, \cdots, x_\ell) \in \Sigma^\ell$ can be represented by a $q \times \ell$ matrix in which the entry (x_j, j) is 1 and the entry (i, j) is 0 if $i \ne x_j$, for every $j, 1 \le j \le \ell$. This matrix is called the *exact matrix* of x. We use x to denote a q-ary word and its exact matrix both when dealing with inner product. The inner product of Π and the word x using its matrix representation and (12) is as follows.

$$\langle \Pi, x \rangle = \sum_{j=1}^{\ell} \pi_{x_j, j}$$

The inner product gives a measure of similarity between the two matrices. For the special case that the two matrices are representations of two q-ary words x_1 and x_2, $\langle x_1, x_2 \rangle = \ell - d_H(x_1, x_2)$ which is the number of components that the two words are the same, and $\langle x, x \rangle = \ell$. This measure is used in [17,16] to give an algebraic soft-decision decoding algorithm that is optimal and minimizes the chance of decoding in error. Given a reliability matrix Π, the output of the decoder is one or more vector(s) that maximize $\langle \Pi, x \rangle$.

Theorem 6. *(Theorem 12, [17]) The algebraic soft-decision decoding algorithm outputs a list of codewords consisting of $u \in \Gamma$ satisfying*

$$\frac{\langle \Pi, [u] \rangle}{\sqrt{\langle \Pi, \Pi \rangle}} \geq \sqrt{k+1} + o(1)$$

where $o(1)$ denotes a function of an integer s that tends to zero as $s \to \infty$.

3.2 Uniquely Decodable Matrices

For a reliability matrix $\Pi = (\pi_{i,j})$, let

$$\pi_j^{max} = \max_{1 \leq i \leq q} \pi_{i,j}$$

$$\bar{\pi}_j^{max} = \max_{i : \pi_{i,j} \neq \pi_j^{max}} \pi_{i,j}$$

$$E_\Pi = \{j : \exists i_1 \neq i_2, \pi_{i_1,j} = \pi_{i_2,j} = \pi_j^{max}\}$$

that is π_j^{max} is the maximum element in column j, $\bar{\pi}_j^{max}$ is the next biggest element (strictly less than the maximum) in that column, and E_Π is the set of columns that more than one element has the maximum value and corresponds to an undecidable position. Although we will use E_Π in our proofs, without loss of generality we can ignore it in comparing our result with hard-detection case because erased positions do not provide any information in either case.

A column in the reliability matrix is a probability distribution on the mark set. More uniform distribution in a column corresponds to more undecidability in detecting a mark. A column with uniform distribution corresponds to an erased position and a column with more than one symbol with maximum probability corresponds to an undecidable position.

We say a word $u = (u_1, u_2, \cdots, u_\ell)$ *matches* a reliability matrix Π in column j if $\pi_{u_j,j} = \pi_j^{max}$. Consider a code Γ with minimum Hamming distance d. A reliability matrix Π is *faithful* to a codeword $u \in \Gamma$ if there is a set $S_\Pi(u) \subseteq \{1, 2, \cdots, \ell\}$ that satisfies [A1], [A2] and [A3] given below.

[A1] $|S_\Pi(u)| > \ell - d + |E_\Pi|$;
[A2] for each $s \in S_\Pi(u)$, $\pi_{u_s,s} = \pi_s^{max}$;
[A3] for each $s \in S_\Pi(u) \setminus E_\Pi$,

$$\pi_{u_s,s} - \bar{\pi}_s^{max} > \frac{1}{d + |S_\Pi(u)| - \ell - |E_\Pi|} \sum_{j \notin S_\Pi(u)} (\pi_j^{max} - \pi_{u_j,j})$$

Informally, a matrix that is faithful to a codeword has at least $\ell - d + |E_\Pi|$ columns that 'match' u and, in each place the 'strength' of the match, $\pi_s^{max} - \bar{\pi}_s^{max}$, is higher than a certain threshold. Denote by Φ_u the set of reliability matrices that are faithful to codeword u.

The following theorem shows that all matrices that are faithful to a codeword will be decoded to that word if soft-decision decoding based on inner product is used, and that codeword is unique.

Theorem 7. *Let Γ be a q-ary code of length ℓ with minimum Hamming distance d, and let $\Pi = (\pi_{i,j})_{q \times \ell}$ be a reliability matrix. If Π is faithful to $u \in \Gamma$, then $\langle \Pi, u \rangle > \langle \Pi, v \rangle$ for all $v \in \Gamma \setminus \{u\}$.*

Proof. Suppose Π is faithful to $u = (u_1, u_2, \cdots, u_\ell) \in \Gamma$ and $S = S_\Pi(u)$ is the set satisfying properties [A1], [A2] and [A3]. Let $v = (v_1, v_2, \cdots, v_\ell) \in \Gamma$ be an arbitrary codeword. Define subsets $J_0, J_e, J_u, J_v \subseteq \{1, 2, \cdots, \ell\}$ as follows.

$$J_0 = \{j : u_j = v_j\}$$
$$J_e = \{j : u_j \neq v_j, \pi_{u_j,j} = \pi_{v_j,j}\}$$
$$J_u = \{j : u_j \neq v_j, \pi_{u_j,j} > \pi_{v_j,j}\}$$
$$J_v = \{j : u_j \neq v_j, \pi_{v_j,j} > \pi_{u_j,j}\}$$

The sets $\{J_0, J_e, J_u, J_v\}$ is a partition of $\{1, 2, \cdots, \ell\}$, and $S \subseteq J_0 \cup J_e \cup J_u$, $J_v \subseteq \{1, 2, \cdots, \ell\} \setminus S$. It follows that $S = (S \cap J_0) \cup (S \cap J_e) \cup (S \cap J_u)$, and we have

$$|S| = |S \cap J_0| + |S \cap J_e| + |S \cap J_u| \tag{13}$$

Note that $|S \cap J_0| \leq |J_0| = \lambda(u, v) = \ell - d_H(u, v)$, and $S \cap J_e \subseteq E_\Pi$ that is $|S \cap J_e| \leq |E_\Pi|$. Then equality (13) gives

$$
\begin{aligned}
|S \cap J_u| &= |S| - |S \cap J_0| - |S \cap J_e| \\
&\geq |S| - (\ell - d_H(u, v)) - |E_\Pi| \tag{14}
\end{aligned}
$$

Since Π is faithful to u, for every $s \in S \setminus E_\Pi$ we have

$$\pi_{u_s,s} - \bar{\pi}_s^{max} > \frac{1}{d + |S| - \ell - |E_\Pi|} \sum_{j \notin S} (\pi_j^{max} - \pi_{u_j,j})$$

This implies that

$$
\begin{aligned}
\sum_{s \in S \cap J_u} (\pi_{u_s,s} - \bar{\pi}_s^{max}) &> \sum_{s \in S \cap J_u} \left(\frac{1}{d + |S| - \ell - |E_\Pi|} \sum_{j \notin S} (\pi_j^{max} - \pi_{u_j,j}) \right) \\
&= |S \cap J_u| \cdot \frac{1}{d + |S| - \ell - |E_\Pi|} \sum_{j \notin S} (\pi_j^{max} - \pi_{u_j,j}) \\
&\geq \sum_{j \notin S} (\pi_j^{max} - \pi_{u_j,j}), \quad \text{(from (14))} \\
&\geq \sum_{j \in J_v} (\pi_j^{max} - \pi_{u_j,j}) \tag{15}
\end{aligned}
$$

The last inequality is because of $J_v \subseteq \{1, 2, \cdots, \ell\} \setminus S$. By definitions of S and J_u, we know that $\pi_{v_s,s} < \pi_{u_s,s} = \pi_s^{max}$ for $s \in S \cap J_u$ and hence $\pi_{v_s,s} \leq \bar{\pi}_s^{max}$, and so $\sum_{s \in S \cap J_u}(\pi_{u_s,s} - \pi_{v_s,s}) > \sum_{s \in S \cap J_u}(\pi_{u_s,s} - \bar{\pi}_s^{max})$ follows. From (15) we obtain that

$$\sum_{s \in S \cap J_u}(\pi_{u_s,s} - \pi_{v_s,s}) > \sum_{j \in J_v}(\pi_{v_j,j} - \pi_{u_j,j})$$

Then we have

$$\sum_{j \in J_u}(\pi_{u_j,j} - \pi_{v_j,j}) \geq \sum_{s \in S \cap J_u}(\pi_{u_s,s} - \pi_{v_s,s}) > \sum_{j \in J_v}(\pi_{v_j,j} - \pi_{u_j,j})$$

That is

$$\sum_{j \in J_u}\pi_{u_j,j} + \sum_{j \in J_v}\pi_{u_j,j} > \sum_{j \in J_u}\pi_{v_j,j} + \sum_{j \in J_v}\pi_{v_j,j} \qquad (16)$$

By definition

$$\langle \Pi, u \rangle = \sum_{j \in J_0}\pi_{u_j,j} + \sum_{j \in J_e}\pi_{u_j,j} + \sum_{j \in J_u}\pi_{u_j,j} + \sum_{j \in J_v}\pi_{u_j,j}$$

$$\langle \Pi, v \rangle = \sum_{j \in J_0}\pi_{v_j,j} + \sum_{j \in J_e}\pi_{v_j,j} + \sum_{j \in J_u}\pi_{v_j,j} + \sum_{j \in J_v}\pi_{v_j,j}$$

When $j \in J_0 \cup J_e$, $\pi_{u_j,j} = \pi_{v_j,j}$. So (16) implies that $\langle \Pi, u \rangle > \langle \Pi, v \rangle$.

Corollary 1. *Let Γ be a code and Π be a reliability matrix. Then Π is faithful to at most one codeword in Γ.*

A geometric interpretation of the above result, as suggested in [16], is by defining the angle $\theta(A, B)$ between two matrices $A = (a_{i,j})$ and $B = (b_{i,j})$ as follows,

$$\cos\theta(A, B) = \frac{\langle A, B \rangle}{\sqrt{\langle A, A \rangle}\sqrt{\langle B, B \rangle}}$$

The following corollary is the direct result of the above theorem and definition (12).

Corollary 2. *Let Γ be a code and $\Pi = (\pi_{i,j})$ be a reliability matrix. If Π is faithful to a codeword $u \in \Gamma$, then $\theta(\Pi, u) < \theta(\Pi, v)$ for all $v \in \Gamma \setminus \{u\}$.*

In hard-decision decoding, given a received word $x = (x_1, x_2, \cdots, x_\ell) \in \Sigma^\ell$, there is at most one codeword u in the ball

$$B_{d/2}(x) = \{w \in \Sigma^\ell : d_H(x, w) < d/2\}.$$

In soft-decision decoding, given a received reliability matrix Π, define

$$\mathcal{B}(\Pi) = \{w \in \Sigma^\ell : \Pi \text{ is faithful to } w\}.$$

The following corollary shows that faithful matrices generalize this ball when soft-decision is used.

Corollary 3. *Let* $x = (x_1, x_2, \cdots, x_\ell) \in \Sigma^\ell$. *Then* $B_{d/2}(x) \subseteq \mathcal{B}(x)$.

Proof. Let $w = (w_1, w_2, \cdots, w_\ell) \in B_{d/2}(x)$. Define a set $S_\Pi(w) = \{j : w_j = x_j, 1 \leq j \leq \ell\}$. We show that [A1], [A2] and [A3] are satisfied for $S_\Pi(w)$. From $d_H(w, x) < d/2$ we have $|S_\Pi(w)| > \ell - d/2$. Observe that $E_\Pi = \emptyset$ for the given Π and we have

$$|S_\Pi(w)| > \ell - d + |E_\Pi|$$

hence [A1] is satisfied. It is clear that $\pi_{w_s, s} = \pi_{x_s, s} = \pi_s^{max}$ for every $s \in S_\Pi(w)$, and so [A2] is satisfied. For every $j \notin S_\Pi(w)$, $w_j \neq x_j$ and so $\pi_{w_j, j} = 0$. Then we obtain that, for each $s \in S_\Pi(w) \setminus E_\Pi$,

$$\pi_{w_s, s} - \bar{\pi}_s^{max} = 1 > \frac{\ell - |S_\Pi(w)|}{d + |S_\Pi(w)| - \ell}$$

$$= \frac{1}{d + |S_\Pi(w)| - \ell - |E_\Pi|} \sum_{j \notin S_\Pi(w)} (\pi_j^{max} - \pi_{w_j, j})$$

The inequality above is because $|S_\Pi(w)| > \ell - d/2$. Therefore [A3] is satisfied. This shows that Π is faithful to w, that is $w \in \mathcal{B}(\Pi)$ and so $B_{d/2}(x) \subseteq \mathcal{B}(\Pi)$.

Corollary 3 shows that if x has at least $\ell - d/2$ in common with a codeword (distance at most $(d-1)/2$), the codeword is unique and that hard-decision decoding using Hamming distance is a special case of soft-decision decoding using inner product as the metric.

4   Tracing Colluders

Reliability matrices represent the set of all possible outputs of the mark detection stage including the cases that the fingerprint is damaged beyond hard tracing. For example if the pirate matrix has uniform or nearly uniform distribution in all columns, the fingerprint has effectively been removed. A pirate matrix Π can always be converted to the most likely pirate word by replacing each column with the symbol that has the maximum probability in that column. This word is called the *hard-detected word* associated with Π. If marks are not damaged beyond recovery, this hard-detected word will be a descendant of the codewords held by the colluders and can be correctly traced. Traditional hard-detection tracing implicitly assumes that the marks are correctly recovered.

Let $\mathcal{P}$ denote the set of all pirate matrices. For a tracing algorithm A, denote by $\mathcal{A}_c \subseteq \mathcal{P}$ the set of all matrices that can be traced to one of up to c colluders. The size of the set $\mathcal{A}_c$ is an indication of the effectiveness of the tracing algorithm. A more powerful algorithm can trace a larger set of pirate matrices. Without loss of generality, for a c-TA codes obtained from error-correcting codes with minimum Hamming distance d, we assume the code cannot tolerate any erased symbols and tracing succeeds if all marks in the fingerprint are correctly detected. Note that c-TA codes Γ may tolerate erasure but this directly translates into higher minimum distance or lower c. Let $\mathcal{D}_c(\Gamma)$ denote the set of all descendants of all colluding sets of size at most c, and $\mathcal{H}_c(\Gamma)$ denote the set of reliability matrices whose hard-detected words are in the set $\mathcal{D}_c(\Gamma)$. This is the set of reliability matrices that can be correctly traced using hard-detection tracing. In the following we will show that using soft-detection allows another set of pirate matrices to be correctly traced. This set has non-empty overlap with $\mathcal{H}_c(\Gamma)$ but includes many matrices that are not in $\mathcal{H}_c(\Gamma)$ and so the set of traceable reliability matrices has been effectively enlarged.

We show that a reliability matrix that is produced by a collusion of size at most c and is faithful to a codeword $u \in \Gamma$ can be correctly traced to u. Assume there are at most e undecidable positions in a reliability matrix. For a collusion $C \subseteq \Gamma$, define the following set

$$T(C) = \left\{ \Pi : \begin{array}{l} \Pi \text{ is faithful to a } u \in C \text{ with a set } S_\Pi(u) \\ \text{satisfying } [A1], [A2], [A3], \text{ and } |S_\Pi(u)| \geq \ell/c, |E_\Pi| \leq e \end{array} \right\} \quad (17)$$

The following theorem shows that the inner product $\langle \Pi, u \rangle$ can be used to correctly trace all matrices in $T(C)$.

Theorem 8. *Let Γ be a code of length ℓ and minimum Hamming distance d over Σ, c and e be non-negative integers. Then $\Pi \in T(C)$ can be traced if*

$$c < \frac{\ell}{\ell - d + e} \quad (18)$$

Proof. Let $\Pi \in T(C)$ be faithful to $u \in C$ and $S_\Pi(u)$ be the set of match columns. Because of $|S_\Pi(u)| \geq \ell/c$, then (18) gives

$$|S_\Pi(u)| \geq \frac{\ell}{c} > \ell - d + e$$

Since $|E_\Pi| \leq e$, then

$$|S_\Pi(u)| > \ell - d + |E_\Pi|$$

From Theorem 7, $\langle \Pi, u \rangle > \langle \Pi, v \rangle$ for all $v \in \Gamma \setminus C$. Hence every $\Pi \in T(C)$ can be traced.

4.1   Tracing Algorithm for Soft-Detection Tracing

Let $\mathcal{T}_c(\Gamma) = \cup_{C,|C| \leq c} T(C)$. Theorem 8 shows that using inner product to measure similarity of a reliability matrix $\Pi \in \mathcal{T}_c(\Gamma)$ and codewords can correctly trace a colluder. We note that $\Pi \in \mathcal{T}_c(\Gamma)$ means that Π is faithful to one of the codewords but its hard-detected word might not be in $\mathcal{D}_c(\Gamma)$. Faithful matrices have high similarity with one of the codewords but they might contain columns that are constructed by other colluders and correspond to undetectable marks. Also note that $\Pi \in \mathcal{H}_c(\Gamma)$ might not be faithful to any codeword as although there will be a codeword with at least ℓ/c matches but the strength of the match might be less than what is required by faithfulness property. To summarize, we have $\mathcal{T}_c(\Gamma) \not\subset \mathcal{H}_c(\Gamma)$ and $\mathcal{H}_c(\Gamma) \not\subset \mathcal{T}_c(\Gamma)$.

Matrices in $\mathcal{H}_c(\Gamma)$ can be hard-detected and traced. For a reliability matrix $\Pi \in \mathcal{T}_c(\Gamma)$, the tracing algorithm must find the codeword u which maximizes $\langle \Pi, u \rangle$ over all codewords. Finding u in general will be computationally expensive with the computational cost growing exponentially with the code dimension $(\log N)$. However using RS codes as the c-TA code allows us to use the soft-decision decoding of [16] to find this codeword and there will be an efficient tracing algorithm. According to theorem 6 the output of the soft-decision algorithm will be a list of codewords for which the inner product is above $\sqrt{k+1} + o(1)$. Among these codewords there will be a unique codeword to which the pirate matrix will be faithful (satisfy [A1], [A2] and [A3]).

Hence, the soft-tracing algorithm will have two steps.

1. Use soft-decision decoding to find a list of suspects.
2. Examine each vector in the suspect list to identify the traitor.

4.2   Codes for Soft-Tracing

In the above we assume that the fingerprinting code is a c-TA code. It was proved [25] that an error-correcting code of length ℓ with the minimum Hamming distance d is a c-TA code as long as $c^2 < \ell/(\ell-d)$. From (18) we have $c < \ell/(\ell-d)$. This means that soft-tracing can trace larger collusions using the same code.

This improvement is because of requiring that the 'strength' of a mark, given by $\pi_{u_s,s} - \bar{\pi}_s$ in a 'matched position' to be higher than

$$\frac{1}{d + |S_\Pi(u)| - \ell - |E_\Pi|} \sum_{j \notin S_\Pi(u)} (\pi_j^{max} - \bar{\pi}_j^{max})$$

Hence, the larger $|S_\Pi(u)|$ requires the smaller strength for matched positions.

5   Conclusion

Tracing pirate media objects by fingerprinting the object can only succeed if we limit the range of possible attacks. We considered a number of attacks that could be used by colluders and gave efficient tracing algorithms that can trace one of at most c colluders if corruption of the pirate fingerprint is below certain level. In this paper we considered the widest (compared to other works) range of attacks against fingerprinting sequences.

The main contributions of this paper are (i) efficient tracing of shortened fingerprints and (ii) efficient tracing of a larger class of corrupted fingerprints.

Shortened fingerprints had already been considered but the construction of codes that protect against r deletions, and efficient tracing of shortened fingerprints had been open problems. Our results provide solutions to both these problems.

For corrupted fingerprints, that is fingerprints for which mark detection stage can not be very reliable, we proposed a combined mark detection and tracing approach to allow useful information from mark detection stage to be used in the tracing stage. Using pirate matrices for tracing provides a generalized setting for tracing and allows various tracing algorithms to be compared in terms of the subset of matrices that they can trace. We showed that the traditional method of hard-detection followed by tracing, referred to as hard-tracing, can be complemented by soft-tracing which allows the subset of pirate matrices that are faithful to a codeword to be traced. Such matrices, although might not be traceable by hard-tracing, but have such a strong similarity to one of the codewords that is possible to correctly trace them. Our definition of similarity follows that used for a recently proposed soft-decision decoding algorithm for RS codes, and so we can use this decoding algorithm to give an efficient soft-decision tracing for faithful matrices. These results can also be extended to other codes such as AG codes that can use this algorithm.

An interesting open question is to find other tracing algorithms that can trace a larger set of pirate matrices. We left combining (i) and (ii) as an open problem. That is, allowing the pirate fingerprint to be shorter than the original one and have corrupted marks and so representable by a pirate matrix with less than ℓ columns.

Finally, characterization of the class of GRS codes that can be used for deletion correction is an open problem.

Acknowledgement

We would like to thank Dr Luke McAven for constructing examples of GRS codes with deletion correcting property using computer searches, which also indicated some errors in an earlier version of this paper. Also our thanks go to Dr Alice Silverberg who proposed the challenge of using soft-decision decoding in tracing.

References

1. D. Boneh and J. Shaw. Collusion-secure fingerprinting for digital data. In *A dvanes in Cryptology - CRYPTO'95, L ecture Notes in Computer Science*, volume 963, pages 453–465. Springer-Verlag, Berlin, Heidelberg, New York, 1995.
2. D. Boneh and J. Shaw. Collusion-secure fingerprinting for digital data. *IEEE Transactions on Information Theory*, Vol. 44, No. 5:1897–1905, 1998.
3. B. Chor, A. Fiat, and M. Naor. T racing traitors. In *A dvanes in Cryptology - CRYPTO'94, Lecture Notes in Computer Scienc e* volume 839, pages 257–270. Springer-Verlag, Berlin, Heidelberg, New York, 1994.
4. I. Cox, M. Miller, and J. Bloom. *Digital Watermarking.* Mulimedia Information and Systems. Morgan Kaufman Publishers, 2002.
5. J. Dittmann, A. Behr, M. Stabenau, P. Schmitt, J. Sc hw enk, and J. Ueberberg. Combining digital w atermarks and collusion secure fingerprinting for digital images. In *Proceedings of SPIE,* volume 3657, pages 171–182, 1999.
6. F. Ergun, J. Kilian, and R. Kumar. A note on the limits of collusion-resistant watermarks. In *A dvanc es in Cryptolgy - EUROCRYPT'99, Lecture Notes in Computer Scienc e* volume 1592, pages 140–149. Springer-Verlag, Berlin, Heidelberg, New York, 1999.

7. A. Fiat and T. Tassa. Dynamic traitor tracing. In *A dvanc esin Cryptology - CRYPTO'99, LectureNotes in Computer Scienc ę* volume 1666, pages 354–371. Springer-Verlag, Berlin, Heidelberg, New York, 1999.

8. Jr. G. D. Forney. Generalized minimum distance decoding. *IEEE Transactions on Information Theory*, Vol. IT-12, No. 2:125–131, 1966.

9. E. Gafni, J. Staddon, and Y. L. Yin. Efficient methods for integrating traceability and broadcast encryption. In *A dvanc es in Cryptolgy - CRYPTO'99, Lecture Notes in Computer Science*, volume 1666, pages 372–387. Springer-Verlag, Berlin, Heidelberg, New York, 1999.

10. V. Guruswami. List decoding of error-correcting codes. Ph.D Thesis, Department of Electrical Engineering and Computer Science, Massachusetts Institute of Technology, USA, 2001.

11. V. Guruswami and M. Sudan. Improved decoding of Reed-Solomon and algebraic-geometry codes. *IEEE Transactions on Information Theory*, Vol. 45, No. 6:1757–1767, 1999.

12. H. Guth and B. Pfitzmann. Error- and collusion-secure fingerprinting for digital data. In *Information Hiding'99, Lecture Notes in Computer Science*, volume 1768, pages 134–145. Springer-Verlag, Berlin, Heidelberg, New York, 2000.

13. H. D. L. Hollmann, J. H. van Lint, J. P. Linnartz, and L. M. G. M. Tolhuizen. On codes with the identifiable parent propert y.*Journal of Combinatorial Theory, Series A*, 82:121–133, 1998.

14. A. Kia yiasand M. Y ung. Self protecting pirates and black-box traitor tracing. In *A dvanes in Cryptology - CRYPTO'01, LectureNotes in Computer Scienc ę* volume 2139, pages 63–79. Springer-Verlag, Berlin, Heidelberg, New York, 2001.

15. A. Kiayias and M. Yung. On crafty pirate and foxy tracers. In *Security and Privacy in Digital Rights Management (SPDRM 2001), Lecture Notes in Computer Science*, volume 2320, pages 22–39. Springer-Verlag, Berlin, Heidelberg, New York, 2002.

16. R. Koetter and A. Vardy. Algebraic soft-decision decoding of Reed-Solomon codes. preprin t, 2000.

17. R. Koetter and A. Vardy. Algebraic soft-decision decoding of Reed-Solomon codes. In *International Symposium on Information Theory (ISIT 2000)*, page 61, 2000.

18. K. Kurosaw a and Y. Desmedt. Optimum traitor tracing and asymmetric schemes. In *Advances in Cryptology - EUROCRYPT'98, Lecture Notes in Computer Science*, volume 1462, pages 502–517. Springer-Verlag, Berlin, Heidelberg, New York, 1998.

19. B. Pfitzmann. T rials of traced traitors. In *Information Hiding, Lecture Notesin Computer Science*, volume 1174, pages 49–64. Springer-Verlag, Berlin, Heidelberg, New York, 1996.

20. R. Safavi-Naini and Y. Wang. Sequential traitor tracing. In *Advances in Cryptology - CRYPTO 2000, Lecture Notes in Computer Science*, volume 1880, pages 316–332. Springer-Verlag, Berlin, Heidelberg, New York, 2000.

21. R. Safavi-Naini and Y. Wang. New results on frameproof codes and traceability schemes. *IEEE T ransactions on Information Theory*, Vol. 47, No. 7:3029–3033, 2001.

22. R. Safavi-Naini and Y. Wang. Collusion secure q-ary fingerprinting for perceptual content. In *Security and Privacy in Digital Rights Management (SPDRM 2001), LectureNotes in Computer Scienc ę* volume 2320, pages 57–75. Springer-Verlag, Berlin, Heidelberg, New York, 2002.

23. P. Sarkar and D. R. Stinson. Frameproof and IPP codes. In *Progress in Cryptology - INDOCRYPT 2001, LectureNotes in Computer Scienc ę* volume 2247, pages 117–126. Springer-Verlag, Berlin, Heidelberg, New York, 2001.

24. A. Silverberg, J. Staddon, and J. Walker. Efficient traitor tracing algorithms using list decoding. In *A dvanc es in Cryptolgy - ASIACRYPT'01, Lecture Notes in Computer Scienc e* volume 2248, pages 175–192. Springer-Verlag, Berlin, Heidelberg, New York, 2001.

25. J. N. Staddon, D. R. Stinson, and R. Wei. Combinatorial properties of frameproof and traceabilit y codes. *IEEE transactions on information theory,* Vol. 47, No. 3:1042–1049, 2001.

26. D. Stinson and R. Wei. Combinatorial properties and constructions of traceability schemes and frameproof codes. *SIAM Journal on Discrete Mathematics*, 11:41–53, 1998.

27. D. R. Stinson and R. Wei. Key preassigned traceabilit y schemes for broadcast encryption. In *Pr oceedings of SAC'98, Lecture Notes in Computer Science*, volume 1556, pages 144–156. Springer-Verlag, Berlin, Heidelberg, New York, 1999.

28. M. Sudan. Decoding of Reed Solomon codes beyond the error-correction bound. *Journal of Complexity*, 13:180–193, 1997.

29. J. H. van Lint. *Introduction to Coding Theory*. Graduate texts in mathematics. Springer-Verlag, New York, 1999.

Evaluating New Copy-Prevention Techniques for Audio CDs

John A. Halderman

Princeton University, Department of Computer Science
35 Olden Street, Princeton NJ 08544, USA
`jhalderm@cs.princeton.edu`

Abstract. Several major record labels are adopting a new family of copy-prevention techniques intended to limit "casual" copying by compact disc owners using their personal computers. These employ deliberate data errors introduced into discs during manufacturing to cause incompatibility with PCs without affecting ordinary CD players. We examine three such recordings: *A Tribute to Jim Reeves* by Charley Pride, *A New Day Has Come* by Celine Dion, and *More Music from The Fast and the Furious* by various artists. In tests with different CD-ROM drives, operating systems, and playback software, we find these discs are unreadable in several widely-used applications as of July 2002. We analyze the specific technical differences between the modified recordings and standard audio CDs, and we consider repairs to hardware and software that would restore compatibility. We conclude that these schemes are harmful to legitimate CD owners and will not reduce illegal copying in the long term, so the music industry should reconsider their deployment.

1 Introduction

Many computer users take for granted the ability to play compact discs in their CD-ROM drives, store and transport music with MP3 compression, and create copies or customized mixes from their CDs. While these technologies have many legal and beneficial applications, they are often used to produce illegal duplicates of copyrighted music and distribute them around the world. The recording industry is extremely concerned about revenue lost to this so-called "consumer piracy" (though the resemblance to murder on the high seas is unclear), and they are battling the issue in the courts and in Congress as well as in the technological arena.

Record companies have been waiting anxiously for the deployment of SDMI (the Secure Digital Music Initiative watermarking system) and other future digital rights management proposals, but these technologies will have little effect on the millions of PCs already capable of copying music. As an interim solution, several record labels and third parties have independently developed a family of copy-prevention techniques that can be implemented immediately and are effective—temporarily, at least—against existing computers. In general, these work by introducing intentional errors into the audio data or other structures on

J. Feigenbaum (Ed.): DRM 2002, LNCS 2696, pp. 101–117, 2003.

compact discs when they are manufactured. The errors are carefully designed to ensure that the discs work correctly in almost all CD players but are unusable in most PCs. A small number of titles incorporating such schemes have been sold this past year, but several labels are considering applying them much more extensively in coming months.

The music industry has an economic interest to reduce infringement, but these new anti-copying measures go beyond the protections granted by the law and pose disadvantages to legitimate record customers and to society. Copyright law creates a careful balance between content producers, who are provided an incentive to create new art, and consumers, who are guaranteed equitable access to a diverse body of works. As part of this compromise, only certain kinds of copying are prohibited. For example, under the doctrine of "fair use," record owners have the right to make copies in many circumstances, such as for backups (in case the original is lost or damaged), for time and space shifting (to play in a car or on a portable MP3 player), and to make personal compilations (by mixing songs from several CDs) [1]. These new schemes make no distinction between legal and illegal copying and block them both indiscriminately. Furthermore, copyright protection is only granted for a limited period of time after which the work passes into the public domain and may be used freely. In contrast, these copy-prevention systems remain in effect indefinitely and create a *de facto* permanent copyright. These extra-legal restrictions significantly reduce the value of the protected recordings to consumers and threaten to upset the balance established by the law.

Users who do attempt to make lawful copies of protected discs face significant hardships ranging from software errors to computer crashes and malfunctioning CD drives. One company marketing copy prevention technology actually holds a patent for a system capable of "damaging audio output circuitry" when copies (even legal ones) are played [2], and Apple Computer reports that another scheme can harm certain iMac systems so severely that they require service [3]. Consumer advocates have complained that labeling these recordings "Compact Discs" is misleading, and Philips, inventor of the CD format, has requested that record producers remove the official CD audio logo [4]. Critics also complain that the new techniques violate principles of good engineering. Their success relies on consistently flawed hardware design and buggy software. The errors they introduce may degrade sound quality and shorten the lifetime of protected discs by compounding the effects of errors caused by normal scratches and dirt. Most importantly, by deliberately violating the compact disc specification, they defeat the central purpose of any standard: interoperability.

Perhaps these severe drawbacks explain why such schemes have been the subjects of more rhetoric than scientific scrutiny. However, sound policy decisions can only be made on the basis of a deeper technical understanding, including answers to a number of interesting questions that we will address in this report:

Are They Effective? Since few albums have been confirmed to use these technologies, accounts on the Internet of uncopyable CDs have become both numerous and unreliable (one site lists over a hundred suspect discs [5]), but further analysis would presuppose that these schemes are reasonably effective. We hope to determine whether they actually do prevent copying with typical PCs, how their effects appear to users, and which systems, if any, are unaffected.

How Do They Work? If they really are effective, these copy-prevention methods warrant further technical study. We wish to know how the modified discs differ from regular albums at the binary level. Few details have been published to date, and producers are guarding their inner workings carefully to provide "security through obscurity." We also want to understand how a simple data carrying medium like a CD can differentiate between playback devices and what features or flaws in these devices facilitate such behavior.

Can They Be Defeated? Policy makers, record labels, and CD owners are interested in whether these techniques can be readily bypassed. If there is no simple work-around today, how easily can hardware and software adapt to cope with protected discs? If the barriers to circumvention are few, it will be only a matter of time before these methods lose their effectiveness, and their disadvantages will more clearly outweigh their limited ability to stop infringement.

2   Discs Studied

Our study was constrained by the small number of recordings known to employ copy-prevention techniques available in early 2002. We tested three titles that used schemes from different manufacturers. These were:

1. Charley Pride, *A Tribute to Jim Reeves*   (Music City Records, 2001)

   Fine print on the back cover reads "... protected by SunnComm MediaCloQ Ver 1.0" and warns: "... designed to play in standard Audio CD players only and not intended for use in DVD players." There are 15 audio tracks and a data track containing a Windows application for downloading compressed, encrypted tracks. The same SunnComm technology is also being evaluated by BMG music. We will refer to this disc as CP-1.

2. *More Music from The Fast and the Furious*   (Universal Music, 2001)

   A sticker on the case says: "This audio CD is protected against unauthorized copying. It is designed to play in standard audio CD players and in computers running Windows... " There are 14 audio tracks and a data track that contains compressed, encrypted copies of the songs and proprietary player software. This title uses copy-prevention technology called 'Cactus Data Shield' marketed by Midbar Technologies, which claims its scheme had been applied to over 10 million CDs by February 2002 [6]. We will refer to this disc as CP-2.

3. Celine Dion, *A New Day Has Come*, UK release   (Columbia/Sony, 2002)

Tersely labeled "will <u>not</u> play on PC/MAC," the disc is reported [7] to use a technique developed by Sony called 'key2audio.' Sony says their technology is used by more than 50 customers with over 10 million units on the market as of January 2002 [8]. The CD contains 17 tracks, but there is no option to download or play encrypted versions. We will refer to this disc as CP-3.

We used two other discs as controls: a normal audio CD, *Made in the USA* by Pizzicato Five, and a multisession CD with audio and data tracks, the *Romeo & Juliet* film soundtrack. All albums were purchased from Amazon.com or the Sam Goody store in Princeton, New Jersey.

3   Testing Effectiveness

Our first goal was to determine under what circumstances the schemes used in these discs effectively prevent playing, "ripping," and copying in PC systems. This will indicate their usefulness for reducing copyright infringement and help reveal their underlying methods of operation.

3.1   Test Procedures

We tested all three CDs with several computer configurations using a variety of operating systems, CD drives, and application programs. The test systems were:

1. Dell Inspiron 3500 Pentium II laptop running Windows 98 with a Toshiba SD-C2202 DVD drive

2. Compaq Presario 5184 AMD K-6 desktop running Windows 2000 Professional service pack 2 with an IBM CD-ROM drive and a Sony CRX0811 CD recorder

3. Dell Dimension XPS Pentium III desktop running Windows 2000 Professional service pack 2 with a Hitachi GD-5000 DVD drive and a Plextor PX-W1210A CD recorder

4. Generic Pentium II desktop running RedHat Linux 7.3 (kernel release 2.4.18) using the same Hitachi and Plextor drives

These machines represent a range of currently deployed hardware and operating systems. Due to architectural similarities, results under Windows 95 or ME would likely be similar to those on Windows 98, and results with Windows XP are expected to resemble those on Windows 2000.

All the drives in our tests connected to the IDE (Integrated Drive Electronics) interface and supported standard ATAPI (AT Attachment Packet Interface) commands. On the Windows systems we used the device drivers included in the operating system or shipped with the computer, except with the Plextor model, which was packaged with its own software. The Linux system used the open-source drivers compiled into the kernel.

We tested with several popular applications for playing, "ripping" (extracting tracks as audio files), and copying CDs. Before each test, we booted the computer, inserted the sample recording into the drive, and waited for the drive's "ready" indicator to come on if one was present. We first tested each configuration with our control CDs to verify correct operation with standards-compliant discs. Tests were declared successful if all tracks played, extracted, or copied correctly. On the Windows systems we tested:

1. *Windows CD Player*, the CD player bundled with Windows 98 and 2000; we tested using the default configuration by attempting to play and seek among the tracks.

2. *MusicMatch Jukebox 7.2*, a popular free application for "ripping" audio tracks in MP3 format; we tested by opening the Record window and clicking the Record button.

3. *Nero Burning ROM 5.5.9.0*, a commercial application for creating and copying CDs that comes bundled with many CD recorder packages; we tested by attempting to copy each disc to an image file on the hard drive using the default copy options.

4. *CloneCD 4.0*, a sophisticated commercial application for making low-level copies of audio and data CDs, including discs with unusual features and subchannel data; we tested by attempting to copy each album to an image file on the hard drive using the 'Audio CD' copy mode.

The first three programs represent typical user applications, and the fourth is a more complex utility intended for advanced users. CloneCD support for Windows 98 was limited, so we tested this program with Windows 2000 only.

On the Linux system we tested three popular open-source applications that are included with many desktop Linux distributions. These were:

1. *CDPlay 0.33*, a basic audio CD player; we tested in interactive mode with the `cdp` command by attempting to play and seek among the tracks.

2. *CD Paranoia III 9.8*, widely regarded as the most robust application for "ripping" CDs under Linux; we tested with the command:
   `$ cdparanoia -d [device] -B`

3. *CDR-DAO 1.1.5*, a command line CD copying application; we tested with the command:
   `$ cdrdao read-cd --device [device] [file]`

We also attempted to play the discs using three regular audio CD players: a Panasonic portable player, model SL-S650; a Technics component system player, model SL-PG4; and a Delco-Bose car CD player. The recordings played correctly in all cases with no apparent loss of fidelity or difficulty seeking among the tracks.

3.2   Test Results

Our test results are summarized in Tables 1 and 2 below. The copy-prevention techniques proved generally effective in these configurations, but there were several notable exceptions.

All our Windows system tests failed to read the CDs with the applications most likely to be chosen by mainstream users: CD Player, MusicMatch, and Nero. On Windows 98 with the Toshiba drive, CD Player complained that CP-1 and CP-2 were not audio CDs, MusicMatch identified CP-1 as a data CD and would not recognize that CP-2 was present in the drive, and Nero began to

Table 1. Summary of test results under Windows system configurations

O.S.	Drive	Album	Software	Results
Windows 98	Toshiba	CP-1	CD Player	Failure: No audio CD in drive
			Music Match	Failure: Data CD detected
			Nero	Failure: Invalid track info
		CP-2	CD Player	Failure: No audio CD in drive
			Music Match	Failure: CD-ROM drive is empty
			Nero	Failure: Invalid track info
		CP-3	—	Failure: Disc won't spin up; drive non-functional until reboot
Windows 2000	Hitachi, IBM and Sony	CP-1	CD Player	Failure: No audio CD in drive
			Music Match	Failure: Data CD detected
			Nero	Failure: Invalid track info
			CloneCD	Success
		CP-2	CD Player	Failure: No audio CD in drive
			Music Match	Failure: CD-ROM drive is empty
			Nero	Failure: Invalid track info
			CloneCD	Success
		CP-3	CD Player	Failure: No audio CD in drive
			Music Match	Failure: CD-ROM drive is empty
			Nero	Failure: Invalid track info
			CloneCD	Failure: Copy contains no data
	Plextor	CP-1	CD Player	Failure: No audio CD in drive
			Music Match	Failure: Data CD detected
			Nero	Failure: Invalid track info
			CloneCD	Success
		CP-2	CD Player	Failure: No audio CD in drive
			Music Match	Failure: CD-ROM drive is empty
			Nero	Failure: Invalid track info
			CloneCD	Success
		CP-3	CD Player	Failure: No audio CD in drive
			Music Match	Failure: CD-ROM drive is empty
			Nero	Failure: Invalid track info
			CloneCD	Success

Table 2. Summary of test results under Linux system configurations

O.S.	Drive	Album	Software	Results
Redhat 7.3	Hitachi	CP-1	CDPlay	Failure: Bad track listing
			CD Paranoia	Success
			CDR-DAO	Failure: Invalid TOC data
		CP-2	CDPlay	Failure: Bad track listing
			CD Paranoia	Failure: Doesn't recognize tracks
			CDR-DAO	Failure: Assertion failure
		CP-3	CDPlay	Failure: Assertion failure
			CD Paranoia	Failure: Doesn't recognize tracks
			CDR-DAO	Failure: Assertion failure
	Plextor	CP-1	CDPlay	Failure: Bad track listing
			CD Paranoia	Success
			CDR-DAO	Failure: Invalid TOC data
		CP-2	CDPlay	Failure: Bad track listing
			CD Paranoia	Success
			CDR-DAO	Failure: Assertion failure
		CP-3	CDPlay	Failure: No audio CD in drive
			CD Paranoia	Success
			CDR-DAO	Failure: Assertion failure

copy CP-1 and CP-2 but immediately aborted with an "invalid track info" error message. We were unable to test CP-3 in this machine because the drive would not accept the disc. It attempted to read CP-3 for several seconds before aborting and signaling an error with its status lights, and after failing it could not read any other disc until the computer was rebooted.

In our Windows 2000 test systems, the Hitachi, IBM, Plextor, and Sony drives encountered similar problems reading CP-1 and CP-2 with CD Player, MusicMatch, and Nero. These drives recognized CP-3, but the software failed with the same errors as with CP-2 on Windows 98. We encountered mixed results with CloneCD. The Hitachi, IBM, and Sony drives successfully copied CP-1 and CP-2. They attempted to copy CP-3, but the copies contained no usable data. The Plextor model copied all three discs successfully.

In our Linux system, the CDPlay software had partial failures with CP-1 and CP-2 on both the Hitachi and the Plextor drives. The discs would begin playing and continue to the end, but the on-screen track listings contained mostly erroneous lengths and showed many tracks as data instead of audio. This severely impaired navigation among the songs. With CP-3, CDPlay crashed with an assertion failure using the Hitachi drive and did not recognize the CD at all with the Plextor model. CDR-DAO also failed in all test cases. Using both drives, it saw invalid track listings for CP-1 and crashed with an assertion failure for CP-2 and CP-3. While CD Paranoia saw invalid track listings too, it successfully read CP-1 with the Hitachi drive and all three discs with the Plextor.

These results indicate that the copy-prevention techniques applied to the test discs are at least temporarily effective for disrupting CD playing, "ripping," and copying operations on many current computer configurations. Out of 75 trials, only 13 were conclusively successful. The distribution of the successes indicates that hardware and software design—or mis-design—is crucial to the operation of these schemes. Drive hardware showed varying degrees of robustness ranging from the Toshiba model, which failed severely with CP-3, to the Plextor, which was the only drive to read all three discs. We also observed two distinct classes of software: program that consistently failed (including the most popular Windows applications) and ones that were usually successful (CloneCD in 9 of 12 cases and CD Paranoia in 4 of 6 cases). Variations in modes of hardware failure with CP-3 using different drives and software failure with the Linux applications also suggest that each disc uses slightly different mechanisms to prevent copying.

4   Technical Analysis

Our second goal was to determine how these copy-prevention techniques work. Their effects seem enigmatic: CD drives support a greater variety of formats than CD audio players, so how can they be *less* compatible with these new recordings? We find the answers in the complex origins of CD standards and the fragile design of many drives and applications.

4.1   CD Data Formats

The compact disc digital audio (CDDA) format was invented by Sony and Philips in the late 1970s as a replacement for vinyl records. Although it stores audio in digital form, CDDA makes no provisions for data applications. In the early 80s, compact disc read-only memory (CD-ROM) was developed to specify discs that could be accessed from a computer and store data as well as audio. These held far more information than PC hard drives at the time, but the discs had to be pressed from glass masters at the factory, so it was impossible for CD drives to write them. Recordable and rewritable CD formats (CD-R, CD-RW) were finally created in the late 80's and early 90's by replacing the pitted aluminum in regular CDs with specialized dyes that could be marked by low-power lasers [9]. To this day the official specifications for CDDA, CD-ROM, and CD-R/W (known as the Red Book, Yellow Book, and Orange Book) remain carefully guarded trade secrets, but many details are publicly available in equivalent international standards (IEC-908 [10] for CDDA and ECMA-130 [11] for CD-ROM) or can be deduced from the programming interfaces for CD drives (such as the SCSI Multimedia Command specification [12]).

The information stored on a compact disc is organized into functional units called *tracks*. A typical audio CD contains one audio track for each song, and CD-ROM discs can contain audio and data tracks. Tracks are subdivided into blocks called *frames*, which hold 1/75 second of audio or around 2048 bytes of digital data along with error correction bits. Multiplexed with the main data stream in each frame are eight *subchannels*. Only two subchannels, designated P and Q, are commonly used. The *P subchannel* marks divisions between tracks.

The *Q subchannel* holds the current track number, the track type (audio or data), and the time signature of the frame relative to the start of the disc. This data is displayed by players and allows seeking to a specific time position. There are two special regions: the *lead-in area* before the first track and the *lead-out area* after the last one. These consist of several empty frames that contain no audio but may include subchannel data describing the rest of the disc. The Q subchannel in the lead-in area holds a *table of contents* (TOC) specifying the number of tracks, their starting positions, and whether each contains audio or data. This is the basic CD format understood by CD audio players and CD-ROM drives. [11,10]

The CD-R and CD-RW writable disc formats have more complicated structures. CD-R media cannot be erased, so the standards were designed to allow data to be written incrementally until the whole disc is filled. One way to do this is to write several *sessions* to the disc, each with its own lead-in, lead-out, and tracks. Every session has its own TOC that describes all of its tracks. A new Q subchannel code is defined to point to the beginning of the previous session area and included in each session's TOC. Discs encoded in this way are called *multisession* CDs [12]. Modern CD drives support the multisession format by starting with the last session TOC and following the links to previous ones, but audio CD players and older CD-ROM devices read only the initial TOC and just see the first session. While the multisession concept was intended for recordable media, many commercial albums now use it to deliver "enhanced" multimedia content on a second session that can be played in PCs.

4.2   Basic Read Mode TOC Errors

The copy-protected CDs in this study retain compatibility with regular CD audio players, so they must incorporate changes at the data level rather than the physical level of disc design. We needed to read the discs to understand how they are protected, but of course this is made intentionally difficult by the copy-prevention technologies. In our tests, the Plextor hardware was the most robust to these schemes and successfully read from all three discs using CloneCD and CD Paranoia, so we analyzed the discs with the Plextor drive. We worked under Linux, but we passed commands directly to the drive, so the results are system independent.

Most of the software we tested encountered problems seeing correct lists of tracks, so we first attempted to read the table of contents from each disc. For various reasons there is no standard method for reading raw TOC data directly with a CD drive. The lead-in area resides in an unaddressable region of the disc, so applications must rely on the drive's firmware to process it. We used the SCSI Multimedia Command interface (which translates directly into ATAPI commands for the IDE drive). The command for returning TOC entries is called READ TOC. It can be called in several modes, of which mode 0 and mode 2 are useful for our purposes.

In mode 0, the READ TOC command returns a processed list of the tracks on the CD with their types (audio or data) and start times. The drive builds this list by reading the TOC from the lead-in area of each session. This is most commonly used by CD player and "ripper" applications, which only need a basic list of tracks [12]. The data returned by READ TOC mode 0 for the test CDs are presented on the left side of Tables 3, 4, and 5 below. The TOC from CP-1 listed all the correct start times, but the first 15 tracks were mis-marked as data instead of audio (track 16 is an actual data track containing the Windows downloading application). CP-2 also reported that its audio tracks contain data, but its start times were incorrect too (except for track 15, which contains the compressed copies of the songs). CP-3 listed false types and start times for some tracks but not others, and which tracks were erroneous seemed to vary each time the disc was inserted into the drive. The incorrect track types in the CP-1 and CP-2 listings explain why some CD player and MP3 extractor applications fail—they simply don't see any audio tracks in the TOC, and this may partially explain the failures for CP-3 in configurations where the drive accepted the disc. We also see why the tracks allowing encrypted versions to be played remained accessible. These results do not show why the discs are uncopyable, since CD copying software will copy data and audio, nor how regular CD players handle the discs correctly.

4.3   Advanced Read Mode TOC Errors

To get a more complete picture of the TOC data, we tested with the READ TOC command in mode 2. In this mode the drive returns Q subchannel entries from each session separately. Besides track start times, mode 2 returns session pointers that link each lead-in area to the next. This mode is used by certain advanced "ripper" applications and most CD copying software, which needs to know the layout of the entire disk. It provides the most detailed information about the multisession TOC that the drive can report.

The entries returned by this method for the test CDs are listed on the right side of Tables 3, 4, and 5. The results for CP-1 aren't very informative. All the times and track types are the same as in mode 0, although we now see that the disc is in multisession format, with the audio portion in session 1 and the data track in session 2. The entries for CP-2 are more revealing. The disc is divided into two sessions like CP-1, and unlike the mode 0 results, those returned in mode 2 appear to be correct for nearly all tracks. The only exception is track 1, which has start time 00:01.74. The CDDA specification requires a pause of at least two seconds before the start of the first track [10], so 00:02.00 is the earliest allowed time. The block addressing scheme used by CD drives actually specifies 00:02.00 as frame 0, so this start time translates to the invalid frame address -1. This will cause many programs to fail while copying the disc or reading track 1, and it made CDR-DAO crash with an assertion failure in some of our tests. Normal CD players do not use this address scheme and are unlikely to be affected.

The mode 2 data from CP-3 warrants extended discussion. These entries list the correct types and start times for all the audio tracks, but strangely they also include multiple sessions with a data-mode track 18 as part of session 2. This CD claims to be completely unusable in PCs, so a real data track would

Table 3. Table of contents entries from disc CP-1

Track†	Type	Start‡	Track†	Session	Type	Start‡
	READ TOC mode 0			READ TOC mode 2		

Track†	Type	Start‡	Track†	Session	Type	Start‡
1	Data*	00:02.00	1	1	Data*	00:02.00
2	Data*	02:21.08	2	1	Data*	02:21.08
3	Data*	05:13.30	3	1	Data*	05:13.30
4	Data*	08:25.54	4	1	Data*	08:25.54
5	Data*	10:51.46	5	1	Data*	10:51.46
6	Data*	13:05.04	6	1	Data*	13:05.04
7	Data*	15:59.74	7	1	Data*	15:59.74
8	Data*	18:08.67	8	1	Data*	18:08.67
9	Data*	21:32.66	9	1	Data*	21:32.66
10	Data*	23:41.49	10	1	Data*	23:41.49
11	Data*	25:58.07	11	1	Data*	25:58.07
12	Data*	28:26.10	12	1	Data*	28:26.10
13	Data*	31:04.41	13	1	Data*	31:04.41
14	Data*	33:31.01	14	1	Data*	33:31.01
15	Data*	35:55.55	15	1	Data*	35:55.55
			0xa2	1	Audio	38:21.42
			0xb0	1	Data	40:51.42
16	Data	40:53.42	16	2	Data	40:53.42
0xaa	Data	40:59.44	0xa2	2	Data	40:59.44

Table 4. Table of contents entries from disc CP-2

Track†	Type	Start‡	Track†	Session	Type	Start ‡
	READ TOC mode 0			READ TOC mode 2		

Track†	Type	Start‡	Track†	Session	Type	Start ‡
1	Data*	00:02.00*	1	1	Audio	00:01.74*
2	Data*	00:06.00*	2	1	Audio	04:10.51
3	Data*	00:10.00*	3	1	Audio	07:32.43
4	Data*	00:14.00*	4	1	Audio	10:28.41
5	Data*	00:18.00*	5	1	Audio	12:13.74
6	Data*	00:22.00*	6	1	Audio	15:32.36
7	Data*	00:26.00*	7	1	Audio	18:56.59
8	Data*	00:30.00*	8	1	Audio	23:11.66
9	Data*	00:34.00*	9	1	Audio	27:01.74
10	Data*	00:38.00*	10	1	Audio	30:20.61
11	Data*	00:42.00*	11	1	Audio	34:34.11
12	Data*	00:46.00*	12	1	Audio	38:12.04
13	Data*	00:50.00*	13	1	Audio	41:15.26
14	Data*	00:54.00*	14	1	Audio	44:39.11
			0xa2	1	Audio	51:14.66
			0xb0	1	Audio	53:44.66
15	Data	53:46.66	15	2	Data	53:46.66
0xaa	Audio	74:00.00	0xa2	2	Audio	74:00.00

Table 5. Table of contents entries from disc CP-3

READ TOC mode 0			READ TOC mode 2			
Track†	Type	Start‡	Track†	Session	Type	Start‡
1	Audio	00:10.00	1	1	Audio	00:10.00
2	Audio	03:40.65	2	1	Audio	03:40.65
3	Audio	07:54.45	3	1	Audio	07:54.45
4	Audio	12:02.60	4	1	Audio	12:02.60
5	Audio	15:28.42	5	1	Audio	15:28.42
6	Audio	19:48.25	6	1	Audio	19:48.25
7	Audio	23:26.00	7	1	Audio	23:26.00
8	Audio	28:45.30	8	1	Audio	28:45.30
9	Audio	34:19.55	9	1	Audio	34:19.55
10	Audio	39:08.12	10	1	Audio	39:08.12
11	Data*	00:08.00*	11	1	Audio	43:25.22
12	Data*	00:08.00*	12	1	Audio	47:42.37
13	Data*	00:08.00*	13	1	Audio	51:52.50
14	Data*	00:08.00*	14	1	Audio	55:44.55
15	Data*	00:08.00*	15	1	Audio	59:14.52
16	Data*	00:08.00*	16	1	Audio	63:04.47
17	Data*	00:08.00*	17	1	Audio	68:47.17
			0xa2	1	Audio	72:32.62
			0xb0	1	Audio	75:02.62
18*	Data*	00:08.00*	18*	2	Data	75:04.62*
19*	Data*	00:08.00*				
0xaa	Data	75:12.62*	0xa2*	2	Data	75:12.62*
			0xb0*	2	Audio	76:42.62*

† Special track number codes—
   Mode 0: 0xaa Final lead-out start time
   Mode 2: 0xa2 Session lead-out start time
          0xb0 Next session start time

‡ Start time from the beginning of the disc in minutes, seconds,
   and frames (75 per second).

* Denotes invalid or erroneous value.

be surprising. We observe that the lead-in time for the second session, 75:02.62, is only a few frames before the last accessible address on the disc, 75:02.68, and that track 18 begins even later. The session 2 TOC also includes a pointer to a *third* session that begins later still than the mysterious track 18.

This elaborate construction is the mechanism behind CP-3's total incompatibility with some configurations we tested. Since the third session begins before the end of the disc but has no TOC or lead-out, it is in an "open" or incomplete state. Sessions on recordable CDs are sometimes left open to allow more tracks to be written later, but most drives cannot recognize the disc until the session is "closed" by writing a complete TOC and lead-out [9]. Some drives, including the Toshiba in our tests, are unable to read open discs because they cannot locate a usable TOC in the final session. Others, like the Plextor used for these readings, are designed to handle open discs and have a more robust failure mode that returns the tracks from sessions 1 and 2 only, as in the mode 2 results. Even on such drives, the non-existent track 18 may cause problems for many CD copying programs which fail when they are unable to read it.

4.4   Concealing Audio Tracks

These TOC errors explain why the protected discs thwart most PC hardware and software, but the question remains how they still work in normal CD players. In fact, this is closely related to why we find different results reading the TOC in mode 0 and mode 2. It's no coincidence all three discs contain multiple sessions (even CP-3, which has no actual content outside of session 1). When a multisession-aware CD drive compiles a list of tracks with READ TOC mode 0, it reads TOCs from the last session to the first, ignoring duplicate track entries. The modified discs could place correct data in the first session TOC and erroneous entries for the same tracks in the second session TOC. The mode 0 results would then contain only the false track listings. In READ TOC mode 2, however, each session's TOC is processed individually and entries referring to tracks outside the current session are discarded, so just the correct session 1 entries would be visible. Audio CD players read only the first session TOC, so they would also be unaffected.

We conducted a simple experiment to test whether the copy prevention schemes for CP-2 and CP-3 use this method to hide their audio tracks. Three small pieces of non-transparent tape were affixed to the data side of discs CP-2 and CP-3 roughly 120 degree apart beginning at the outer edge and extending inward radially for approximately 3/4 inch. This prevented the drive from reading the TOC in the second session, which begins in the region under the tape, so we expected that the drive would now return only the correct TOC entries from session 1. When the taped discs were examined with READ TOC mode 0, the audio tracks were listed with the proper types and start times as in mode 2 without the tape, confirming our theory. Unfortunately, the tape covered portions of later audio tracks too, so the discs were not entirely usable. This multisession trick also explains why DVD players, video game systems, and certain car audio systems reportedly fail to read the discs, since many of these devices are multisession aware and read the later TOCs just like computer CD drives. Last May, several weeks after we completed these tests, reports appeared in the popular press that writing around the outer edge of certain discs with a felt-tipped marker would defeat the copy protection [13]. This works by obscuring the last session TOC just like the tape but leaves the audio tracks accessible when carefully applied.

We did not test CP-1 in this way because the entries returned by READ TOC in either mode were the same for the audio tracks on this disc. The start times were all correct, but the tracks were marked as data instead of audio. The designers of the scheme used on this disc relied on the fact that most audio CD players ignore the track types listed in the TOC and use types from the track subchannels instead. This variation makes this particular scheme more likely to defeat CD reader software that uses the READ TOC mode 2 method and may confuse CD copying software that will attempt to treat the audio tracks as data. It represents a different trade off between greater copy resistance and increased chances of incompatibility with audio CD players.

4.5   Other Errors

In addition to TOC errors, copy prevention schemes may place errors in the track data area, either in the subchannel codes or in the audio data and its error correction bits. For instance, the makers of the protection technology applied to CP-2 hold a patent describing one such scheme that injects corrupt audio samples but conceals them from audio CD players using bits in the P subchannel [2]. Other proposed techniques involve writing corrupt audio samples along with incorrect error correction codes to simulate scratches on the disc. These errors are unrecoverable, so audio CD players interpolate over them. Most CD drives designed for data access have no audio interpolation capability and would return the faulty samples instead.

To test for subchannel errors we used the PLAY CD command to seek to each frame and then called READ SUBCHANNEL to retrieve the data. We found no invalid entries in the P or Q subchannels for these discs. This either indicates that the discs contain no such errors or that the drive firmware recognized and corrected them before returning the samples. We listened to copies made by CloneCD for evidence of faulty error correction codes, but they contained no noticeable loss of fidelity compared to the output from an audio CD player. However, another study reports an unusually high C1 error rate in the audio portion of the CP-2 disc [14]. These are low-level errors corrected by drive hardware and not normally visible to applications, but at the reported frequency certain drives might be unable to read the audio data, drastically slow down during copying, or return reduced quality samples.

5   Repairing Broken Hardware and Software

Our third and final goal was to determine whether hardware and software can be adapted to read discs with copy-prevention technology. As we have shown, these schemes take advantage of bugs and poor error handling in existing hardware and software. Now that these problems have been pointed out, we expect manu-facturers to improve such fragile designs and produce more robust products that will gradually reduce the effectiveness of these methods.

Hardware compatibility is essential for reading the CDs successfully, since the worst case hardware failures (as illustrated by CP-3 in the Toshiba model) prevent the drive from accepting the disc at all. Our tests reveal that many current CD drives are poorly designed to cope with unusual conditions, but the robustness of the Plextor model demonstrates that greater compatibility is possible today. In addition to handling the TOC errors gracefully, well-built drive hardware should correct errors in the audio data stream during reading as CD players do or report specific data and subchannel errors to applications using the C2 and C3 feedback mechanisms [9] so that errors can be corrected in software. The Plextor drive and other recent models optimized for audio extraction do both. These changes are not specific to copy-prevention systems but improve operation with all damaged or poorly recorded discs.

Software can adapt more easily to changing conditions, and we expect future applications will fix problems that prevent them from supporting discs like these with almost any drive that does not reject them outright. As for hardware, the most important improvements for software are increased robustness and better modes of failure. For maximum compatibility, CD reading and copying programs should be modified to detect and correct data errors and to recover gracefully even when certain tracks or frames are unreadable. Obvious subchannel and TOC errors should simply be ignored. Since many drives might not report TOC information correctly even with READ TOC mode 2 and future copy-prevention techniques may include more persistent faults, applications for reading audio data should include an option to ignore the TOC entirely and derive a table of contents directly from the track data like some audio CD players do. Analyzing individual frames shows whether they contain audio data or are a transition between songs, and a simple binary search can reveal where each track begins and ends. This approach and improved error correction would allow playback under nearly any copy-prevention scheme that remains usable in audio CD players.

How easily can existing software be repaired to work with these CDs? To find out, we examined the source code of the CDR-DAO copying program [15]. Debugging revealed that our test CDs caused errors in just a few procedures, mostly related to reading the TOC. The program combines READ TOC mode 0 and mode 2 results, but the differences between them caused problems in logic for detecting the format of the start times. This could be corrected by using mode 2 data only or by using a subchannel scan to derive the correct TOC. The invalid start time of 00:01.74 on CP-2 was caught by a safety check and forced the program to abort. A better recovery would have been to guess the earliest valid start time, 00:02.00. Audio tracks incorrectly reported as data caused faults when CDR-DAO tried to read frames from the disc, but the actual types could instead be determined from the track subchannel codes or by analyzing data in the track. Finally, unreadable frames such as the contents of track 18 on CP-3 caused the whole copy operation to abort. This error could be changed to a warning and the invalid frames replaced by empty ones. All these modifications would be straightforward for someone familiar with the source code. Of course, other software would require different changes that might be more challenging, but it is unlikely that any would require significant rewriting to achieve compatibility with copy-protected CDs.

Recent developments indicate that changes like these are already being implemented. In May, the makers of two "ripper" applications released new versions with specific fixes for working around copy-prevention schemes. Feurio 1.64 adds special routines for defective CDs [16], and EAC 0.9x can detect CD structure by track subchannel analysis, bypassing the TOC [14]. Both already supported extended error correction mechanisms. Version 4.0 of the CloneCD copying software includes a special mode for audio CDs, and this greatly improved its success rate in our tests compared to earlier releases. Although all these programs are more obscure than MusicMatch, Nero, and other mainstream applications, they demonstrate that greater compatibility is possible through better software design. Drive hardware is adapting too. Philips is reportedly considering adding support for reading and copying these discs to future versions of its products [17], and market demand may induce competing manufacturers to do the same.

Hardware and software are becoming more resistant to these copy-prevention techniques even before they have been widely adopted. Given the relatively simple modifications needed to achieve full compatibility, it seems unlikely that these schemes will enjoy lasting effectiveness. Record producers might also adapt their practices to changing technology, but their options are limited by the need to maintain compatibility with audio CD players. Once more robust CD hardware becomes dominant, support for any new protection mechanism will require only software upgrades, which can be delivered easily using the Internet, and this will permanently undermine the usefulness of audio CD copy prevention. It may be proposed to prohibit such adaptations through legislation, but to do so would be to mandate buggy software and poor hardware design.

6   Conclusions

The development of inexpensive, user-friendly computer recording devices has pitted the technology industry versus the music industry in a battle for consumer dollars. Yet there is more at stake than economics. These copy-prevention schemes threaten fair use and the future of the public domain, and pressure to preserve their effectiveness by prohibiting circumvention could limit the freedom of hardware and software developers to improve their products and correct bugs.

While the techniques we studied prevented copying and playback in a high percentage of our test systems, it seems they have done little to reduce "piracy." A quick search on the Kazaa and Gnutella file trading networks in May 2002 revealed copies of nearly every track freely available for downloading. Instead of combating copyright infringement, these schemes harm legitimate record owners. Their inflexible copy controls prevent many legal uses, they cause hardware and software errors, and they threaten to damage PCs and stereo systems. As long as just a few computer configurations can read new CDs, they will inevitably be redistributed, and with so many disadvantages for consumers, these measures may actually encourage users to resort to illegal copying instead of purchasing CDs.

The concept of audio CD copy-prevention is fundamentally misguided. It is based on the false premise that specific deviations within the framework of a standard data format could result in lasting incompatibility. Yet hardware and software adaptation is an inevitable and natural extension of improved design and bug fixing. These ill-conceived schemes will amount to little more than a temporary speed bump for copyright infringement and promise to further alienate customers from the record industry.

Acknowledgments

I am grateful to Andrew Appel for his guidance throughout this project, and to Edward Felten, Brian Kernighan, and Scott Aaronson for valuable comments and support.

> *One likes to believe in the freedom of music,*
> *But glittering prizes and endless compromises*
> *Shatter the illusion of integrity.*
>
> —Rush, "The Spirit of Radio"

References

1. Stanford University: Copyright and fair use web site. http://fairuse.stanford.edu/.
2. Sinquin, P., Selve, P., Alcalay, R.: Anti-counterfeit compact disc. US Patent 6,208,598 (2001) Assignee: Midbar Tech Ltd.; filed Jan 13, 1999.
3. Apple Computer: Mac OS cannot eject copy protected audio disc. AppleCare Knowledge Base article 106882 (2002)
4. Lettice, J.: Philips moves to put 'poison' label on protected CDs. (The Register; January 18, 2002)
5. Campaign for Digital Rights: Corrupt audio discs web site. http://uk.eurorights.org/issues/cd/bad/.
6. Midbar surpasses 10 million milestone. Midbar press release (2002)
7. Bickers, J.: Copy-protected CDs: Piracy defense or rip-off? (USA Today; June 20, 2002)
8. Sony DADC reaches production milestone with 10 million key2audio-protected CD-audio discs. (Sony press release, 2002)
9. McFadden, A.: comp.publish.cdrom FAQ (2002) http://www.cdrfaq.org/.
10. International Electrotechnical Commission: Compact disc digital audio system. IEC standard 60908 (1999)
11. ECMA: Data interchange on read-only 120 mm optical data discs (CD-ROM). ECMA standard 130 (1996)
12. NCITS: SCSI multimedia commands 3 (MMC-3). Working draft, revision 10g (2001)
13. Reichert, K., Troitsch, G.: Kopierschutz mit filzstift knacken. (Chip.de; May 2002)
14. CDR-Info: Essay: Cactus data shield 200 (2002) http://www.cdrinfo.com/Sections/News/Details.asp?RelatedID=1926.
15. Mueller, A.: CDR-DAO program source. Version 1.1.5 (2001) http://cdrdao.sourceforge.net/.
16. Feurio version history, 1.64 http://www.feurio.com/English/history_1_64.shtml.
17. CD creator burns copy-protection efforts. (Reuters; January 17, 2002)

Towards Meeting the Privacy Challenge: Adapting DRM*

Larry Korba[1] and Steve Kenny[2]

[1] National Research Council of Canada, 1500 Montreal Road, Ottawa, Canada K1A 0R8
Larry.Korba@nrc.ca
[2] Independent Consultant, Den Haag, The Netherlands
Stephen_MH_Kenny@yahoo.com

Abstract. Achieving the privacy needs for applications as expressed in law is complex. Currently there is no commonly accepted technical approach for meeting these privacy requirements. An often-fruitful way for uncovering solutions to challenges such as this is to examine how technologies used in quite different applications may be adapted for the purpose. In this paper, we examine the prospect of adapting systems designed for Digital Rights Management for the purpose of Privacy Rights Management for European Community. We begin by outlining the legal requirements for privacy under the European Union Data Directive. After an overview of digital rights management systems, we describe adaptations for transforming a DRM system into a privacy rights management system. We also detail the strengths and weaknesses of this approach.

1 Introduction

Privacy issues facing developed societies today are made complex because of incompatible ideologies and policies between the different countries, the Internet, and the growth of new technologies in general. In this context, the complexity is extended from a technological perspective due to Directive 95/46/EC of the European Parliament and the Council of 24 October 1995. This legislation, referred to as The Directive [1], describes the protection of individuals regarding the processing and free movement of their personal data. Many of the provisions of this Directive have the potential to become global de facto standards for e-business.

In this paper we investigate the potential of adapting ideas from Digital Rights Management (DRM) systems for the purpose of managing personal data held and controlled by organizations. For the purposes of this work, we define Privacy Rights Management (PRM) as the management of personal information according to the requirements of The Directive. The purpose of this work is to develop a framework for a broader integration of privacy services that would mitigate certain privacy-concerning characteristics of e-commerce systems in general. As well, through this exploration we uncover pertinent research issues that must be addressed in order to develop effective, robust and comprehensive privacy-enhancing technologies.

---

* NRC paper number: NRC 44956

J. Feigenbaum (Ed.): DRM 2002, LNCS 2696, pp. 118–136, 2003.

1.1   Legislative Imperative

The right to privacy in the EU is defined as a human right under Article 8 of the 1950 European Convention of Human Rights and Fundamental Freedoms (ECHR). The implementation of this Article can be traced to The Directive. Similar legislation and enforcement structures to the European model exist in Canada, Australia, Norway, Switzerland and Hong Kong.

The Directive applies to all sectors of public life, with some exceptions. It specifies the data protection rights afforded to "data subjects", plus the requirements and responsibilities obligated for "data controllers" and by association "data processors" [2]. This triad structure of entities balances data subject fundamental rights against the legitimate interests of data controllers (see Fig. 1). The Directive places an obligation on member states to ratify national laws implementing its requirements. The implicit principles and constructs of The Directive define the enforcement and the representation of data protection. The terms privacy and data protection are often used interchangeably, though we are aware that in other contexts the two terms are not necessarily equivalent.

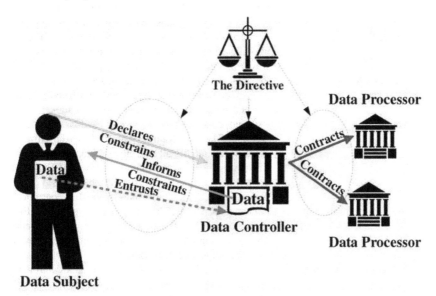

Fig. 1. A schematic representation of the roles of the three entities defined in the Directive.

The data subject is a natural person who can be identified by reference to one or more pieces of data related to his physical, physiological, mental, economic, cultural or social identities. Even data associated with an individual in ambiguous ways may be deemed reasonable personally identifiable information. Following Article 1 of the ECHR, the fundamental right to data protection falls not to the nationality of the data subject, but as an obligation to a relying party of the data subject [3]. The relying parties are the data controller and, by association, the data processor.

The data controller is an entity that determines the purpose and means of processing personal data, and is defined as the holder of ultimate accountability as it relates to the correct processing and handling of the information from the data subject. The data processor is an entity that processes personal data on behalf of the data controller.

Privacy principles (Table 1) abstracted from the complexities of legislation have been developed to simplify compliance with privacy regulations. Analyzing an approach using the principles as a guide, offers a fruitful means for determining the effectiveness and pitfalls of the approach. We thus use these principles to consider the appropriateness of adapting systems and ideas currently used in DRM for PRM.

Table 1. European Union Privacy principles.

Principle	Description
1. Reporting the processing	All non-exempt processing must be reported in advance to the National Data Protection Authority.
2. Transparent processing	The data subject must be able to see who is processing his personal data and for what purpose. The data controller must keep track of all processing it performs and the data processors and must make it available to the user.
3. Finality & Purpose Limitation	Personal data may only be collected for specific, explicit, legitimate purposes and not further processed in a way that is incompatible with those purposes.
4. Lawful basis for data processing	Personal data processing must be based on what is legally specified for the type of data involved, which varies depending on the type of personal data.
5. Data quality	Personal data must be as correct and as accurate as possible. The data controller must allow the citizen to examine and modify all data attributable to that person.
6. Rights	The data subject has the right to improve his or her data as well as the right to raise certain objections regarding the execution of these principles by the data controller.
7. Data traffic outside EU	Exchange of personal data to a country outside the EU is permitted only if that country offers adequate protection. The data controller assures appropriate measures are taken in that locality if possible.
8. Data processor processing	If data processing is outsourced from data controller to processor, controllability must be arranged.
9. Security	Measures are taken to assure secure processing of personal data.

1.2   Business Imperative

DRM systems are not without controversy regarding privacy. Since DRM systems track what users purchase, how often they access material, when they use it, it is clear that these systems may be used to track detailed activity of subscribers [4]. Currently, divisions are opening between content providers and technology developers regarding intellectual property protection, versus privacy protection. Technology providers are faced with attempting to please their corporate customers, i.e. content providers, who are losing revenue due to copyright abuses, versus the potential alienation tracking solutions generate within their customers.

DRM mechanisms for capturing and tracking of personal data have incited concern from data protection bodies. It is clear that design assumptions such as extensive notification of organizational privacy policies coupled with controllability via external privacy auditing from reputable firms will be insufficient to quell concern.

Our position is that, notwithstanding the privacy issues with DRM systems, aspects of DRM architecture have features that would allow the development of a system-based approach to data protection compliance, i.e. Privacy Rights Management. Privacy Rights Management offers a solution for the paradox in which content deliverers find themselves. It embeds The Directive into a technology framework for protecting data subject information. Such an architecture may be applied to the management of personal data for many types of e-commerce applications. By implementing European style data protection rights ubiquitously through PRM, individuals are able to engage personalized content-provision business models, such as pay per play, in confidence that all their personal data is being processed legitimately.

The rest of this paper is organized as follows. In section 2 we state the problem we are addressing in this work, followed by a description of a basic DRM system. In Section 3 we describe the architecture of a PRM system, drawing parallels between its components and their counterparts in a DRM system. We describe the changes required to transform a DRM system into a PRM system. Section 4 describes mechanisms to express privacy using ODRL. Section 5 proffers a discussion on this analysis, describing the issues that must be addressed for this approach to be successful.

2   Problem Statement

Under The Directive, the data controller has a major data protection compliance responsibility. There are currently no technical solutions that would meet all aspects of The Directive. The problem focus of this paper is the development and analysis of a PRM architecture that meets the requirements indicated by the privacy principles of The Directive. Interestingly, Digital Rights Management technology, developed for protecting intellectual property rights, appears to offer the potential as a foundation for meeting these requirements. The next three sections of this paper describe how a generic DRM system may be adapted to offer Privacy Rights Management. We first start with an overview of digital rights systems.

2.1   DRM Overview

Originally conceived to facilitate controlled distribution of digital content and to combat breaches of copyright law, digital rights management (DRM) involves all aspects of content distribution, ranging from content locking mechanisms, through content metering, to payment processes, and record keeping. DRM architectures support description, trading, protection, monitoring and tracking of the use of digital content. DRM technologies can control file access (number of views, lengths of views), altering, sharing, copying, printing, and saving. These technologies may be contained within operating systems, program software (e.g. specialized viewers), or in the hardware of a device. Fig. 2 illustrates a simplified DRM system. In order to present the concept of privacy rights management we adopt the client-server rather than the peer-to-peer architecture for reasons of simplicity.

As illustrated in Fig. 2, a DRM system operates in the following fashion. An owner or distributor submits its electronic property to a packager that encodes the property into an appropriate format for eventual end use. The packager encrypts the content to guard against unauthorized use, and adds metadata concerning the content. The metadata not only specifies the content, but also may hold information regarding how a user may gain access to the content. The DRM Server, sometime known as the Rights Fulfillment Server, manages assets stored within various databases. An important concept that forms a foundation for DRM is the separation between the content and the rights for access to the content. Rights describe precisely what a user is allowed to do with the content. Typically some sort of language is used to express those rights (for example: XrML [5], and ODRL [6]). The Rights Management Language implements the business model for the commercial distribution of the content, providing details concerning different types of purchase models, use models, etc.

In order to view or play DRM managed content, the user must deploy client software on his computer. This client software handles user authentication and provides secured access to the content. The intention here is to ensure that only those entitled to a file will be able to access it. A challenging element of DRM is to ensure that the content may not be directed to other uses when it is available in the clear for legitimate processing (e.g. viewing an e-book, or video file, or listening to an audio file and saving the data for later reuse).

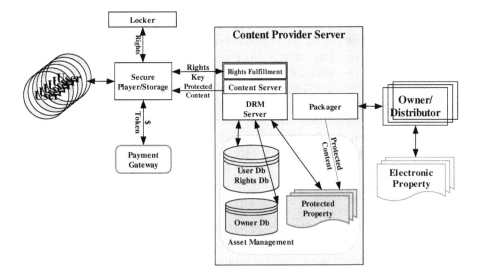

Fig. 2. A simplified DRM system focusing on client-server architecture.

3   Privacy Rights Management

As is clear from the description of privacy principles in Table 1, there are many demanding requirements placed upon the data controller. In order to examine the possibility of meeting these requirements, we propose the system shown in Fig. 3.

Key participants for the system include the data subject, the data controller (in this case a single data controller) and one or more data processors. PRM manages personal data from the data subject, the originator and the owner of the personal data. The Directive defines the authorities and boundaries of the relationships between each of the participants.

The data controller manages gathering, storage and processing of data subject data. The responsibility is enforceable through both national data protection authorities and the importance of preserving data controller reputation. There may be many data processors associated with a PRM system. A data processor may be an element operating under direct management of the data controller, or it may operate as a separate entity, under a contractual arrangement with the data controller. Since the data controller enlisted the data processor to render services, liability ultimately falls to the data controller for correct data processor operations. In this PRM system there may be many data processors dealing with data from many different data controllers. This situation is very similar to the DRM case where a user may interact with many different content providers.

When comparing Fig. 2 and Fig. 3, definite parallels may be drawn between the PRM and DRM system components. Table 2 outlines these comparisons.

The PRM server block provides base PRM services. Personal data in a PRM system plays a similar role to that of Protected Property in a DRM system (see Table 2).

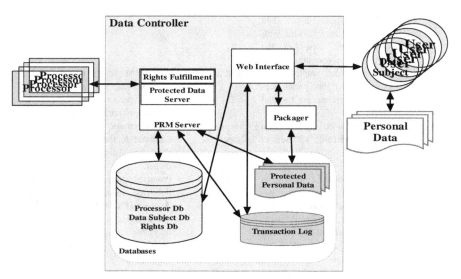

Fig. 3. A simplified privacy rights management system showing the three participants: data subject, data controller, and data processor.

The Data Subject owns the data, and entrusts it to the PRM server wherein it is protected and managed by the data controller. Data subject profiles are treated as electronic property assets in DRM. In order to perform its functions, the server block must maintain and use different sets of data. As well, it will manage data exchanges with processors to meet potentially a wide variety of processing objectives.

The PRM server maintains several databases. A rights database provides information regarding how personal data is managed within the system. There are also data-

Table 2. DRM and PRM system component parallels.

PRM Component	PRM Comments	DRM Component	DRM Comments
Data Subject	The Data Subject entrusts a relatively small amount of data for management by the data controller. The data controller manages the data, including its distribution to data processors.	Owner	The Owner entrusts its electronic property to the DRM server for distribution. In contrast to its PRM counterpart, the Data Subject, there are relatively few Owners as compared to Data Subjects.
Data controller Web Server	The data controller acts as the enforcer of usage requirements associated with personal data, with accountability provided through detailed logging. The web server provides an interface providing data subjects with several views such as the 'objection view' where they can access, rectify, revoke and maintain their personal data. Data controllers are provided with management views of the PRM system operation.	Content Provider Web Server	The Content Provider Web Server provides an interface allowing owners to maintain personal data and for management of the system. The Owners may track usage and other information regarding the their data.
PRM Server(s)	Privacy rules implementing triad entity rights, preferences and requirements are handled here.	DRM Server	The DRM server contains rules implementing the way in which owners' property and subscribers' interactions are managed.
Personal Data	Data provided by the data subject traceable to them in some way.	Electronic Property or Asset	The electronic property (content) entrusted to the DRM system for controlled distribution by the owner.
Protected Personal Data	PRM protected property is personal information entrusted to the data controller, held and distributed using data protection. The number of entities among which the property is shared (data controller and data processors) is smaller than in the DRM protected property scenario.	Protected Property	Protected property is held and delivered using data protection. Access to the property is controlled via a rights usage policy. There may be a very large number of people gaining access to the protected property.

bases containing processor and data subject reference information, as well as activity logs for collecting information regarding system operation. Interestingly, while there is the potential for unbridled user tracking in a DRM system, when adapting DRM to PRM, the tables are turned where the activities of both data controller and data processor are monitored. PRM data subject tracking would be strictly in accordance with the stipulations of The Directive's Article 7.

At the organizational level, there are also important distinctions between DRM and PRM. System elements within DRM models may well be operated by different legal entities. Thus the partner selection criteria for a privacy-conscious firm will naturally consider the degree of trust a potential partner presents regarding its privacy practices. One foresees several ways to achieve that credential, with the most obvious being extensive notification of organizational privacy practice, augmented with strong controllability via external privacy auditing. One aspect of interpretation of the security stipulations from The Directive from the perspective of Dutch data protection law is that contracts between data controller and data processor must provide assurance that data processors will enforce a security policy as rigorous as the one to which the data controller is subject. Service Level Agreements with bi-lateral audit rights would be appropriate here.

3.1   DRM Evolution to PRM

The three aspects of DRM functionality of interest to PRM are Asset Creation, Asset Management and Asset Usage.

Asset Creation (as illustrated in Fig. 4) supports rights creation and validation. Rights validation ensures content may only be created from *existing* content if the rights exist to do so. Rights creation allows rights to be assigned to content. Below we schematically illustrate asset creation.

The driving purpose behind DRM - content distribution management - relates easily to data protection constructs, constraining the exchange of personal data. Article 6 (d) of The Directive builds arguments related to the responsibility of data quality on the part of the data controller and, by association, the data processor. Similarly, Article 12 (b) will require the data controller to provide the data subject with opportunity to amend his or her personal data. In addition, the data must be of consistent quality in all its instances. As well, a retention period of personal data that is either based upon legitimate grounds or consented to must be upheld.

Asset Management supports the access and retrieval of both content and metadata in distributed databases. Asset Management also provides logging functionality. Article 6 (c) requires data controllers to process volumes of personal data that are minimized for the task at hand. More centrally, PRM asset management maintains data subject's rights over their data, which would be managed by a PRM asset management rules engine. The rules engine also codifies data controller interests so that, for instance, a data subject objection to a processing request, may not be complied with by the data controller, if the data subject has not explicitly consented to the processing.

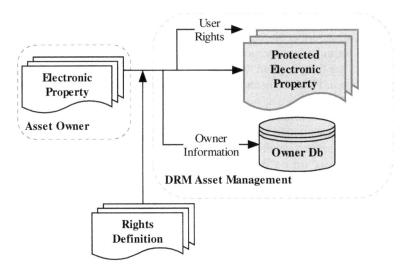

Fig. 4. DRM asset creation.

The PRM system must implement a high degree of monitoring of subject data usage. As well, the monitoring process itself must be protected. With multiple data processors operating on personal data, the data controller is in a high-risk position if any data processor engages in illegitimate processing. A data controller requirement will therefore be for each contractually engaged data processor to maintain cryptographically protected log files [8] relating to the operations on al personal data. In addition to meeting the requirements of The Directive, it would offer the data controller a means for data controller monitoring of privacy performance via log analysis.

Asset Usage supports permission management and (depending upon definition) audit trail functionality that permits the usage environment to honor rights associated with content. This offers a means for monitoring and tracking content use. Below we illustrate some functional elements of a DRM system especially required for content usage monitoring.

The PRM server must extend the core logic associated with DRM server asset usage so as to support the PRM operational context: a large number of different owners of electronic property, many distributed data processors, as well as major responsibilities under The Directive (see Fig. 5). Three key entities contained within a DRM server are the Content Server (CS), the Rights Fulfillment Server (RFS) and the Usage Clearing Server (UCS). These entities are present, but reconfigured, in a PRM server. In DRM, the CS standard task is to distribute cryptographically packaged content, accessible by retrieving content and rights keys. In PRM, the CS manages the controlled distribution of personal data assets. A significant difference in a PRM secure container however is that it may have a varied granularity level of asset protection and auditing requirements based upon role-based rules the requirements of Article 7 of the Directive.

The functionality provided by the RFS in DRM ranges from providing payment receipts to recording asset accesses and device sets. In PRM, the RFS enables the tracking of processor use of subject data. The Asset tracking databases must be tamperproof, to prevent unauthorized changes to the tracking records. Article 6 (b) of The Directive may be implemented by appending a retention period to personal data. This retention period is transfer-independent. If the period agreed to is 30 days, and the data controller passes this data to a data processor after 15 days, the data processor must conform to the remaining 15-day retention period. Once the retention period is exhausted, all instances of the personal data must be erased. Given this requirement, RFS functionality may be extended to coordinating asset usage information databases. This extension is required to meet Article 6 (b) of the Directive. To support temporal semantics, a secure timing mechanism linked to the database is required.

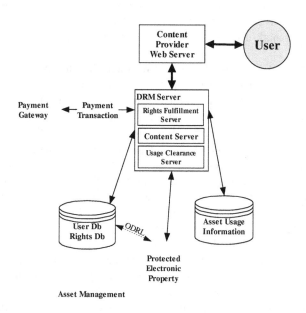

Fig. 5. DRM asset usage.

Basic UCS functions include recording and analyzing transaction data. From Fig. 5, the PRM server is advised by the rights database of the degree to which personal data may be disclosed to other parties, according to original data controller data capture conditions. There must be sufficient granularity in the operation of the usage clearance server to link different purpose specifications to different parts of data subject data. This permits implementation of both Article 6 (b) through the ability to identify which (element of) data is needed for each purpose, and Article 6 (d) via the retroactive and proactive updates necessary to assure data accuracy (plus audit trails) in the relationship between data protection concepts such as purpose specification and the personal data itself.

Underlying these PRM requirements is a concept of data subjects controlling their personal data in much the same way that content owners or distributors control and monitor access and use of their digital content using DRM approaches. Interestingly, DRM systems gain maximum leverage from personal data through tracking consumer activity and subjecting that output to data mining at a clearing agency. In PRM, data subjects are able to visualize and influence the amount, quality and granularity of tracking information generated from their data.

4   Expressing Privacy

In this section, we describe entity modeling for a PRM system based upon the Open Digital Rights Language (ODRL). ODRL is a standard vocabulary for expressing the terms and conditions for the use of assets [6]. Our approach may also be applied to extensible rights mark-up language (XrML) [5]. The XrML approach is described elsewhere [7].

Modeling content is necessary in a PRM system because personal data is a non-homogeneous asset, in terms of its sensitivity, post processor download control, and also in terms of the data subject's ability to control some part of the asset. Since both personal data and usage tracking data are personally identifiable, they are, in the sense of data protection, one and the same thing. Since one can think of granularity as being descriptive metadata about a data subject herself in addition to usage information available at different levels of granularity to the asset viewer, then a standard vocabulary for the degree of granularity regarding both content and tracking information is a need which vendors and indeed standards bodies would do well to consider, though we do not consider further here.

DRM rights describe permissions, constraints and obligations between users and contents. DRM business models such as pay per play rely on client software receiving rights, formatted in rights languages that express the number of times a song can be played for instance. Rights metadata defines control over that content. For instance, a client may *view* but not *edit* a document. In PRM, these rights are configured to allow the data subject to exert control over personal data as permitted by data protection legislation. The data controller, when dealing with content, interprets and enacts those rights. It follows that the rights entity in a PRM system is a relevant target for privacy expression.

ODRL Specification 1.0 proposes a base set of semantics useable for PRM proposes including rights holders and the expression of permissible usages of assets. Consider below a DRM entity model for ODRL.

In terms of parties' expression, PRM is primarily interested in multiple processors all of whom must enforce and be advised of the processing preferences and requirements for assets. These preferences and requirements may be denoted by, for instance, jurisdictional origin and self determination metadata constructs appended to those assets. In a PRM system, the jurisdictional requirement regarding rights implies that a bi-directional operator would replace the unidirectional attribution between parties and rights in Fig. 6 as rights for any personal data must match the legal requirements of the country of origin for the data subject.

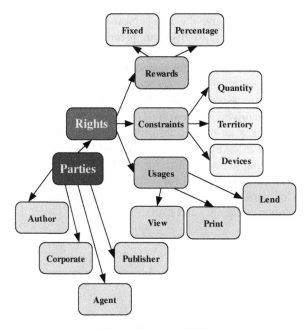

Rights and Parties for ODRL

Fig. 6. ODRL rights and parties model.

In terms of rights expression, there is a need to consider a vocabulary translated from The Directive to describe ODRL access rights for profiles, data subject metadata profiles in terms of granularity and tracking extensiveness, and also the contingent responsibilities passed to interacting processors. The current forms of ODRL *agreement*, *permissions and constraints* abstract elements, as they relate to the rights entity in the specification's data dictionary possess syntax that may be applied to a PRM system. The *agreement* element represents a concatenation of the entity's asset, context, party and permissions so as to express agreements between processors for specific rights over the assets of personal data. Specifying expression containers and linkages may be effectively used to generate data protection service level agreements (SLAs) between different legal entities operating under a PRM system.

Within the permissions abstract element two abstract entities have particular value to PRM systems: reuse and transfer permissions.

\<Permissions\> Abstract Element

Reuse	*Transfer*
\<Modify\>	\<Sell\>
\<Copy\>	\<Lend\>
\<Annotate\>	\<Give\>
	\<Lease\>

These metadata definitions give the data subject an unprecedented level of control over the processing of their data by disparate processors within a PRM system. The reuse abstract entity offers syntax applicable to reuse of some part of personal data, while the transfer abstract entity implies temporal constraints applied to personal data actions. This can be instantiated in expression fragments through ODRL-defined expression linking. In this aspect we find the semantic basis to realize, in part, our earlier description of finality as required by The Directive. Once a retention period is exhausted, a processor has an obligation to delete, or to make anonymous the personal data related to the asset. Further, the *modify and lend* abstractions would be key to instantiating versioning accountability for the data controller, for managing revisions of the personal information and for enforcing the responsibility to maintain an accurate version of personal to every implicated processor. This latter aspect is clearly related to notions of quality and data subject rights.

\<Constraints\> Abstract Element

Bounds	Temporal	Spatial	Aspect	Target
\<Count\>	\<DateTime\>	\<Country\>	\<Quality\>	\<Interval\>
\<Range\>	\<Accumulated\>		\<WaterMark\>	

The *bounds* abstraction may be applied for the benefit of the data controller, to model control of onward transfers of personal data. Indeed, the data subject herself may also make use of this, and in doing so, would be provided with a new level of control. In fact, the level of control could exceed that prescribed by The Directive.

The *temporal* abstraction represents important definitions for a PRM system, in view of the need for a timestamp tag. Ideally maintenance of this tag should be independent of any processor's infrastructure. The retention period functionality discussed earlier would be a timestamp abstraction.

The *spatial* abstract entity is an important tag for designating the country of origin of the data subject in PRM. As an indication of EU nationality, personal data must conform to the control and processing restrictions related to EU Community law – as we have illustrated through the simplification of *principles* (Table 1). For instance, if this entity indicates US citizenship, then in effect since there is currently no legal requirement to execute PRM system functionality for that user.

The *aspect* abstract entity appears to be the ideal focus of The Directive's data quality requirements and the requirements of data controllers to enforce these in processing. The *target* abstract entity is particularly interesting because of Article 8 of The Directive, regarding national implementation. Such an entity would limit the transfer of assets, even within the same legal entity, to uses similar to the original purpose of processing. In Fig. 7 we summarize the key changes needed to DRM metadata for PRM.

In addition to the expression technology for access rights to an asset, the P3P protocol also offers a ready-made data transfer platform that, in terms of data subject privacy preference expression, is generally judged to be sufficiently rich.

Because the rights attribute encapsulates semantic expression over assets, and because the Data controller, when dealing with assets, interprets and enacts rights, it follows that the rights entity in a PRM system is a key component of the PRM server's data controller and data processor management activities. Clearly this system element holds the assurance responsibility of enforcing legitimate processing, which may be realized through periodic examination of processor log files. A computational map of the appearance of legitimate processing for a given scenario is the main prerequisite for automated analysis of this crucial controllability parameter.

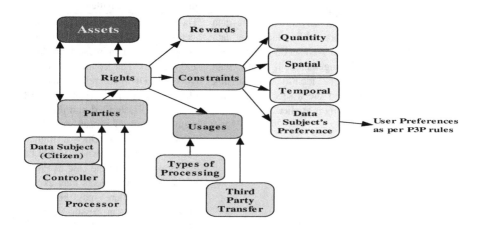

Fig. 7. PRM entity model.

5   Discussion and Conclusions

To clearly understand the potential of how effective adapting DRM to meet the demanding requirements for PRM would be, we analyze PRM requirements and implementation challenges with respect to the facilitation principles (Table 3).

It appears from Table 3 that adapting DRM systems holus bolus would accommodate PRM functionality with relative ease, forming a technical implementation of the privacy principles. However, there are areas that require further research and development. For instance, protection against unlawful processing and data traffic outside of the EU are two key areas potential technology development.

In the former case, a means for tracking the actual processing performed by a data processor is needed. A DRM system is well suited to track the time a data processor requests and receives data for processing, however it is not designed to restrict, track and record the actual processing performed. Once a data processor receives the data in the clear for an expressed purpose, the data processor may simply do what it wishes with the data. This information "leakage" by data controllers or data processors would be difficult to detect. To remedy this situation at least two approaches may be taken. One involves development of a means for determining the actual processing done by the data processor. Another involves deploying a reputation management and reporting system to assess over time which data processors may be most trusted to deal with personal data. Another possibility for accomplishing processing management might be a specialized type of sandbox wherein the personal data would be entrusted to the processor only if the processing to be performed by the subject may be verified before and after processing operations.

Table 3. PRM requirements and implementation challenges in meeting the privacy facilitation principles.

Principle	PRM Requirements	Implementation Challenges
1. Reporting the Processing	The PRM server tracks the data processors with which the data controller web server has processing arrangements. It tracks: data processor identity, processing type, and the assets upon which processing is applied.	There are many possible data subjects (many millions) and data processors (many hundreds, both local and remote). This contrasts dramatically with DRM wherein the number of content owners (Data Subject counterpart) is limited and there are many millions of subscribers (Processor counterpart). Only a limited number of content owners would be active at a time. In the case of PRM, all of the Data Subjects may expect reports, and there may be many hundreds of data processors active at any time. Therefore despite individual asset size (i.e., Data Subject personal information) being small, highly scalable approaches are required to manage the logging and reporting processes required in PRM in order to meet scalability requirements for the PRM server.
2. Transparent Processing	The PRM server provides data subjects the ability to view data controller / processor operations on subject data on an "on demand" basis.	DRM systems are designed to meter usage of content. In a PRM system, adaptation of usage tracking through secure distributed logging techniques is required. Centralized management via asset usage monitoring is the common approach in DRM for asset metering. However, this approach may not scale well. A major challenge for implementing this principle is that it is not currently possible to determine exactly what a processor is doing or what it has done with the personal data it has received.

Principle	PRM Requirements	Implementation Challenges
3. Finality and Purpose Limitation	When adapted for PRM, DRM means for specifying and enforcing requirements on processing of tangible assets may similarly protect personal data such as data subject consented retention periods.	There are many data subjects, each with potentially different rights specifications especially with regards to rights specifications for processing. Scalability challenges present themselves here if the data controller holds the rights, and there are many distributed data processors that must access each data subject's rights for processing. One way to mitigate this challenge would be to distribute rights as well as the personal data. Functionally (if not legally), this distributes responsibility for data protection enforcement from the PRM server to the data processor. A means for maintaining data controller-linkable responsibility is facilitated by the rights granting model specified by ODRL. For instance, personal data can travel separately with only information on where to get permission to process. At the time of processing, a request would be made to the Data controller, which would in turn return an ODRL "License". The "License" would contain the permissions and the conditions (time, territory, tracking state, etc) for processing. DRM systems support similar functionality for e-media distribution.
4. Lawful basis for data processing	The data controller may only process personal data on certain grounds. These grounds which must be replicated in all data processors of personal data.	The central problem of processing enforcement has yet to be solved. Considering DRM, It is difficult to ensure that once a user receives a license to use electronic material, that it is not processed in a manner that was not intended (for instance, in the case of music, making copies, or converting to other formats). The first step, however, is to standardize a data protection definition language as a starting point so as to control parsing. For instance, there may be an exchange of credentials between the data processor must possess in order to grant permissions. In this

Principle	PRM Requirements	Implementation Challenges
		case, the effectiveness of this approach depends upon the trust between the data controller and data processor. Since once the data is in the clear at the data controller, any sort of processing is possible.
5. Data Quality	Quality relates to specified attributes the asset must maintain. Effectively it must be as correct and accurate as possible for all who deal with the data.	If the data controller maintains a central repository of subject data and controls access for each data processor request, there is a reasonable likelihood data quality may be maintained. However, this approach is not scalable. On the other hand, if the personal data is distributed to provide scalability, the data must first of all be protected, and secondly, it must be possible to assure the data is consistent throughout should the data subject requires amendments.
6. Rights	The data subject has the right to determine and maintain the correctness of the relevant personal data held by the data controller. The data subject also has the right to raise objections as to the behaviour of the data controller and processors. For a PRM system, this requires editing provisions and a communication channel for raising objections.	In DRM asset management, owners may transfer content to the server for distribution. Content editing is performed by the owner offline, on a master copy of the content. To support an on-line editing function, some sort of online editing tools would be required. As well, access to the editing function must be authorized. Also, a communication channel for raising objections is required. An effective tool for raising objections would also include data mining tools of processing transactions. The objective would be to provide evidence of contract, or privacy breaches.
7. Data traffic outside the EU	The PRM server block should enforce grounds for data transfer on the basis data adequacy and exceptions – for EU nationals of different member states, as well as say American nationals who express a self-determination for EU data protection applied by a PRM system.	This requires the ability to identify the nationality of the data controller, and data processors, and the enforcement of suitable logic appropriate to origin. Unfortunately, there are currently no foolproof technologies to determine geographic location of users (although Quova Inc. [9] purports to have a solution). As well, rules systems to support multiple countries would be extraordinarily complicated.

Principle	PRM Requirements	Implementation Challenges
8. Processor processing.	The PRM server must decide when it will outsource data processing, and on the correct grounds in a dynamic arrangement. Key for this operation is the enforcement of data controller rules.	It is clearly challenging for the data controller to enforce processing among widely distributed data processors, apart from recourse to third party auditing. Negotiation techniques between data controller and data processor could determine a likelihood of compliance, but not enforcement.
9. Security	The data controller is responsible for ensuring data processors apply uniform security standards across all data controllers.	DRM secures content for distribution – PRM builds on this in an adaptive way as data protection prescribes – such as relating authentication to data sensitivity.

With respect to the issue of data traffic outside the EU, one aspect of this issue is the ability to determine geographical location of data controller and processor representations. There have been techniques and at least one service [9] developed to determine geographical location. Unfortunately, these approaches are far from foolproof. One means of circumvention involves the deployment of dynamic proxies. A further complication to dealing with data traffic outside the EU is that privacy laws do not have consistent electronic implementations that would facilitate any sort of automatic negotiation or decision-making around how to deal with subject data.

Other challenges exist regarding adoption of DRM architecture for PRM: third party tracking, scalability, and DRM purpose. Regarding third party tracking and scalability, DRM was developed to support delivery and protection of potentially vast amounts of electronic property from typically just a few owners or distributors. In PRM, relatively small amounts of data are collected from a very large number of citizens, where the citizen entrusts information to a data controller. All Data subject data must be tracked for use. This data must be managed, kept confidential and must be editable by the data subject to assure accuracy. A PRM system is designed to keep data protected as well as track the sharing of personal data. It is clear that conventional DRM systems potentially require extensive redesign to support this demanding application. Incorporating a Trusted Third Party approach wherein, a data controller or processor must "check out" information each time it is used may appear to offer a solution to this issue. Unfortunately, this approach adds considerable overhead to data controller and processor activities as well as being a single point of failure. An alternate approach might be the delegation of the use-tracking function to the data controller. While this would distribute the tracking function load, it would also require a high degree of *trust* between the data subject and the data controller.

Given that DRM systems may be used to profile individuals, one may question the value of considering such systems to implement privacy rights management to uphold data subjects' privacy. It is important to understand that in the PRM architecture we describe, the tables are turned; the digital material of value is user data. It is treated like the immaterial goods controlled in DRM. Rather than tracking purchasers of immaterial goods (music video, etc.) our system tracks the use of personal data by data controllers.

As we have illustrated, simply protecting data in storage and transit is no longer enough when considering The Directive. In our approach, we propose an adaptation of DRM functionality to provide privacy rights management for individuals. Given the embryonic commercial status of the privacy market and its projected economics in a commercial environment placing increased value in integrity, a PRM investment appears extremely worthwhile both in terms of what is necessary to come close to achieving compliance with current legislative requirements, and what is required to meet corporate privacy policies towards building a stronger trust relationship with clients. On the other hand, while the application of digital rights management appears to offer promise for privacy rights management, a fully scalable delivering an implementation to support The Directive would be challenging.

References

1. Official Journal L 281, 23/11/1995, 0031 – 0050
2. Deitz, L.: Privacy and Security – EC's privacy directive: protecting personal data and ensuring its free movement, Computers and Security Journal, V. 17, N. 4, (1998) 25-46
3. Council of Europe Convention 108: Convention for the Protection of Individuals with regard to Automatic Processing of Personal Data. Available at:
   http://conventions.coe.int/treaty/EN/Treaties/Html/108.htm
4. J. Feigenbaum, M. Freedman, T. Sander, A. Shostack: Privacy Engineering for Digital Rights Management Systems, Proc. of the ACM Workshop on Security and Privacy in Digital Rights Management 2001, Philedelphia, Nov. (2001). Available at:
   http://citeseer.nj.nec.com/feigenbaum01privacy.html
5. XrML is being contributed to the standards body OASIS Rights Language Technical Committee as its foundation technology. More information can be found at http://www.oasis-open.org/committees/rights/ or at http://www.xrml.org
6. Open Digital Rights Language (ODRL) Available at: http://www.odrl.net
7. Kenny, S., Korba, L.: Adapting Digital Rights Management to Privacy Rights Management, Computers & Security, V. 21, N. 7, (2002) 648-664
8. Schneier, B., Kelsey, J.: Secure audit logs to support computer forensics, ACM Trans. on Information and System Security, Vol. 2, No. 2, (1999) 159-176
9. Quova, Inc. at: http://www.quova.com/

Implementing Copyright Limitations
in Rights Expression Languages

Deirdre Mulligan[1] and Aaron Burstein[2]

[1] Director, Samuelson Law, Technology & Public Policy Clinic and
Acting Clinical Professor of Law, University of California School of Law (Boalt Hall)
Berkeley, CA, 94720
dmulligan@law.berkeley.edu
http://www.samuelsonclinic.org
[2] J.D. Candidate, Class of 2004, Samuelson Law, Technology & Public Policy Clinic
University of California School of Law (Boalt Hall), Berkeley, CA, 94720
burstein@boalthall.berkeley.edu

Abstract. Drafters of rights expression languages (RELs) claim that RELs will
form the basis for generic, content-neutral expressions of rights in digital objects, suitable for a broad range of contexts. Generally modeled on access control languages, RELs are structured predominantly as permission languages -
meaning that no rights exist in an object until they are affirmatively and specifically granted. The permissions-based exclusivity likely to result from existing
RELs and digital rights management (DRM) contrasts with the myriad limitations on exclusivity in the Copyright Act. Unless REL designers and DRM system implementers consider these limitations, DRM systems will alter the copyright balance in the direction of copyright holder exclusivity. In this paper we
propose changes to RELs that would approximate the copyright balance more
closely than current DRM technologies do.

1   Introduction

1.1   The Relationship between Rights and Rights Expression Languages

Simply put, current RELs reduce the expression of legal rights which may be: a)
given by the object's owner, b) conveyed clearly by a legal instrument, or c) asserted
by the individual (and reviewed after the fact for legal validity); to the granting of
"permissions" by the owner/rights holder of the digital object. Theoretically it is
possible for a third-party (government) or the user to grant rights, but it is difficult to
imagine either occurring for a mix of political and practical reasons. We acknowledge
that the term "rights" in RELs encompasses more than legal rights. Nevertheless,
when implemented to manage copyrighted works the rights defined in RELs will have
the practical effect of supplanting legal rights. Thus in the context of copyrights,
RELs and the DRMs in which they are deployed will replace the balance of rights
holders' and users' rights with self-enforcing, machine readable rule sets reflecting
the desires of copyright holders exclusively.

The exclusivity likely to result from existing RELs and DRM is in contrast with the
myriad limitations on exclusivity in the Copyright Act. To the extent DRM systems

J. Feigenbaum (Ed.): DRM 2002, LNCS 2696, pp. 137–154, 2003.

supplant the existing copyright rules with machine enforced licenses defined by copyright holders they will alter the copyright balance in the direction of copyright holder exclusivity.

If RELs are to be agnostic as to legal context they must at least support the expression of the exceptions and limits on exclusivity found in copyright policy. To do so, several additional steps must be taken to better align RELs, and thereby DRMs, with copyright policy. First, the REL must be supported by a messaging protocol that enables statements of "rights" in multiple directions and from multiple sources, and resolves conflicting assertions of rights. The messaging protocol and REL must allow for the assertion and exercise of rights not yet granted or recognized and their later resolution. Second, recognized social norms regarding the use of works should be easy to reflect in RELs. Third, recognizing that RELs alone cannot address the imbalance that DRM can introduce protocols for processing and enforcing REL-based rules should provide a buffer between rights holders and the users of copyrighted works. This separation would both alleviate some of the concerns relating to DRM technology and privacy and protect the kinds of unauthorized but fair use that the Copyright Act allows.

We consider how to implement these goals in the context of a particular REL, XrML (the eXtensibleRights Markup Language)[1].

1.2   The Differences between Permissions and Rights

The phrase "rights expression language," then, encapsulates a great deal of promise and controversy. The notion of a machine-readable statement that accurately expresses the rights of both copyright holders and users is a beguiling one. Such statements could aid in providing greater clarity to copyright terms, and even allow for works to be provided on terms more generous than those dictated by copyright law. Reliable enforcement of these statements could promote wider use and distribution of works in digital form [18]. Such distribution could be of benefit to the general public, if it allowed new opportunities to view, study, learn from, comment upon, copy, re-use and transform the works. This is the promise.

The controversy arises from the strong likelihood that DRM systems in which RELs are deployed give rights holders too much control over the terms of use for copyrighted works [32]. Indeed, the "rights" in DRM may have no relationship to legal rights, and are more accurately described as "permissions." Machine-readable rules that control access to digital works could inhibit, restrict, or altogether prevent many legally authorized uses. This creates a substantial likelihood that these machine-readable rule sets, written by rights holders and offered on an accept/reject basis to purchasers, could supplant copyright law [30]. As a result, the balance remaining in our copyright policy,-reflecting the interests of many groups, including copyright holders, creators, and purchasers of that content-would be replaced with contracts and machine-readable, machine-enforceable "code constraints" that reflect the interest of the rights holders alone [21].

Instances of this kind of control have already appeared. For example, Adobe eBooks may have licenses that forbid all copying, printing, lending, and even reading

---

[1] We choose to discuss XrML because it is a published language which can serve as the basis for a concrete discussion about REL capabilities.

aloud [9]. Neither readers of books nor listeners of music nor viewers of films encounter analogous controls with audio or visual media. Machine-enforced use restrictions, in other words, frequently defy the "real space norms" that have developed around the use of copyrighted works [10]. Some of these norms, enshrined in the Copyright Act itself, are legally protected. Moreover, copyright law leaves the private use of copyrighted materials essentially unregulated [20]. The Act does not empower copyright holders to require readers, viewers, or listeners to seek authorization before using a work privately[2]. Privacy is crucial to the full exploration of purchased works. Privacy is protected by the structure of the Copyright Act, the "real space norms" regarding the use of copyrighted works, and the constitutional protections for speech, freedom of association and access to information [38]. Preserving the privacy of readers, viewers, and listeners also has a practical benefit to copyright holders. There is substantial evidence from the digital environment that collecting usage information, especially when this data contains personally identifying information, repels people from the use of expressive materials [15, 18].

The limitations on copyright's exclusivity also extend to activities that affect the commercial value of a work. The "first sale" doctrine, for example, allows purchasers of legal copies of works to dispose of them in any manner they choose [5]. Copying, even for the purpose of publishing excerpts in a commercial product, receives substantial protection under the "fair use" statute [3]. Fair use is an especially open-ended part of the Copyright Act. Determining whether a use is fair often requires fact-intensive litigation, but this flexibility has contributed to copyright's ability to accommodate new technology and to protect the kinds of expression that the Copyright Act is meant to promote [23].

We do not claim that it is necessary or even possible for a REL to provide for "fair use" statements or that DRM systems be designed to act as a "judge on a chip" [23]. Instead, we highlight the fact that the Copyright Act leaves wide varieties of activity unregulated and allows for the flexible evolution of "fair use." The evolution of fair use depends on, and the exercise of exceptions to copyright presupposes that, users may determine for themselves whether to seek "permission" for a given use. The Copyright Act provides a framework that allows "rights" to flow from several sources - the owner of the object (or copyright holder), a third party (including the government), and the user.

Unfortunately, the limitations on the exclusive grants given to rights holders under the Copyright Act, the breathing room required for "fair use," and the various entities who can grant or claim rights do not appear to have prompted consideration of analogous limits and supports in RELs. Instead, common RELs take the exclusive rights of copyright [2] as an unqualified baseline and then provide the means for rights holders to make the work available under issuer-defined access models. XrML and other rights languages can do more to reflect the balance between "exclusive rights" and "unrestrained public access" that copyright law seeks to create [24]. In addition, RELs lack the ability to provide key contextual clues that would allow the REL, and DRM

---

[2] In certain contexts courts have enforced contractual restrictions on a purchaser's rights under copyright [26]. Whether such restrictions will be enforceable in all circumstances is uncertain. This uncertainty arises from the minimal requirements for assent that "clickwrap" and "browsewrap" licenses rely upon and from concern that these licenses violate public policy by restricting the dissemination of uncopyrightable material.

systems, to more closely approximate "fair use" and identify exceptions to exclusive rights.

Considering the concrete, statutory limitations on copyright provides one method of expressing this balance. We also suggest that REL designers include instances of familiar "real space" works in REL vocabularies, with semantics that approximate the real space uses of these works. We suggest the inclusion of several elements designed to provide contextual inputs to support "fair use" modeling. We recommend the inclusion of a rights messaging protocol to ensure that grants and claims of right can be made by parties other than the copyright holder. We present these ideas in detail in Section 3. A REL that approximates real space norms does not address the privacy-based objections unique to DRM systems. Specifying a license enforcement protocol that allows users to choose license processing systems not controlled by the copyright holder would substantially reduce the incentive to gather personal information from license processing transactions. Limiting the information collection supported by the REL to pseudonyms will further reduce the privacy concerns of DRM. Section 4 contains a practical discussion of how RELs, and the protocol for evaluating REL-based licenses, could be designed to better protect privacy.

2   Rights Expression Languages

Current RELs use an access control-based approach to managing all kinds of content. The result of this model is that a top-down, unidirectional flow of rights inheres in all communications of usage rules. XrML, which we briefly describe, adopts this approach. The access control model is manifestly unsuited to the kinds of communication that must take place if a REL is to facilitate any reasonable approximation to copyright law. In Section 2.2, we suggest an approach to RELs that will at least allow users to claim the rights they have under existing law.

2.1   The Present: XrML

XrML is an XML-based [34] rights expression language. Its substance is defined in two specifications: the Core Specification and the Standard Extension Specification [13, 14][3]. These specifications are expressed in the form of XML Schemas [35]. XrML was contributed to the Rights Language Technical Committee of the standards body OASIS as the basis for a REL specification [25]. A highly simplified representation of the XrML Core Schema is given in Figure 1. Branches that are at the same depth on the tree form a valid sequence under the schema.

2.2   The Future: RELs That Allow Bi-directional Communications

Copyright law grants certain rights to purchasers and other users of copyrighted works. It is neither a legal nor a practical requirement for users to declare (or claim) these rights *explicitly* in order to enjoy them. While the public's legal rights cannot be

---

[3]   Earlier versions (through Version 2.0) of XrML included a Content Extension, which defined such a number of concrete rights and methods for expressing metadata.

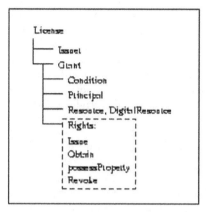

Fig. 1. A simplified representation of the XrML hierarchy.

altered by DRM systems *per se*, we can imagine scenarios in which DRM systems may require users to make these kinds of declarations, in order to work around inherent technical limitations. It is therefore essential that a rights expression language (REL) provide the vocabulary necessary for individuals to express, in a straightforward way, the rights that copyright law grants them to use materials. The user's claim of right would provide the essential information for a usage-rights issuing agency to give the user the technical capability to use the work in a particular way.

For the purposes of this discussion we will set aside the question of whether contract law may qualify (or narrow) the rights that a recipient of a work has under copyright law, acknowledging that there are contexts in which a party may wish to narrow the rights it grants to the recipient of a work. Outside the context of the relationships created by copyright between rights holders and users, there are contractual relationships that the REL must also support. For example an employer may want to control employee use of company information. In many instances it is important that both parties in the relationship be able to assert their rights and/or desired terms. True negotiation between parties requires that, at a minimum, the REL provide the vocabulary and syntax to support bi-directional exchanges. Otherwise, the rights transaction reduces to the mere request for and acceptance of an offer of permissions asserted by the rights holder.

At a minimum, recipients of works must have the ability to assert their rights as recognized under copyright law, and have these assertions reflected in their ability to use the work. Extending an REL to support a broader range of statements that reflect current law is, however, insufficient. The *rights messaging protocol* (RMP) layer must also be extended to accommodate both the downstream and upstream assertion of rights [39]. We recognize that the RMP layer is not currently within the scope of this discussion, but we believe that the assumption of a one-way expression of rights has in part led to the deficiencies in the RELs that are currently available.

3   Copyright

The Constitution grants Congress "power...to promote progress of science and useful arts, by securing for limited times to authors and inventors the exclusive right to their respective writings and discoveries" [33]. The Copyright Act is one manifestation of this power [1][4]. The Act specifies, in 17 U.S.C. § 106, that copyright is the exclusive right of authors of original works to reproduce, distribute, publicly perform and publicly display their works. Copyright holders also have the exclusive right to prepare derivative works. As holders of a certain kind of property-"intellectual" property-copyright holders can contract with others to perform engage in some of these activities. Copyright holders can also transfer their rights to others.

3.1   Statutory Limitations on Exclusive Rights

The exclusive rights in section 106 are not as simple as they appear. Some performances, reproductions, displays, and derivative works do not infringe the exclusive rights in a work, because parts of the Copyright Act explicitly carves these uses out of the copyright. In other words, engaging in these activities is not a defensible infringement, but simply not an infringement at all. A good deal of the Copyright Act's prolixity[5] is attributable to these exemptions, whose contours reflect political bargaining more than a coherent approach to copyright [22].

For example, the Act establishes the "first sale" doctrine, which limits the right to distribute copies of a work to the first sale of a work from a copyright holder [5]. Non-profit and governmental agencies that produce copies of published works in "specialized formats [braille, audio, or digital text] exclusively for use by blind or other persons with disabilities" do not infringe the derivative work right, because the Copyright Act does not grant this right in the first place [8]. Teachers, students, religious organizations, persons performing for audiences of the disabled, and many other non-profit groups may perform or display copyrighted works without infringing the public performance rights of the copyright holder [6]. Additionally, the Copyright Act grants libraries, rather than copyright holders, the right to make a copy of a work for noncommercial purposes, and three copies for preservation purposes [4]. Finally, copyright holders do not have the right to control the licensing of their works under all circumstances, as compulsory licenses govern the terms for live performances of musical compositions [7] and for the transmission of musical recordings in restaurants and stores [6]. Thus, the Copyright Act places bright-line, statutory constraints on the very definition of the copyright grant and also limits copyright holders' control over the alienability of some of their exclusive rights. The exceptions to copyright listed above are framed, non-exhaustively, in terms of role, audience, use, and purpose. To support copyright-consistent statements, a REL should allow for statements about these and other variables.

Despite the statutory limitations on copyright, it is still an expansive, and expanding, right. In the 1990s Congress buttressed copyright protection by defining new criminal provisions, extending the term of copyright protection, and by passing the Digital Millennium Copyright Act (DMCA). It is a violation of the DMCA to circumvent access controls, or to provide tools to others that circumvent access controls. The

---

[4] The ultimate limit of Copyright Clause power is the subject of a case that is under review by the Supreme Court of the United States at the time of this writing [17].

[5] Our discussion of statutory limitations is far from exhaustive. We highlight in our discussion those limitations that are most relevant to RELs aimed at the mass-market distribution of digital works.

DMCA places no duty on rights holders to ensure that their access control systems reflect users' rights, constitutional or otherwise. At the same time, the DMCA states that nothing in the act "shall affect rights, remedies, limitations, or defenses to copyright infringement, including fair use." Substantial question remains over whether or not courts will interpret the traditional defenses to copyright infringement as defenses to the anti-circumvention provisions as well. By making the circumvention prohibitions distinct from copyright infringement, defendants can be held liable for circumventing an access control measure even if the uses made of the work are held not to infringe on the rights of the copyright owner. The anti-circumvention provisions of the DMCA coupled with narrow RELs will essentially replace the broad contextual defense of fair use, discussed below, with a narrow set of carve outs to an otherwise absolute right of copyright owners to control access to and use of works.

If REL designers decide that the expression of legal rights is best left to semantic domains that are not part of the core REL, compliant implementations of the REL must support these semantic domains. A place to begin designing a REL that supports these rights is the fair use statute, which we discuss in the following section.

3.2   Fair Use

In addition to recognizing that certain communities have needs that are best served by limitations on copyright exclusivity, Congress recognized that original works form the basis for more than passive enjoyment. Works are praised, criticized, parodied - in general, transformed - in unanticipated ways. To restrict these transformative uses by requiring authorization from the copyright holder is to extinguish vast amounts of creative activity. Thus, fair use, along with the limitations on exclusivity discussed in Section 3.1, form the foundation for the public's rights which DRM systems[6], and the DMCA's protection of them, will "dramatically alter[ ]" [28]. In the following section we give an overview of the fair use statute, which has been central heretofore in setting the balance between copyright holders and the public. We then explore ways to reconcile some of the tension between fair use and DRM.

3.2.1 The Structure of the Fair Use Statute. Section 107 states that "the fair use of a copyrighted work, including such use by reproduction in copies or phonorecords or by any other means specified by that section, for purposes such as criticism, comment, news reporting, teaching (including multiple copies for classroom use), scholarship, or research, is not an infringement of copyright." Section 107 then lists four non-exclusive factors that are to be balanced in determining whether a use is fair:

1. the purpose and character of the use;
2. the nature of the copyrighted work
3. the amount and substantiality of the portion used in relation to the copyrighted work as a whole; and
4. the effect of the use upon the potential market for or value of the copyrighted work.

---

[6] Although the fair use statute itself does not tie the defense to the First Amendment, courts have done so. Courts have also established the idea-expression dichotomy as a framework for curbing copyright's limitations on speech.

A few features of the fair use statute deserve emphasis. First, Section 107 draws attention to certain kinds of uses – "criticism, comment, news reporting, teaching, scholarship, or research" - that weigh in favor of a finding of fair use. Second, fair uses of copyrighted works involve uses that are within the exclusive rights of the copyright holder[7], but a fair use "is not an infringement of copyright." Third, Section 107 presents four broad factors rather than bright-line rules. Fair use analysis therefore requires a fact intensive, case-by-case approach. This inquiry is necessary to set the correct balance between the exclusivity of a copyright and the public interest in being able to freely discuss others' works. Although the fair use statute mentions specific uses that are likely to be considered fair, the statute does not link *uses* to *roles*, though a role may be one of the facts that a court considers in determining fairness. Finally, the four factors are non-exclusive, leaving courts free to consider other factors in determining whether a use is fair. In summary, a fair use is

1. an unauthorized use
2. within the exclusive rights of the copyright holder
3. but which requires no compensation to the copyright holder.

3.3   Reducing DRM's Interference with Fair Use

The broad factors that determine whether a use of a copyrighted work is fair do not lend themselves to automated decision-making. It is impractical to expect the rights expression language component of a DRM system to support the machine-readable expression of a fair use. Focusing too heavily on the REL leads us astray and excludes many possibilities to ease the threat to fair use, so future RELs should be developed with an eye toward the REL's role in a DRM system. To illustrate the importance of the integrated development, consider the printing of a few pages from a digital book at home. Most RELs would express this proposed action as "print," the quantity printed, and identification of the resource printed. An enforcement engine would then allow or deny the request. If the REL-based rules allow the printing, the engine will allow it to proceed.

But what happens if the rules do not grant printing permission? The printing, if it could occur, would almost certainly be a fair use. In order to exercise this (legal) right, however, the owner of the book must (1) express the request in the REL and (2) communicate the request to the enforcement engine. Unless the REL is tied to a rights messaging protocol, as discussed in Section 2.2, the owner of the book is stuck, as he would be with current RELs. Moreover, expressions of the overall context of the use are required to more closely approximate fair use, even in this simple case, where the fact that the printing occurs for personal use is highly significant. In some cases, contextual inputs will include the recipients (audience) of the copied material, and in others the distinction between parody and satire.

We suggest three broad methods through which RELs and therefore DRM systems could reduce the burden of making fair use of a copyrighted work: (1) defining concrete syntax and semantics for certain kinds of rights, (2) creating a robust sphere for private use, and (3) designing limitations on copyright holders' abilities to extract

---

[7] We thank one of our reviewers for suggesting this phrasing.

payments for fair uses. Implementing these features would help preserve the extremely limited relationship between a copyright holder and a downstream purchaser, established by the Copyright Act, in particular the first sale doctrine. Since first sale arises from a separate statute, however, we delay discussion of it until Section 3.4.

A more detailed example will illustrate some of the challenges that fair use presents to DRM systems, and particularly RELs, as well as ways in which a REL can better accommodate fair use. Suppose a music critic has purchased an album which he plans to review. Instead of submitting this review for national radio broadcast, as is his custom, our critic plans to publish this review on his Web site. This critic's reviews always include excerpts of the work under review. Sometimes his reviews are favorable, but often they are searingly critical. Our critic wishes to keep this essential part of his reviews alive on the Web, so he decides to provide links to a few streaming audio files which contain the parts of the album that are relevant to his review. This critic has panned this band's last four albums and, after listening to the new work, plans to do the same in the present review. To complete his review, the critic must:

1. Copy portions of the album into streaming audio files. Seeking permission from the record label would be fruitless, the critic decides, because the label is unlikely to contribute to a negative review. To simplify the publishing and reading of his review, the critic decides to encode the album excerpts in an existing streaming format.
2. Publish his review.
3. Allow his readers to read his review. He does not charge a fee for access to his writings.

Thus, the critic's activities include rather extensive uses of the album, all of which would likely be found to be fair uses of the recording: limited copying without authorization, a change in file format, and access to the streaming audio files by anyone who wishes to read the review. These are difficult cases for a REL, but they are representative of the kinds of problems that must be analyzed under 17 U.S.C. § 107. We find that the general fair use problems that this scenario illustrates point to deficiencies of existing RELs in expressing fair use. The difficulty extends beyond any REL, however. DRM systems that are unrevised access control systems are unlikely ever to allow the kinds of uses that the Copyright Act recognizes[8].

3.3.1 Define Concrete Rights. Although certain elements of the XrML Core and Standard Extension would be useful in making fair use statements, XrML provides no means of making fair use the "default" for a License. Part of this problem arises from XrML's striving to be a general REL, one which makes no assumptions and imposes no limits on the kinds of resources to which the REL can restrict access. This generality leaves the Right element abstract, except for a limited number of Rights "which are related to the domain of XrML2 itself" (i.e., Issue, Revoke, Pos-

---

[8] Note that we do not state that these systems are "unlikely ever to implement all parts of the Copyright Act." Aside from being impractical, such an end may not even be desirable. Conceiving of copyright as a "copy" "right," for example, limits many solutions from the outset. Perhaps a more realizable goal is, to paraphrase the IETF, rough consensus, working code, and a balance of rights.

`sessProperty`, and `Obtain`). In a related problem, XrML provides few ways to identify a work. The Core Specification specifies a `DigitalResource` element, which allows the `License` to mark "arbitrary binary data" as being the "target object of relevance within the `Grant`."

To address these shortcomings, XrML could define more specific elements for digital works that correlate specific kinds of works with specific `Rights`. Developers of data dictionaries have undertaken the data modeling part of this work [16, 19]. The fact that metadata projects are, in large part, separate from other aspects of DRM system development raises doubt about the scope of relationships that will become part of the final DRM system [27]. A new element that provides some of the human-readable convenience of `Title` with the semantic power of `DigitalResource` would facilitate `Licenses` that grant these permissions. In particular, the XrML could define a "`Work`" element, which would have concrete descendants, such as "`Book`," "`Film`," or - as or music critic would want – "`MusicalAlbum`."

Although this level of specification would contrast with the emphasis that XrML places on being applicable to any kind of digital work, the neutrality that XrML claims as to the underlying content comes at a cost: the language imposes an access control model on all rule sets. To specify a few concrete kinds of `Works` does not suggest that a `License` should be required to use one of these concrete types, or a `Work` element mandatory in a `License`. Such a correlation between specific kinds of content and rights might call for a more flexible model of relationships than access control languages allow. This additional coordination of data modeling, language definition, and systems design could go a long way toward accommodating purchasers and rights holders who are concerned with maintaining vibrant fair use activities. The discussion in Section 3.3 indicates that a purchaser must be able to play the work without restriction, and also to copy parts of it. Thus, if a `Work` is a `MusicalAlbum`, the default interpretation of the `License` must be that the `Principal` - the music critic, who bought the album - must be able to play the album without restriction, and to copy arbitrary parts of the album. This suggests that a concrete `Work` would impose certain default `Rights`, which would be granted by a given kind of concrete `Work`. In the case of a `MusicalAlbum`, this would include "`Play`," "`Rewind`," "`Seek`," and "`Excerpt`" or "`Copy`" `Rights`. Similar default `Rights` can be specified for different kinds of `Works`.

3.3.2 Maintain (at least) an Arm's Length between Rights Holders and Purchasers.
These suggestions would help to ensure that purchasers of works will be able to use works in ways that approximate some uses of physical works, but XrML and other RELs must go further still to ensure that these uses remain uncompensated. Some integration of the `Fees` currently described in the XrML Standard Extension in the `Work` would likely be adequate to express the expectation that the use of a lawfully obtained work is not subject to oversight by the copyright holder.

To keep with the example of the music critic, we confine our attention here to the purchase of a `MusicalAlbum`. In this case, the `Fee`'s `PaymentAbstract` should be set to `PaymentFlat` by default. Thus, the purchaser of a `MusicalAlbum` would make a one-time payment for the recording, and would then have full use of the recording as specified above. Furthermore, all that the REL should require for a processing system's decision to allow or prohibit a proposed use of a `Work` is a comparison of the exercise with the exercises contained in the statement associated with the `Work` (i.e., the `MusicalAlbum` should grant `Play` permission), and verification that the required one-time fee has been paid. The processing system should make no inquiry into the extent or frequency with which the user seeks to exercise the rights.

This example in turn suggests that instances of a concrete `Work` should trump the effect of other XrML elements. In particular, elements such as `TrackReport`, `TrackQuery`, `SeekApproval`, and various flavors of `ValidityIntervals` should be given no effect by the processing system in the context of copyright[9]. By associating default rule sets with particular kinds of concrete `Work` trump these potentially invasive inquiries into the uses of a DRM-restricted work, the REL would render fruitless attempts by rights holders to reach beyond the provisions of copyright law in monitoring the uses of the `Works`. Finally, XrML and other RELs must address the distribution of works that fairly use other copyrighted works. In the music critic example, this problem arises in the context of the critic's readers, who must be allowed to play streams of the excerpts that the critic wishes to discuss in his review.

The XrML Core Specification provides some support for this end in the form of the `forAll` option in `Grants`. We suggest that concrete `Work` types provide a `LicensePart` granting universal use permissions appropriate to the kind of `Work`. A `MusicalWork` could contain a `LicensePart`, referring to the excerpts that the critic includes in his review, which would permit any user to play the excerpts. This requirement imposes similar overrides of

XrML elements that could be used to restrict access to the excerpts in a manner that is inconsistent with fair use. Alternatively, RELs could include an element that allows purchasers to change the format of the work. Although this kind of permission places some risk on the right holder of copying beyond the limits of fair use, that risk is explicitly placed on the copyright holder by the fair use statute. Other concrete `Works` require similar permissions for users of works that incorporate the copyrighted original, but we do not discuss them here.

It could be argued that the critic could obtain these `Rights` by negotiating with the entity that issues the rules. Indeed, some commentators have suggested that this kind of private ordering is more efficient than fair use and would increase access to informational works [39]. Others have pointed out, however, equating "social efficiency" (the optimization of progress and access) with "allocative efficiency" overlooks "the public-good nature of creative and informational works and the unpredictable pathways of creative progress" [36]. The "unpredictab[ility] of creative progress" is central to understanding how licensing usage rights, even if a DRM system reduces the burden of doing so relative to current transactional options, severely interferes with the values that Section 107 codifies. First, a purchaser would need to declare the uses that he plans to make of the work. In general purchasers cannot make these predictions. Our music critic, for example, has no way to know which segments of the album he will use in his review before he buys the album and listens to it. But even if he were equipped with precise plans for his use of a copyrighted work, requiring him to declare and license those uses is inconsistent with a fundamental purpose of fair

---

[9] The XrML Standard Extension also defines a Territory element, which presents the possibility that parties to a transaction would be able to apply a specific national law to their agreement.

use: permitting unauthorized uses that might be chilled if copyright law required that the fair user seek approval from the copyright holder. The music critic who plans to issue a negative review of an album provides a particular example of how critical uses of copyrighted material are likely to suffer if fair uses are replaced by declared, licensed uses.

3.3.3 Creating Private Sphere Use. As discussed above, copyright law grants certain rights to purchasers and other users of copyrighted works. It is neither a legal nor a practical requirement for users to declare (or claim) these rights *explicitly* in order to enjoy them. Thus the structure of copyright law is in tension with the access control model of RELs and DRM. One important aspect of the structure of copyright law is that private use of works is generally unregulated. Thus the ability of a REL to aid in distinguishing private use from, regulated public uses, such as distribution and sale, would better align with copyright law. For example, many of the "verbs" discussed above as being desirable closely track private uses (privately displaying or performing a work is different from sending or transmitting it) and could form the basis for the concept of private sphere use. Implementing such distinctions requires cooperation of the REL, the application, and the policy enforcement engine. The private sphere is a conceptual framework that if modeled in RELs could ease decisions about fair use.

Paradoxically, distinguishing between public and private use could diminish privacy. Plausible DRM implementations designed to make this distinction might: a) require declaration of when private use is being made; b) require that works be registered for use with certain pieces of hardware; or c) might require GUID/tracking of works. While there are methods of mitigating against the identification, data collection, and data reuse threats posed by these options they do not reflect the current norm of no data collection once a work is purchased. As others have noted, Fair Information Practice Principles, particularly collection limitation, disaggregation of identifying and transactional data, and data destruction should inform the design and implementation of all aspects of DRM [18]. We do not attempt to resolve the privacy concerns here, but rather to call attention to the competing requirements placed upon RELs and DRM.

3.4   First Sale

As indicated in Section 3.1, Section 109 of the Copyright Act authorizes a person who has lawfully obtained a copy of a work to "dispose of the possession of that copy" by sale or otherwise. Thus, the copyright holder retains no control over the distribution of copies after the "first sale" to a purchaser. First sale encourages people to explore new works by using them as they see fit, and then transferring possession to another party. When this transfer involves a sale, the seller recovers some money to apply to another purchase, if she wishes. The buyer obtains a copy of a work, perhaps at a lower price than the original buyer paid. XrML and other RELs should define language elements that permit analogous post-first sale transfers of digital works.

A workable implementation of Section 109 requires not only (1) that no permission be obtained from, nor any compensation paid to, the copyright holder but also (2) that the seller no longer be able to use the copy that she has sold. Thus, the basic problem for a DRM system is to record the current owner of a copy without collecting data about the entire history of the copy, or providing the right holder with an opportunity to interfere with the transfer. Collecting information that defines the state of a copy also raises privacy concerns, which are best handled by a broader consideration of a license processing protocol. The need for careful consideration of users' privacy is especially important in light of proposals to embed "traitor tracing" marks in informational works [40, 41]. Although the ostensible purpose of such tracing is to identify parties who illegally share information, tracing technology also provides a powerful mechanism by which a rights holder could collect detailed information about the use of copies without necessarily gaining a more effective enforcement tool than those provided by current law and technology. A more complete discussion of this point is in Section 4. Here, we outline REL vocabulary that lays the foundation for a license processing protocol that builds upon privacy protections for users.

3.4.1 Create a Transfer Right. Within the context of XrML, the core `Rights` should include a "Transfer" `Right`. `Transfer` should be part of all `Licenses` by default. Although `Transfer` may be inconsistent with certain kinds of transactions, such as rentals, overriding the `Transfer Right` should be left to those particular situations. Exercising a `Transfer Right` would trigger a mandatory response from the processing system, as described below.

3.4.2 Require That Processing Systems Issue New Licenses for Transfers. License processing systems must honor `Transfer` exercises. As Section 109 makes plain, a copyright holder has no right to restrict the alienability of copies of a work after the first sale. To preserve this separation between rights holders and users, processing systems must not reject `Transfer` requests. In effect, we suggest that processing servers be required to issue new rule sets upon the request of a holder of the current rule set, with the effect that the previous license is terminated. Mark Stefik has already described how this information could be recorded by maintaining a record of keys or digital signatures that are valid (or invalid) for use with a given work [31]. If a right holder wishes to restrict transfers of copies of the work, he must do so by reaching some agreement with the purchaser that removes the default `Transfer Right` from the `License`. Such a transaction requires recording of information about the work as an incident of transfer, but not about the buyer or seller. Furthermore, and in contrast to Stefik's proposal, neither the REL nor the DRM system should assign the copyright holder the default right to collect a royalty on each transfer of a work. Allowing the purchaser to specify a processing system would help to enforce this behavior, as discussed in Section 4.

3.5   Some Materials Are Not Copyrightable

It is crucial that REL designers recognize that not all expressions receive the protection of copyright. Two important examples are facts (as opposed to the expression of a fact) and works that reside in the public domain, either because the author dedicated the work to the public domain, or because copyright protection on the work has expired. XrML and other RELs should specify elements in the REL that help to identify such works.

3.5.1 Facts. The `DigitalResource Resource` (see Section 3.3 above) of an XrML Grant would appear to lend itself to an expression of where a fact is located within a work. We suggest that XrML contain a sibling `Fact Resource`, which could be used to mark the parts of a work that the copyright on the work as a whole does not protect. Although adding this markup to rule sets would involve some effort and expense, this effort would introduce tremendous value by marking information that can be freely shared, without a cloud of uncertainty as to copyrights claimed in the information. Use of the `Fact` element could be especially conducive to automated markup when a copyrighted work contains segments of data that are not themselves copyrightable, and the author wishes to signal that the data are not protected by copyright.

3.5.2. Public Domain. The access restrictions that DRM systems place on copyrighted works must not be used to restrict access to works in the public domain. XrML and other RELs would likely meet with wider approval if they provided a robust mechanism for marking public domain works. This specification could be quite simple. We propose a `Grant` sibling, `PublicDomain`, which would grant permission to all Principals to exercise all `Rights` relevant to the `Resource`. These children of `PublicDomain` should be the only possible children; since the work is in the public domain, there is no basis for imposing stricter access control to the work. A `PublicDomain` would contain no `Conditions` restricting its use. Such `Works` could, however, be incorporated into new copyrighted works. In other words, we propose that `Fact` and `PublicDomain` elements serve more of a data description function, rather than an enforcement function.

4   Privacy

When a person buys, rents, or borrows a copy of a creative work fixed in a tangible medium, he does not expect that his use of that work will be monitored by the seller or the rights holder. An author, for example, cannot count how many times a reader flips to a given page, nor can a movie studio determine how many times a home viewer watches a given scene. Purchasers of physical copies of works also expect that any intermediaries, such as retailers or libraries, will not reveal data about who has bought which work. These expectations are admittedly somewhat different on the Web, where it is well known that many sites collect detailed data about how visitors use a site. But the more applicable set of expectations here are those of "physical" purchase or borrowing, that is, of transactions between two parties that involve an explicit agreement about what each party is providing the other[10]. There may be some

---

[10] Of course, privacy concerns also affect how people use the Web [15]. The privacy problem maybe somewhat less acute on the Web, because a) frequently tracking occurs without name, address or other personally identifiable information; b) there are often several sites that provide similar information; and, c) Web sites have come under regulatory and public pressure to create better privacy policies. Copyrighted works in contrast to Web sites are more likely to be unique. Thus copyright holders may have a stronger position than a Web site to demand access to private information as a condition of access to a work.

revelation of personal information at the time of purchase, but that exchange of information is incidental to the transaction, not somehow tied to the purchaser's use of the work. Purchasers of digital works will expect that DRM systems do not diverge from these boundaries.

4.1   The Rights Expression Language Must Minimize Expressions of Personally Identifying Information

One way in which a REL can limit the expression of personal information is to specify a concrete implementation of the `Principal` element, rather than leaving the `Principal` abstract. The `Principal` should identify only the work, not the individual who purchased it. Thus, the `Principal` need be no more complicated than some unique alphanumeric string. The specification should prohibit extensions in the copyright domain that allow the expression of information that is tied to the person who purchases the work.

Threats to users' privacy may also arise from elements that are necessary to enforce certain rules. Creating a rule set with an "expiration date," for example, obviously requires that the REL be able to express the time interval during which the work may be used. XrML should specify, however, that the program evaluating the license may use such elements only for the purpose of rendering a ternary decision-granting or denying permission to use the work in the way the user requests, or granting permission of no other `Condition` exists preventing its exercise. The processing system must not store or otherwise use this kind of information outside the context of transient decisions about use permissions. Although it may be impossible to include this restriction in a REL itself, the REL could still make honoring such a restriction a condition of compliance with the REL's specification.

Another way to discourage storage of data about users' actions is to remove from the basic REL the capacity of the right holder unilaterally to terminate or otherwise modify the license. The `RevokeRight`, is one example of an element that invites monitoring of the uses of protected digital works for purposes other than ternary yes/no/maybe decisions. Including a `RevokeRight` in a license provides an incentive to determine whether users are attempting to exceed the terms of their licenses, which in turn provides an incentive to monitor and store information. For example, an `Issuer` should not be allowed, upon discovering that a purchaser has tried 15 times within the last half-hour to copy all of a work, to terminate the license to view the work. There is no need, and no basis in copyright law, for a license processing system to permit a right holder or rule issuer to monitor and track attempted uses of a work. While such a `RevokeRight` may be appropriate in other domains its existence in the core invites misuse in the copyright domain. Finally, REL designers should note that intermediaries can protect individual privacy, a role RELs and the protocols that use them should exploit [11, 18]. A right holder generally has no direct access to the personal information that intermediate parties might be able to collect about purchasers, and the specification should preserve this state of affairs. While the preceding discussion provides suggestions which, if implemented, would severely restrict rights holders' access data that becomes available as a byproduct of DRM restrictions, the REL should do even more. The following sections contains more specific suggestions for how the REL can promote user privacy.

4.2   The REL Must Allow Users to Select License Processing Systems

The need for a vertical approach to DRM again becomes apparent when one examines the role of enforcement systems. Both rule makers and the purchasers of digital works must be able to trust the entity that processes usage rules. While a rule issuer has an obvious interest in ensuring that the terms of a license are executed, the purchaser of a work also will also require that the processing system does not use personal information about the user for any purpose other than rendering a yes/no/maybe decision on the proposed use of a work. It is therefore essential that the REL allow users be able to control the choice of processing system, whether the user possess a physical copy of a work or accesses it via a "locker services," which permit users to access works upon authentication and authorization [29].

XrML's support for multiple Issuers of Licenses suggests an analogous construction for license processors. In particular, the REL should contain a Processor entity, which would specify the location of a trusted (by the Issuer and the end user) license processing system. The Processor must not be assumed, by default, to be identical to the Issuer. The License must be able to contain multiple Processors. Furthermore, the REL must allow the user to select this processing system, and to change it at any time after purchase. Finally, RELs should specify that the processing system may not store any data related to a use request beyond the time required to render a ternary yes/no/maybe decision. It is expected that this time will be very short, lasting only as long as the rule evaluation. REL specifications should also require that information generated as an incident of transactions not be shared with any entity outside the processing system.

5   Conclusion

The vocabulary and structure of a REL is of central importance to a DRM system. Creating a REL robust enough to support copyright-consistent rule sets is a significant challenge. To do so, REL developers must consider the limitations on copyright exclusivity. This challenge must be confronted by REL designers for DRM systems to be useful in the copyright context and gain public acceptance. The fact that published works can be examined and used as their lawful possessors see fit - without authorization and without surveillance by rights holders - is the basis for much of the demand for these works and, more importantly, is a central feature of cultural participation and development. RELs should provide a platform that supports rule sets and access to copyrighted works in a fashion that tracks social norms and the limitations of copyright law itself.

References

1. 17 U.S.C. § 101 et seq.
2. 17 U.S.C. § 106 (enumerating exclusive grants in copyright)
3. 17 U.S.C. § 107 (codifying fair use)
4. 17 U.S.C. § 108.
5. 17 U.S.C. § 109(a) (defining the first sale limitation to the distribution right)

6. 17 U.S.C. § 110
7. 17 U.S.C. § 115
8. 17 U.S.C. § 121
9. Therien, J.R.: Exorcising the Specter of a "Pay-Per-Use" Society: Toward Preserving Fair Use and the Public Domain in the Digital Age. Berkeley Tech. Law J. 16 (2001) 979, 1030-31, n.268 (citing an eBook license, one of whose terms is "Read Aloud: This book cannot be read aloud")
10. Bartow, A.: Electrifying Copyright Norms and Making Cyberspace More Like a Book. Presented at the "Fair Use by Design?" Workshop at Computers, Freedom, and Privacy. San Francsico, CA, April 16, 2002. Available at http://www.cfp2002.org/fairuse/bartow.pdf
11. Burk, D. and Cohen, J. E.: Fair Use Infrastructure for Rights Management Systems. Harvard J. of Law & Tech. 15 (2001) 41
12. Committee on Intellectual Property Rights and the Emerging Information Infrastructure: The Digital Dilemma: Intellectual Property in the Information Age. National Academy Press, Washington, D.C. (2000)
13. ContentGuard: eXtensible Rights Markup Language Core Specification, Version 2.1. Available as part of a ZIP archive at
    http://www.oasis-open.org/committees/rights/documents/xrml200205.zip
14. ContentGuard: eXtensible Rights Markup Language Standard Extension Specification, Version 2.1. Available as part of a ZIP archive at
    http://www.oasis-open.org/committees/rights/documents/xrml200205.zip
15. Cranor, L. F., Reagle, J, and Ackerman, M.S.: Beyond Concern: Understanding Net Users Attitudes About Online Privacy. AT&T Labs-Research Technical Report TR 99.4.3. Available at http://www.research.att.com/resources/trs/TRs/99/99.4/99.4.3/report.htm
16. Dublin Core Metadata Initiative. http://dublincore.org/
17. Eldred v. Ashcroft, 255 F.3d 849 (D.C. Cir. 2001), cert. granted 122 S. Ct. 1062 (2002)
18. Feigenbaum, J., Freedman, M., Sander, T., and Shostack, A.: Privacy Engineering for Digital Rights Management Systems. In: Proceedings of the 2001 ACM Workshop on Security and Privacy in Digital Rights Management. Springer-Verlag. Berlin (2002)
19. Interoperability of Data in E-commerce Systems (<indecs>) Project. See
    http://www.indecs.org/
20. Lessig, L.: The Future of Ideas: The Fate of the Commons in a Connected World. Random House. New York. (2001)
21. Lessig, L.: The Law of the Horse: What Cyberlaw Might Teach. Harvard Law Rev. 113 501, 529 (1999).
22. Litman J.: Digital Copyright. Prometheus Books, Amherst, New York (2001) 70-74.
23. von Lohmann, F.: Reconciling DRM and Fair Use: Preserving Future Fair Uses? Presented at the "Fair Use by Design?" Workshop at Computers, Freedom, and Privacy, San Francsico, CA, April 16, 2002. Available at http://www.cfp2002.org/fairuse/lohmann.pdf
24. Netanel, N.W.: Copyright and a Democratic Civil Society. Yale Law J. 106 283 (1996)
25. OASIS Rights Language Technical Committee.
    http://www.oasis-open.org/committees/rights/
26. ProCD v. Zeidenberg, 86 F.3d 1447 (7th Cir. 1996)
27. Röscheisen, R.M.: A Network-Centric Design for Relationship-Based Rights Management. Ph.D. dissertation, Stanford University (1997)
28. Samuelson, P. and Scotchmer, S.: The Law and Economics of Reverse Engineering. Yale Law J. 111 1575 (2002)
29. Sander, T. and Garnett, N.: What DRM Can and Cannot Do - and what It Is or Isn't Doing Today. Presented at the "Fair Use by Design?" Workshop at Computers, Freedom, and Privacy, San Francsico, CA, April 16, 2002. Available at
    <http://www.cfp2002.org/fairuse/garnett.pdf>
30. Sommer, J. H.: Against Cyberlaw. Berkeley Tech. Law J. 15 1145 (1999)
31. Stefik, M.: Shifting the Possible: How Trusted Systems and Digital Property Rights Challenge Us to Rethink Digital Publishing. Berkeley Tech. Law J. 12 137, 145-46 (1997)

32. "User" comments to the United States Senate Committee on the Judiciary. April 15, 2002. Available at http://judiciary.senate.gov/special/input_form.cfm
33. United States Constitution, Article I, § 8, clause 8. ("To promote the Progress of Science and useful Arts, by securing for limited Times to Authors and Inventors the exclusive Right to their respective Writings and Discoveries.")
34. World Wide Web Consortium, Extensible Markup Language (XML) 1.0 (Second Edition). Available at http://www.w3.org/TR/2000/REC-xml-20001006
35. World Wide Web Consortium, XML Schema Part 1: Structures, http://www.w3.org/TR/2001/REC-xmlschema-1-20010502/, and XML Schemas Part 2: Datatypes, http://www.w3.org/TR/2001/REC-xmlschema-2-20010502/
36. Cohen, J.E.: Lochner in Cyberspace: The New Economic Orthodoxy of Rights Management. Michigan Law Rev. 97 (1998) 462
37. Cohen, J.E.: A Right to Read Anonymously: A Closer Look at "Copyright Management" in Cyberspace. Connecticut Law Rev. 28 (1996) 981
38. Erickson, J.S.: OpenDRM: A Standards Framework for Digital Rights Expression, Messaging and Enforcement, available at http://www.ait.utk.edu/drmworkshop/opendrm_20sep02.pdf
39. Hardy, I.T.: Property (and Copyright) in Cyberspace. Univ. of Chicago Legal Forum 1996 217
40. Safavi-Naini, R. and Wang, Y.: Traitor Tracing for Shortened and Corrupted Fingerprints, available at http://crypto.stanford.edu/DRM2002/drm02.pdf.
41. Biddle, P., England, P., Peinado, M. and Willma, B.: The Darknet and the Future of Content Distribution. Available at http://crypto.stanford.edu/DRM2002/darknet5.doc

The Darknet and the Future
of Content Protection

Peter Biddle, Paul England, Marcus Peinado, and Bryan Willman

Microsoft Corporation*
Redmond, WA 98052, USA
(peterbi,pengland,marcuspe,bryanwi)@microsoft.com

Abstract. We investigate the darknet – a collection of networks and technologies used to share digital content. The darknet is not a separate physical network but an application and protocol layer riding on existing networks. Examples of darknets are peer to peer file sharing, CD and DVD copying, and key or password sharing on email and newsgroups. The last few years have seen vast increases in the darknet's aggregate bandwidth, reliability, usability, size of shared library, and availability of search engines. In this paper we categorize and analyze existing and future darknets, from both the technical and legal perspectives. We speculate that there will continue to be setbacks to the effectiveness of the darknet as a distribution mechanism, but ultimately the darknet genie will not be put back into the bottle. In view of this hypothesis, we examine the relevance of content protection and content distribution architectures.

1 Introduction

People have always copied things. In the past, most items of value were physical objects. Patent law and economies of scale meant that small scale copying of physical objects was usually uneconomic, and large scale copying (if it infringed) was stoppable using policemen and courts. Today, things of value are increasingly less tangible: often they are just bits and bytes or can be accurately represented as bits and bytes. The widespread deployment of packet switched networks, and the huge advances in computers and codec technologies, have made it feasible (and indeed attractive) to deliver such digital works over the Internet. This presents great opportunities and great challenges. The opportunity is low cost delivery of personalized, high quality content. The challenge is that such content can be distributed illegally. Copyright law governs the legality of copying and distribution of such valuable data, but copyright protection is increasingly strained in a world of programmable computers and high speed networks.

For example, consider the staggering burst of creativity by authors of computer programs that are designed to share audio files. This was popularized

---

* Statements in this paper represent the opinions of the authors and not necessarily the position of Microsoft Corporation.

J. Feigenbaum (Ed.): DRM 2002, LNCS 2696, pp. 155–176, 2003.
© Springer-Verlag Berlin Heidelberg 2003

by Scour and Napster, but today several popular applications and services offer similar capabilities. In addition, CD-writers have become mainstream, and DVD-writers may well follow suit. Hence, even in the absence of network connectivity, the opportunity for low cost, large scale file sharing exists.

1.1   The Darknet

Throughout this paper, we will call the relevant items (e.g. software programs, songs, movies, books, etc.) objects. We will use the term to copy to refer to the duplication of objects in circumvention of copyright. The persons who copy objects will be called users of the darknet, and the computers used to copy objects will be called hosts. The idea of the darknet is based upon three assumptions:

1. Any widely distributed object will be available to a fraction of users in a form that permits copying.
2. Users will copy objects if it is possible and interesting to do so.
3. Users are connected by high bandwidth channels.

The darknet is the distribution network that emerges from the injection of objects according to assumption 1 and the distribution of those objects according to assumptions 2 and 3.

One implication of the first assumption is that any content protection system will leak popular or valuable content into the darknet, because some fraction of users – possibly experts – will overcome any copy prevention mechanism or because the object will enter the darknet before copy protection is applied.

The term "widely distributed" is intended to capture the notion of mass market distribution of objects to thousands or millions of practically anonymous users. This is in contrast to the protection of military, industrial, or personal secrets, which are typically not widely distributed and are not the focus of this paper.

Like other networks, the darknet can be modeled as a directed graph with labeled edges. The graph has one vertex for each user/host. For any pair of vertices (u, v), there is a directed edge from u to v if objects can be copied from u to v. The edge labels can be used to model relevant information about the physical network and may include information such as bandwidth, delay, availability, etc. The vertices are characterized by their object library, object requests made to other vertices, and object requests satisfied.

To operate effectively, the darknet has a small number of technological and infrastructure requirements, which are similar to those of legal content distribution networks: The static hardware requirements to support a darknet are:

1. The *injection* requirement comprises technologies, devices and mechanisms that convert objects into a form, in which they can be transmitted and consumed in a darknet. Examples include audio and video compression algorithms and tools, CD and DVD readers, and programs that circumvent content protection systems (cracks). Injection provides darknets with new objects.

2. Mechanisms for *storage* and *replication* are required to allow users to make and keep copies of objects and to support the store and forward model of peer to peer networks. Examples include tapes, CDs, DVDs, and computer hard disks.
3. *Ubiquitous rendering devices* required to allow consumption of objects. Examples include portable music players, computers and consumer electronics DVD players and television sets.

The following core network related requirements correspond roughly to the components of the graph model outlined above:

1. Any darknet requires nodes that operate as object *sources*. These correspond to users who let at least some other users copy objects available to them.
2. Similarly, any darknet will contain *destination nodes* – users who want copies of objects. Often, nodes operate as both sources and destinations.
3. *Transmission links* are necessary to move copies of objects from source nodes to destination nodes. The Internet is the link that supports today's peer to peer networks. The postal service and hand carried CDRs (sneakernet) support other darknets.
4. *Search engines* or other introduction mechanisms allow new and existing users to find objects on the darknet.

The dramatic rise in the efficiency of the darknet can be traced back to the general technological improvements in these infrastructure areas. At the same time, most attempts to fight the darknet focus on limiting or auditing one or more of the infrastructure items. Legal action has traditionally targeted search engines and source nodes. As we will describe later in the paper, this has been partially successful. The drive for legislation on mandatory watermarking aims to deprive the darknet of rendering devices. We will argue that watermarking approaches are technically flawed and unlikely to have any material impact on the darknet. Similarly, most content protection systems are meant to prevent or delay the injection of new objects into the darknet. However, no such system constitutes an impenetrable barrier; later, we will discuss the merits of some popular systems.

We see no technical impediments to the darknet becoming increasingly efficient (measured by aggregate library size and available bandwidth). However, the darknet infrastructure is under legal attack. In this paper, we trace the historical and current attacks on darknets and speculate on the technical and legal future of sharing technologies, concentrating particularly, but not exclusively, on peer to peer networks.

The rest of this paper is structured as follows: Section 2 analyzes different manifestations of the darknet with respect to their robustness to attacks on the infrastructure requirements described above and speculates on the future development of the darknet. Section 3 describes content protection mechanisms, their probable effect on the darknet, and the impact of the darknet upon them. In Sect. 4 and 5, we speculate on the situations in which the darknet will be effective, and how businesses may need to behave to compete effectively with it.

2   The Evolution of the Darknet

We classify the different manifestations of the darknet that have come into existence in recent years with respect to the five infrastructure requirements described and analyze weaknesses and points of attack.

As a system, the darknet is subject to a variety of attacks. While legal action, aimed at deterring widespread infringement, continues to be the most powerful challenge to the darknet, the darknet is also subject to a variety of other common threats (e.g. viruses, spamming) that, in the past, have lead to minor disruptions of the darknet. They threaten to become considerably more damaging.

In this section we consider the potential impact of legal developments on the darknet. Most of our analysis focuses on system robustness, rather than on detailed legal questions. We regard legal questions only with respect to their possible effect: the failure of certain nodes or links (vertices and edges of the graph defined above). In this sense, we are investigating a well known problem in distributed systems.

2.1   Early Small Worlds Networks

Prior to the 1990s, copying was organized around groups of friends and acquaintances[1]. The copied objects consisted mainly of music on cassette tapes and computer programs. The rendering devices were widely available tape players and the computers of the time (see Fig. 1). Content injection was trivial, since most objects were either not copy protected or, if they were equipped with copy protection mechanisms, the mechanisms were easily defeated. The distribution network was a "sneaker net" of floppy disks and tapes (storage), which were exchanged in person by members of a group or were sent by postal mail. The bandwidth of this network – albeit small by today's standards – was sufficient for the objects of the time. The main limitation of the sneaker net, with its mechanical transport layer, was latency: It could take days or weeks to obtain a copy of an object. Another serious limitation of these networks was the lack of a sophisticated search engine.

There were some attempts to prosecute individuals who were trying to sell copyrighted objects they had obtained from the darknet (commercial piracy). However, the darknet as a whole was never under significant legal threat. Reasons may have included its limited commercial impact and the protection from legal surveillance afforded by sharing amongst friends.

The sizes of object libraries available on such networks are strongly influenced by the interconnections between the networks. For example, schoolchildren may copy content from their "family network" to their "school network" and thereby increase the size of the darknet object library available to each. Such networks

---

[1] Prior to this, some early computer users had access to ftp servers, usenet, and bulletin boards. These provided high bandwidth access to computer programs, and later to objects, such as images scanned in violation of copyright. However, the size of the communities served by these darknets was negligible.

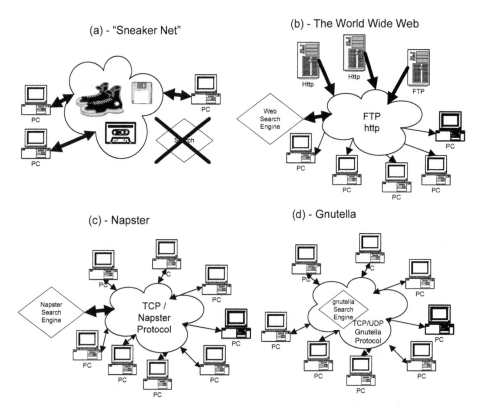

Fig. 1. Historical evolution of the Darknet. We highlight the location of the search engine (if present) and the effective bandwidth (thicker lines represent higher bandwidth). Network latencies are not illustrated, but are much larger for the sneaker net than for the IP-based networks

have been studied extensively and are classified as "interconnected small worlds networks" [1]. There are several popular examples of the characteristics of such systems. For example, most people have a social group of a few score of people. Each of these people has a group of friends that partly overlap with their friends' friends, and also introduces more people. It is estimated that, on average, each person is connected to every other person in the world by a short chain of people from which arises the term "six degrees of separation." These findings are remarkably broadly applicable (e.g. [2,3]). We suspect that these findings have implications for copying on darknets, and we will return to this point when we discuss the darknets of the future later in this paper.

The small worlds darknet continues to exist and indeed remains dominant for certain types of content. However, a number of technological advances have given rise to new forms of the darknet that have superseded the small worlds manifestation for some object types (e.g. audio).

2.2   Central Internet Servers

By 1998, a new form of the darknet began to emerge from technological advances in several areas. The internet had become mainstream, and could be used by anyone seeking to connect users with a centralized service or with each other. The continuing fall in the price of mass storage together with advances in compression technology had also crossed the threshold at which storing large numbers of audio files was no longer an obstacle to mainstream users. Additionally, the power of computers had crossed the point at which they could be used as rendering devices for multimedia content. Finally, "CD ripping" (from unprotected CDs) became a convenient, broadly available method for content injection.

The first embodiments of this new darknet were central internet servers with large collections of MP3 audio files. A fundamental change that came with these servers was the use of a new distribution network: The internet displaced the sneaker net – at least for audio content. This solved several problems of the old darknet.

Firstly, latency was reduced drastically. Secondly, and more importantly, discovery of objects became much easier because of simple and powerful search mechanisms – most importantly general purpose world wide web search engines. The local view of the small world was replaced by a global view of the entire collection accessible to all users. The main characteristic of this form of the darknet was centralized storage and search – a simple architecture that mirrored mainstream internet servers.

Centralized or quasi-centralized distribution and service networks make sense for legal online commerce. Bandwidth and infrastructure costs tend to be low, and having customers visit a commerce site means the merchant can display adverts, collect profiles, and bill efficiently. Additionally, management, auditing, and accountability are much easier in a centralized model. However, centralized schemes work poorly for illegal object distribution because large, central servers are large single points of failure: If the distributor is breaking the law, it is relatively easy to force him to stop. Early MP3 Web and FTP sites were commonly "hosted" by universities, corporations, and ISPs. Copyright holders or their representatives sent "cease and desist" letters to these website operators and web owners citing copyright infringement and in a few cases followed up with legal action [4]. The threats of legal action were successful attacks on those centralized networks, and MP3 web and FTP sites disappeared from the mainstream shortly after they appeared.

In the language of the model of Sect. 1, the centralized server darknet succumbed to a legal attack on its source nodes, whose small number made the attack tractable.

2.3   Peer to Peer Networks

The realization that centralized networks are not robust against attack has provided part of the impetus for the evolution of peer to peer networking and file sharing technologies. In this section, we examine architectures that have evolved. Early systems were flawed because critical components remained centralized (Napster) or because of inefficiencies and lack of scalability of the protocol (gnutella) [5]. It should be noted that the problem of object location in a massively distributed, rapidly changing, heterogeneous system was new at the time peer to peer systems emerged. Efficient, highly scalable protocols have been proposed since then [6,7].

Early Internet Protocols. Simple peer to peer-like systems have existed on the internet for a long time. The main example is Usenet, which predates the central server darknets described above. While certain parts of Usenet have been and are still being used to distribute certain types of objects illegally, Usenet never became a mainstream darknet and never faced many of the attacks the more recent darknets are exposed to. We note, however, that the problem of endpoint anonymity arose in connection with Usenet. This resulted in work on anonymizing remailers and legal attacks on them.

Napster. Napster was the service that ignited peer to peer file sharing in 1999 [8]. There is little doubt that a major portion of the massive (for the time) traffic on Napster was of objects being transferred in a peer to peer model in violation of copyright law. Napster succeeded where central servers had failed by relying on the distributed storage of objects not under the control of Napster. This moved the injection, storage and replication, source nodes, network distribution, and consumption of objects to users.

However, Napster retained a quasi-centralized database with an index searchable on the file name. The centralized database itself became a legal target [4]. Napster was first enjoined to deny certain queries (e.g. "Metallica") and then to police its network for copyrighted content. As the size of the darknet indexed by Napster shrank, so did the number of users. This illustrates a general characteristic of darknets: there is a correlation between the size and bandwidth of the object library and the appeal of the network for its users. This translates into positive feedback in the number of users: an efficient service quickly gains new users, and vice versa.

Gnutella. The next technology that sparked public interest in peer to peer file sharing was Gnutella. In addition to distributed object storage, Gnutella uses a fully distributed database described more fully in [9]. Gnutella does not rely upon any centralized server or service – a peer just needs the IP address of one or a few participating peers to (in principle) reach any host on the Gnutella darknet. Second, Gnutella is not really "run" by anyone: it is an open protocol and anyone can write a Gnutella client application. Finally, Gnutella and its descendants have substantial non-infringing uses. This changes its legal standing markedly and places it on a similar legal footing with email. Because email has substantial non-infringing use, it is not under direct legal threat in the jurisdiction of the authors of this paper, even though it may be used to transfer material unlawfully.

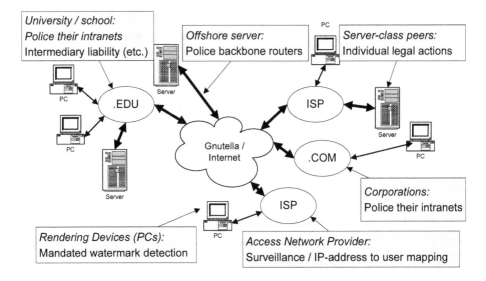

Fig. 2. Policing the darknet. Gnutella-style networks appear hard to police because they are highly distributed, and there are thousands or millions of peers. Looking more closely there are several potential vulnerabilities

2.4 Robustness of Fully Distributed Darknets

Fully distributed peer to peer systems do not present the single points of failure that led to the demise of central MP3 servers (injection) and Napster (search). It is natural to ask how robust these systems are and what form potential attacks could take. We observe the following weaknesses in Gnutella-like systems:

- Free riding
- Lack of anonymity

Free Riding. Peer to peer systems are often thought of as fully decentralized networks with copies of objects uniformly distributed among the hosts. While this is possible in principle, in practice it is not the case. Recent measurements of libraries shared by gnutella peers indicate that the majority of content is provided by a tiny fraction of the hosts which we term "super peers" [10]. Although gnutella appears to be a homogeneous peer to peer network of cooperating hosts, in actual fact it has evolved to effectively be another largely centralized system (Fig. 2). Free riding (i.e. downloading objects without sharing them) by many gnutella users appears to be main cause of this development. Widespread free riding removes much of the power of network dynamics and may reduce a peer to peer network into a simple unidirectional distribution system from a small number of sources to a large number of destinations. Of course, if this is the case, then the vulnerabilities that we observed in centralized systems (e.g. FTP-servers) are present again. Free riding and the emergence of super-peers have several causes:

Peer to peer file sharing assumes that a significant fraction of users adhere to a post-capitalist ideal of sacrificing their own resources for the "common good" of the network. Apparently, most free riders do not seem to adopt this ideology. For example, with 56 kbps modems still being the network connection for most users, allowing uploads constitutes a tangible bandwidth sacrifice. One approach is to make collaboration mandatory. For example, Freenet [11] clients are required to contribute some disk space. However, enforcing such requirements without a central infrastructure is difficult.

Existing infrastructure is another reason for the existence of super peers. There are vast differences in the resources available to different types of hosts. For example, a T3 connection provides the combined bandwidth of about one thousand 56 kbps telephone connections.

Lack of Anonymity. Users of gnutella who share objects they have stored are not anonymous. Current peer to peer networks permit the server endpoints to be determined, and if a peer-client can determine the IP address and affiliation of a peer, then so can a government agency. Users who share objects illegally face the threat of legal action. This appears to be another motivation for free riding.

2.5   Attacks

In this section, we analyze the robustness of distributed darknets with global databases. We consider how a variety of counter measures might apply to each of the technological and infrastructure requirements we identified in Sect. 1. These measures can be broadly classified as:

Legal: Filing lawsuits against users of the darknet or the operators of its infrastructure. Such attacks remove users from the darknet, but more importantly discourage participation of a much larger group of potential users.

Content protection: A collection of technical measures ranging from hindering injection (DRM) to attempts to make rendering devices reject darknet objects (watermark screening) and forensics (fingerprinting). These techniques are discussed in more detail in Sect. 3.

Network attacks: Like any other network, the darknet is subject to well known attacks, such as denial of service (DoS), spamming and viruses. We do not investigate the legal status of these attacks, but simply note that they are, in principle, possible and, to a very limited degree, appear to have taken place in the past.

Much of the static infrastructure (injection, storage, replication, rendering) has substantial non-infringing uses. Examples of such dual use technologies include audio and video compression tools, CD and DVD players, computers, monitors and television sets. These technologies appear largely immune to legal action. Furthermore, network attacks do not appear to apply in most cases. This leaves content protection as the main class of measures against the static darknet infrastructure. We analyze the effectiveness of these techniques in detail in Sect. 3. It appears unlikely that content protection measures alone will have a significant impact on the darknet.

The case of injection is different in the sense that injection tools that circumvent content protection mechanisms are subject to legal action – possibly under the Digital Millennium Copyright Act (DMCA). However, the most relevant recent example of such legal action appears to have been largely unsuccessful. DVD "ripping" tools that circumvent the CSS copy protection system are easily available on the internet.

Attacks against the network infrastructure of the darknet fall mostly into the categories of legal action and network attacks.

Sources. Source nodes of the darknet (i.e. hosts that make objects available to users in violation of copyright law) are subject to legal action. Lack of endpoint anonymity makes these hosts identifiable. Because of the prevalence of super peers the darknet depends on a relatively small set of powerful hosts, and these hosts are promising targets for attackers.

Darknet hosts owned by corporations are typically easily removed. Often, these hosts are set up by individual employees without the knowledge of corporate management. Generally corporations respect intellectual property laws. This together with their rational aversion to lawsuits, and their centralized network of hierarchical management, makes it relatively easy to remove darknet hosts in the corporate domain.

While the structures at universities are typically less hierarchical and strict than those of corporations, similar rules often apply.

If the .com and .edu OC-3 and OC-12 lines were pulled from under a darknet, the usefulness of the network would be impaired. Today, this would leave DSL, ISDN, and cable modem users as the high bandwidth servers of objects. We believe limiting source hosts to this class would present a far less effective piracy network today from the perspective of acquisition because of the relative rarity of high bandwidth consumer connections, and hence users would abandon this darknet. However, consumer broadband is becoming more popular, so in the long run it is probable that there will be adequate consumer bandwidth to support an effective consumer darknet.

The obvious next legal escalation is to bring direct or indirect (through the affiliation) challenges against users who illegally share large libraries of material. This is already happening and the legal actions appear to be successful [12]. This requires the cooperation of ISPs in identifying their customers, which appears to be forthcoming due to requirements that the carrier must take to avoid liability and, in some cases, because of corporate ties between ISPs and content providers. Once again, free riding makes this attack strategy far more tractable.

In addition to legal action, sources are subject to different kinds of denial of service attacks. These attacks become also more viable in the presence of widespread free riding.

Destination Nodes. Destination nodes suffer from the same endpoint anonymity problem as source nodes. In principle, similar legal attacks apply. In practice, destination nodes are better protected by their larger numbers.

Transmission. Attacks on transmission typically take the following forms. First, there have been attempts to identify and block darknet traffic on the internet. While such attacks may succeed with today's peer to peer systems, they are easily prevented by encrypting the darknet traffic. A second type of countermeasure is to limit the upload bandwidth of users who are suspected of providing large amounts of data into the darknet. While measures of this type may work against darknets with a relatively small set of super peers, they appear significantly less effective in darknet environments with more broadly distributed source nodes.

Search Engine. In Gnutella-style darknets, the search engine is integrated into the nodes. Thus, legal measures against the search engine are largely equivalent to legal measures against source and destination nodes, as described above. However, the global search engine has important implications for the feasibility of legal measures, as it removes endpoint anonymity and makes nodes globally identifiable. That is, the identity (IP address) of any source node is exposed through the global search engine to any client.

There are some technological workarounds to overcome the vulnerability presented by the lack of endpoint anonymity: anonymizing routers, overseas routers and object fragmentation complicate the effort required by law enforcement to determine the original source of unlawfully transferred bits. For example, Freenet tries to hide the identity of the hosts storing any given object by means of a variety of heuristics, including routing the object through intermediate hosts and providing mechanisms for easy migration of objects to other hosts. Similarly, Mnemosyne [13] organizes object storage such that individual hosts may not know what objects are stored on them. It is conjectured in [13] that this may amount to common carrier status for the host. A detailed analysis of the legal or technical robustness of these systems is beyond the scope of this paper. However, all such systems introduce the possibility of intermediary liability for the individuals who provide the "final hop."

Conclusions. The most relevant attacks we have identified exploit the lack of endpoint anonymity and are aided by the effects of free riding. We have seen effective legal measures on all peer to peer technologies that are used to provide global access to copyrighted material. Centralized web servers were effectively closed down. Napster was effectively closed down. Gnutella and Kazaa are under threat because of free rider weaknesses and lack of endpoint anonymity.

Should Gnutella-style systems become unviable as darknets, systems such as Freenet or Mnemosyne might replace them. It is hard to predict further escalation, but we note that the DMCA is a far reaching (although not fully tested) example of a law that is potentially quite powerful. We believe it probable that there will be ongoing technical efforts to sidestep existing laws, followed by new laws, or new interpretations of old laws, in the next few years. The rapid build out of consumer broadband, the decreasing price of storage, and the fact that personal computers are effectively establishing themselves as centers of home entertainment are technical developments that will continue to drive darknet demand.

Lack of endpoint anonymity is a direct result of the globally accessible global object database, and it is the existence of the global database that most distinguishes the newer darknets from the earlier small worlds. At this point, it is hard to predict whether the darknet will be able to retain this global database in the long term, but it seems clear that legal setbacks to global index peer to peer will continue.

2.6   Small Worlds Networks Revisited

In this section we try to predict the evolution of the darknet should global peer to peer networks be effectively stopped by legal or other means. The globally accessible global database is the only infrastructure component of the darknet that can be disabled in this way. The other enabling technologies of the darknet (injection, distribution networks, rendering devices, storage) will not only remain available, but will rapidly increase in power. We stress that the networks described in this section (in most cases) provide poorer services than the global network.

In the absence of a global database, small worlds networks could again become the prevalent form of the darknet. However, these small worlds will be more powerful than they were in the past. With the widespread availability of cheap CD and DVD readers and writers as well as large hard disks, the bandwidth of the sneaker net has increased dramatically, the cost of object storage has become negligible and object injection tools have become ubiquitous. Furthermore, the internet is available as a distribution mechanism that is adequate for audio for most users, and is becoming increasingly adequate for video and computer programs. In light of strong cryptography, it is hard to imagine how sharing could be observed and prosecuted as long as users do not share with strangers.

Students in dorms will establish darknets to share content in their social group. These darknets may be based on simple file sharing, DVD-copying, or may use special application programs or servers: for example, a chat or instant messenger client enhanced to share content with members of your buddy list. Each student will be a member of other darknets: for example, their family, various special interest groups, friends from high school, and colleagues in part time jobs (Fig. 3). If these small worlds are sufficiently well connected, we can anticipate that content will rapidly diffuse between darknets. Since the legal exposure of such sharing is quite limited, we believe that sharing amongst socially oriented groups will increase.

The limited exposure of sharing with strangers does not imply that such sharing will become universal. Non-technical admonitions will continue to discourage users from sharing. Such counsel may originate from parents, employers, or educators. The associated threats and possibility of discovery will factor into each individuals decision to share.

Small worlds networks suffer from the lack of a global database; each user can only see the objects stored by his small world neighbors. This raises a number of interesting questions about the network structure and object flow:

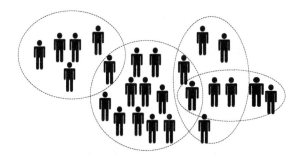

Fig. 3. Interconnected small worlds darknets. Threats of surveillance and prosecution may discourage participation in global darknets. In response, darknets form around social groups for which surveillance of illicit activity is unlikely. These darknets will use high bandwidth, low latency communications (intranets and the internet) and are supported by search engines. Custom applications, Instant Messenger style applications or simple shared file systems host the darknet. People's social groups overlap so objects available in one darknet diffuse to others: in the terminology used in this paper, each peer that is a member of more than one darknet is an introduction host for objects obtained from other darknets

- What graph structure will the network have? For example, will it be connected? What will be the average distance between two nodes?
- Given a graph structure, how will objects propagate through the graph? In particular, what fraction of objects will be available at a given node? How long does it take for objects to propagate (diffuse) through the network?

Questions of this type have been studied in different contexts in a variety of fields (mathematics, computer science, economics, physics, and biology). A number of empirical studies seek to establish structural properties of different types of small world networks, such as social networks [2] and the world wide web [3]. These works conclude that the diameter of the examined networks is small, and observe further structural properties, such as a power law of the degree distribution [14]. A number of authors seek to model these networks by means of random graphs, in order to perform more detailed mathematical analysis on the models [15,16,17,18] and, in particular, study the possibility of efficient search under different random graph distributions [19,20]. We will present a quantitative study of the structure and dynamics of small worlds networks in an upcoming paper, but to summarize:

- For popular titles, small worlds darknets can be extremely efficient: very few peers are needed to satisfy requests for "top 20" books, songs, movies or computer programs. If darknets are interconnected, we expect the effective injection rate (injection from other networks) rate to be large. If darknet clients are enhanced to seek out new popular content, as opposed to the user demand based schemes of today, small worlds darknets could become very efficient.

- Less popular titles, will be harder or impossible to find, depending on the network parameters.
- Time sensitive objects will not be available.

For popular titles, small world darknets may provide a quality of service that matches that of peer to peer networks with global databases; for less popular titles, they may suffer from a reduced library size and latency.

3   Introducing Content into the Darknet

Our analysis and intuition have led us to believe that efficient darknet replication and propagation will remain a fact of life. In this section we examine rights management technologies that are being deployed to limit the introduction rate of content into the darknet.

3.1   Conditional Access Systems

A conditional access system is a simple form of rights management system in which subscribers are given access to objects based (typically) on a service contract. Digital rights management systems often perform the same function, but typically impose restrictions on the use of objects after unlocking.

Conditional access (CA) systems such as cable, satellite TV, and satellite radio offer little protection against objects being introduced into the darknet from subscribing hosts. A conditional access system customer has no access to channels or titles to which they are not entitled, and has essentially unencumbered use of channels that he has subscribed or paid for. This means that an investment of $100 (at time of writing) on an analog video capture card is sufficient to obtain and share TV programs and movies. Some CA systems provide post unlock protections but they are generally cheap and easy to circumvent.

Thus, conditional access systems provide a widely deployed, high bandwidth source of video material for the darknet. In practice, the large size and low cost of CA-provided video content will limit the exploitation of the darknet for distributing video in the near term.

The same can not be said of the use of the darknet to distribute conditional access system broadcast keys. At some level, each head end (satellite or cable TV head end) uses an encryption key that must be made available to each customer (it is a broadcast), and in the case of a satellite system this could be millions of homes. CA system providers take measures to limit the usefulness of exploited session keys (for example, they are changed every few seconds), but if darknet latencies are low, or if encrypted broadcast data is cached, then the darknet could threaten CA system revenues.

We observe that the exposure of the conditional access provider to losses due to piracy is proportional to the number of customers that share a session key. So, cable operators are in a safer position than satellite operators because a cable operator can narrowcast more cheaply.

3.2   DRM Systems

A classical DRM system is one in which a client obtains content in protected (typically encrypted) form, with a license that specifies the uses to which the content may be put. Examples of licensing terms that are being explored by the industry are "play on these three hosts," "play once," "use computer program for one hour," etc.

The license and the wrapped content are presented to the DRM system whose responsibility is to ensure that:

- The client cannot remove the encryption from the file and send it to a peer.
- The client cannot "clone" its DRM system to make it run on another host.
- The client obeys the rules set out in the DRM license.
- The client cannot separate the rules from the payload.

Advanced DRM systems may go further. Some such technologies have been commercially very successful – the content scrambling system used in DVDs, and (broadly interpreted), the protection schemes used by conditional access system providers fall into this category, as do newer DRM systems that use the internet as a distribution channel and computers as rendering devices. These technologies are appealing because they promote the establishment of new businesses and reduce distribution costs. If costs and licensing terms are appealing to producers and consumers, then the vendor thrives. If the licensing terms are unappealing or inconvenient or the costs are too high then the business will fail. The DivX "DVD" rental model failed on most or all of these metrics, but CSS-protected DVDs succeeded beyond the wildest expectations of the industry.

On personal computers, current DRM systems are software only systems using a variety of tricks to make them more or less hard to subvert. DRM enabled consumer electronics devices are also beginning to emerge.

In the absence of the darknet, the goal of such systems is to have comparable security to competing distribution systems – notably the CD and DVD – so that programmable computers can play an increasing role in home entertainment.

DRM systems strive to be BOBE (break once, break everywhere)-resistant. That is, suppliers anticipate that individual instances (clients) of all security systems, whether based on hardware or software, will be subverted. If a client of a system is subverted, then all content protected by that DRM client can be unprotected. If the break can be applied to any other DRM client of that class so that all of those users can break their systems, then the DRM-scheme is BOBE-weak. If, on the other hand, knowledge gained breaking one client cannot be applied elsewhere, then the DRM system is BOBE-strong.

Most commercial DRM systems have BOBE exploits, and we note that the darknet applies to DRM hacks as well. The CSS system is an exemplary BOBE weak system. The knowledge and code that comprised the De-CSS exploit spread uncontrolled around the world on websites, newsgroups, and even T shirts, in spite of the fact that, in principle, the Digital Millennium Copyright Act makes it a crime to develop or distribute these exploits.

A final characteristic of existing DRM systems is renewability. Vendors recognize the possibility of exploits, and build systems that can be field updated.

It is hard to quantify the effectiveness of DRM systems for restricting the introduction of content into the darknet from experience with existing systems. Existing DRM systems typically provide protection for months to years; however, the content available to such systems has to date been of limited interest, and the content that is protected is also available in unprotected form. The one system that was protecting valuable content (DVD video) was broken very soon after compression technology and increased storage capacities and bandwidth enabled the darknet to carry video content.

3.3   Software

The DRM systems described above can be used to provide protection for software, in addition to other objects (e.g. audio and video). Alternatively, copy protection systems for computer programs may embed the copy protection code in the software itself.

The most important copy protection primitive for computer programs is for the software to be bound to a host in such a way that the program will not work on an unlicensed machine. Binding requires a machine ID: this can be a unique number on a machine (e.g. a network card MAC – media access control – address), or can be provided by an external dongle.

For such schemes to be strong, two things must be true. First, the machine ID must not be "virtualizable." For instance, if it is trivial to modify a network card driver to return a different MAC address, then the software-host binding is easily broken. Second, the code that performs the binding checks must not be easy to patch. A variety of technologies that revolve around software tamper resistance can help here [21].

We believe that binding software to a host is a more tractable problem than protecting passive content, as the former only requires tamper resistance, while the latter also requires the ability to hide and manage secrets. However, we observe that all software copy protection systems deployed thus far have bee broken. The definitions of BOBE strong and BOBE weak apply similarly to software. Furthermore, once software is broken, the hacks or patched software are just as much subject to the dynamics of the darknet as passive content.

4   Policing Hosts

If there are subverted hosts, then content will leak into the darknet. If darknet propagation is efficient, then content will be available to all interested peers. In this section we evaluate technologies proposed for limiting output, or provide forensic information that allows users who inject objects in violation of copyright or contract to be identified.

4.1   Watermarking

Watermarking embeds an "indelible" invisible mark in content. A plethora of schemes exist for audio/video and still image content and computer programs.

There are a variety of schemes for exploiting watermarks for content protection. These schemes are implemented in output devices. Consider a rendering device that locates and interprets watermarks. If a watermark is found then special action is taken. For example, the output device may:

Restrict behavior: For example, a bus adapter may refuse to pass content that has the "copy once" and "already copied once" bits set.

Require a license to play: For example, if a watermark is found indicating that content is rights-restricted then the renderer may demand a license indicating that the user is authorized to play the content.

Such systems were proposed for audio content – for example the secure digital music initiative (SDMI) [22], and are under consideration for video by the copy protection technical working group (CPTWG) [23].

There are several reasons why it appears unlikely that such systems will ever become an effective anti-piracy technology. From a commercial point of view, building a watermark detector into a device renders it strictly less useful for consumers than a competing product that does not have one, and such detectors impose a "tax" in performance and cost on consumers who are using devices for perfectly lawful activities. Hence watermarking schemes are unlikely to be widely deployed, unless mandated by legislation. The recently proposed Hollings bill is a step along these lines [24]. Even with legislation, they are likely to meet severe resistance.

We contrast watermark based policing with classical DRM: If a general purpose device is equipped with a classical DRM system, it can play all content acquired from the darknet, and have access to new content acquired through the DRM channel. This is in stark distinction to reduction of functionality inherent in watermark based policing.

Even if watermarking systems were mandated, this approach is likely to fail due to a variety of technical inadequacies. The first inadequacy concerns the robustness of the embedding layer. We are not aware of systems for which simple data transformations cannot strip the mark or make it unreadable [25]. Marks can be made more robust, but in order to recover marks after adversarial manipulation, the reader must typically search a large phase space, and this quickly becomes untenable. In spite of the proliferation of proposed watermarking schemes, it remains doubtful whether robust embedding layers for the relevant content types can be found.

A second inadequacy lies in unrealistic assumptions about key management. Most watermarking schemes require widely deployed cryptographic keys. Standard watermarking schemes are based on the normal cryptographic principles of a public algorithm and secret keys. Most schemes use a shared key between marker and detector. In practice, this means that all detectors need a private key, and, typically, share a single private key. It would be naïve to assume that these keys will remain secret for long in an adversarial environment. Once the key or keys are compromised, the darknet will propagate them efficiently, and the scheme collapses. There have been proposals for public key watermarking systems. However, so far, this work does not seem practical and the corresponding schemes do not even begin to approach the robustness of the cryptographic systems whose name they borrow.

A final consideration relates to the location of mandatory watermark detectors in client devices. On open computing devices (e.g. personal computers), these detectors could, in principle, be placed in software or in hardware. Placing detectors in software would be largely meaningless, as circumvention of the detector would be as simple as replacing it by a different piece of software. This includes detectors placed in the operating system, all of whose components can be easily replaced, modified and propagated over the darknet.

Alternatively, the detectors could be placed in hardware (e.g. audio and video cards). In the presence of the problems described this would lead to untenable renewability problems – the hardware would be ineffective within days of deployment. Consumers, on the other hand, expect the hardware to remain in use for many years. Finally, consumers themselves are likely to rebel against "footing the bill" for these ineffective content protection systems. It is virtually certain that the darknet would be filled with a continuous supply of watermark removal tools based on compromised keys and weaknesses in the embedding layer. Attempts to force the public to "update" their hardware would not only be intrusive, but impractical.

In summary, attempts to mandate content protection systems based on watermark detection at the consumer's machine suffer from commercial drawbacks and severe technical deficiencies. These schemes, which aim to provide content protection beyond DRM by attacking the darknet, are rendered entirely ineffective by the presence of even a moderately functional darknet.

4.2   Fingerprinting

Fingerprint schemes are based on similar technologies and concepts to watermarking schemes. However, whereas watermarking is designed to perform a-priori policing, fingerprinting is designed to provide a-posteriori forensics.

In the simplest case, fingerprinting is used for individual sale content (as opposed to super-distribution or broadcast – although it can be applied there with some additional assumptions). When a client purchases an object, the supplier marks it with an individualized mark that identifies the purchaser. If the marked content appears on a darknet, a policeman can identify the source of the object and the offender can be prosecuted or other action can be taken.

Fingerprinting suffers from fewer technical problems than watermarking. The main advantage is that no widespread key distribution is needed – a publisher can use whatever secret or proprietary fingerprinting technology they choose, and is entirely responsible for the management of their own keys.

Fingerprinting has one problem that is not found in watermarking. Since each fingerprinted copy of a piece of media is different, if a user can obtain several different copies, he can launch collusion attacks (e.g. averaging). In general, such attacks are very damaging to the fingerprint payload.

It remains to be seen whether fingerprinting will act as a deterrent to theft. There is currently no legal precedent for media fingerprints being evidence of crime, and this case will probably be hard to make since detection is a statistical process with false positives, and opportunity for deniability. However, we anticipate that there will be uneasiness in sharing a piece of content that may contain a person's identity and that ultimately leaves that person's control.

Note also that, with widely distributed watermarking detectors, it is easy to see whether a watermark has been successfully removed. There is no such assurance for determining whether a fingerprint has been successfully removed from an object because users are not necessarily knowledgeable about the fingerprint scheme or schemes in use. However, if it turns out that the deterrence of fingerprinting is small (i.e. everyone shares their media regardless of the presence of marks), there is probably no reasonable legal response. Finally, distribution schemes in which objects must be individualized will be expensive.

5   Conclusions

There are no inherent technical impediments to darknet based object sharing technologies growing in usability, library size, aggregate bandwidth and efficiency, but the legal future of darknet technologies is less certain. We have described successful or partially successful legal attacks on all network based object sharing technologies in widespread use today. We anticipate further escalation of attacks and of darknet technologies to remove the vulnerabilities that were exploited in previous attacks. We have analyzed the infrastructure components necessary to support arbitrary darknets, and have argued that, while some of the infrastructure components appear immune to legal or technological attack, some vulnerabilities will remain.

The largest vulnerability arises from the exposure of a user's identity, either directly or indirectly, to law enforcement masquerading as a peer. This vulnerability arises if users share with unknown or anonymous peers, and is a consequence of registering hosts and objects with a global database or other database without user access control. Should the threat of legal action make sharing among anonymous users too risky for average users, then we have argued that darknets will form around smaller, access controlled small worlds groups for which the risk of surveillance is smaller.

The reduced exposure afforded by small worlds darknets to their users may come at the price of diminished quality of service. The library size, availability, and latency of a small world darknet will always be inferior to that of a global darknet. This will almost certainly mean that small worlds darknets will be impractical for sharing less popular objects and time sensitive objects. On the other hand, even moderately efficient small worlds darknets are likely to provide high quality of service for the most popular objects.

It is our conjecture that darknets will survive, but the efficiency and size of these future darknets is uncertain. In the remainder of this section we speculate on the technical and business implications of the continued existence of darknets of varying levels of efficiency on the commerce of digital goods.

5.1 Technological Implications

Darknets replicate objects. An efficient darknet replicates objects rapidly, and makes the original and its replicas available to an expanding group of users. If the darknet is an efficient global darknet then all users can access an object immediately after it is introduced. If architectural deficiencies or attacks reduce the efficiency of a global darknet then significant time and effort may be required to obtain a copy of an object. If no global darknet exists, but a user is a member of one or more small worlds darknets then users must wait until an object reaches their small world – either by diffusing from an interconnected small world, or through direct injection.

Classical DRM systems inhibit the injection of objects into darknets. However, we must always assume that a fraction of DRM systems are subverted, or objects are introduced into the darknet through other channels. In light of the arguments in the previous paragraph we conclude that DRM systems will be effective in limiting the widespread availability of objects for isolated small worlds darknets, but will be ineffective security measures in the presence of efficient global darknets.

The interesting cases arise between these two extremes – in the presence of a darknet which is connected but in which factors such as latency, limited bandwidth or the absence of a global database limit the speed with which objects propagate. It appears that quantitative studies of the effective "diffusion constant" of different kinds of darknets and objects would be highly useful in elucidating the dynamics of DRM systems and the darknet.

Proposals for systems involving mandatory watermark detection in rendering devices try to impact the effectiveness of the darknet directly by trying to detect and eliminate objects that originated in the darknet appear flawed. In addition to severe commercial and social problems, these schemes suffer from serious technical deficiencies, which argue against their future value. We conclude that such schemes are doomed to failure.

5.2 Business in the Face of the Darknet

Darknets are a competitor to legal commerce, and the normal rules of competition apply. The level of competition of a darknet for an industry depends on its efficiency and effective price compared to the convenience and price of the competing legal channels (as well as other social factors like the price sensitivity and honesty of the users).

Historically, the efficiency of a darknet has been affected by the legal and technical attacks upon it. We have argued that global darknets have inherent vulnerabilities that can be exploited to reduce library size and aggregate bandwidth. Clearly, the level of competition provided by a darknet depends on the attacks it is exposed to, and we assume that businesses will continue to invest in such attacks. We have argued that these attacks may reduce the quality of service of darknets, even if they may not completely eliminate them.

A moderately efficient darknet will provide pressure on the price and convenience of legal channels for businesses. There are many technical and social factors that determine the competitiveness of a darknet, and we will list those that seem particularly important. First, the size of the shared objects: Current peer to peer darknets appear adequate for audio, but are not adequate for video for most users. Second, the behavior of the customers: corporate customers are unlikely to engage in widespread sharing of digital objects in violation of contract or copyright. However, it appears that many people share audio files without compunction. Third, the distribution size: mass market media is widely distributed and widely interesting. This implies many potential injection hosts, and high demand driving darknet replication. In contrast, personalized documents or premium business reports are far less likely to be introduced and replicated. Fourth, the convenience of the legal channel: convenience can take many forms: a DRM-protected object may be less convenient than an unprotected object; a native digital representation of an object from a darknet may be more appealing to some users than an object embedded in a physical artifact (e.g. a CD). Fifth, time: if darknets are only moderately efficient then there will be a delay before a new object is widely available. Of course the price of the object is a huge factor, and there are many others.

We do not believe that darknets will drive the cost of all digital goods to zero, but it appears likely that the effects on some types of mass market digital commerce will be significant.

Acknowledgements

We are grateful to Cormac Herley, Rico Malvar, John Manferdelli and Yacov Yacobi, for many useful comments, ideas, and discussions.

References

1. Watts, D., Strogatz, S.: Collective dynamics of small world networks. Nature **393** (1998) 440–442
2. Milgram, S.: The small world problem. Psychology Today **2** (1967) 60–67
3. Albert, R., Jeong, H., Barabási, A.L.: Diameter of the world-wide web. Nature **401** (1999) 130–131
4. http://www.riaa.com
5. Javanović, M., Annexstein, F., Berman, K.: Scalability issues in large peer-to-peer networks – a case study of gnutella. Technical report, ECECS Department, University of Cincinnati (2001)
6. Stoica, I., Morris, R., Karger, D., Kaashoek, M.F., Balakrishnan, H.: CHORD: A scalable peer-to-peer lookup service for internet applications. In: Proceedings of the ACM SIGCOMM 2001 Conference (SIGCOMM-01). (2001) 149–160
7. Dabek, F., Brunskill, E., Kaashoek, M.F., Karger, D., Morris, R., Stoica, I., Balakrishnan, H.: Building peer-to-peer systems with Chord, a distributed lookup service. In: Proceedings of the Eigth IEEE Workshop on Hot Topics in Operating Systems (HotOS-VIII). (2001) 81–86
8. http://www.napster.com
9. http://www.gnutelladev.com/protocol/gnutella protocol.html

10. Adar, E., Huberman, B.: Free riding on Gnutella. Technical report, Xerox-PARC (2000)
11. Clarke, I., Sandberg, O., Wiley, B., Hong, T.: Freenet: A distributed information storage and retrieval system. In: International Workshop on Design Issues in Anonymity and Unobservability. (2000)
12. Clarke, R.: A defendent class action law suit.
    http://www.kentlaw.edu/perritt/honorsscholars/clarke.html
13. Hand, S., Roscoe, T.: Mnemosyne: peer-to-peer steganographic storage. In: Proceedings of the first International Workshop on Peer-to-Peer Systems. (2000)
14. Barabási, A.L., Albert, R.: Emergence of scaling in random networks. Science **286** (1999) 509–512
15. Aiello, W., Chung, F., Lu, L.: Random evolution in massive graphs. In: Proceedings of the 42nd Annual IEEE Symposium on Foundations of Computer Science. (2001) 510–519
16. Cooper, C., Frieze, A.: A general model of web graphs. In: Peoceedings of the 9th Annual European Symposium on Algorithms. (2001) 500–511
17. Newman, M.: Small worlds: the structure of social networks. Technical Report 99-12-080, Santa Fe Institute (1999)
18. Newman, M., Watts, D., Strogatz, S.: Random graph models of social networks. Proc. Natl. Acad. Sci. USA **99** (2002) 2566–2572
19. Kleinberg, J.: Navigation in a small world. Nature **406** (2000)
20. Kleinberg, J.: Small-world phenomena and the dynamics of information. Advances in Neural Information Processing (NIPS) **14** (2001)
21. Aucsmith, D.: Tamper-resistant software: An implementation. In Anderson, R., ed.: Information hiding: first international workshop, Cambridge, U.K. Volume 1174 of Lecture Notes in Computer Science., Springer-Verlag (1996) 317–333
22. http://www.sdmi.org
23. http://www.cptwg.org
24. Hollings, F.: Consumer broadband and digital television promotion act
25. Kirovski, D., Petitcolas, F.: Replacement attack on arbitrary watermarking systems. In: Proceedings of the 2002 ACM Workshop on Digital Rights Management, Springer-Verlag (2003)

Replacement Attack
on Arbitrary Watermarking Systems

Darko Kirovski[1] and Fabien A.P. Petitcolas[2]

[1] Microsoft Research, One Microsoft Way, Redmond, WA 98052, USA
[2] Microsoft Research, 7 J. J. Thomson Avenue, Cambridge, CB3 0FB, UK
{darkok,fabienpe}@microsoft.com

Abstract. Billions of dollars allegedly lost to piracy of multimedia have recently triggered the industry to rethink the way music and movies are distributed. As encryption is vulnerable to re-recording, currently all copyright protection mechanisms tend to rely on watermarking. A watermark is an imperceptive secret hidden into a host signal. In this paper, we analyze the security of multimedia copyright protection systems that use watermarks by proposing a new breed of attacks on generic watermarking systems. A typical replacement attack relies upon the observation that multimedia content is often highly repetitive. Thus, the attack procedure replaces each signal block with another, perceptually similar block computed as a combination of other similar blocks found either within the same media clip or within a library of media clips. Assuming the blocks used to compute the replacement are marked with distinct secrets, we show that if the computed replacement block is at some minimal distance from the original marked block, large portion of the embedded watermark is irreversibly removed. We describe the logistics of the attack and an exemplary implementation against a spread-spectrum data hiding technology for audio signals.

1 Introduction

Significantly increased levels of multimedia piracy over the last decade have put the movie and music industry under pressure to deploy a standardized anti-piracy technology. The goal is to enforce copyright protection via content screening on client media players. A media player would refuse to play copyright protected content for which the user does not hold a license. A content screening platform, for example, aims at disabling free downloads from centralized and peer-to-peer file-sharing networks – e.g., Napster alone had orchestrated almost 3 billion downloads of sound clips in February 2001. Several industry-wide initiatives have had little success in establishing a content screening standard [1,2,3].

1.1 Content Screening

The problem of ensuring copyright at the client side lies in the fact that traditional data protection technologies such as encryption or scrambling cannot

J. Feigenbaum (Ed.): DRM 2002, LNCS 2696, pp. 177–189, 2003.

be applied as they are prone to digital or analog re-recording (copying). Thus, almost all modern copyright protection mechanisms tend to rely to a certain extent on **watermarks**, imperceptive marks hidden in host signals. In a typical content screening system, the client's media player searches the content for hidden information. If the secret mark is found, the player must verify, prior to playback, whether it has a license to play the content. By default, unmarked content is considered as unprotected and is played without any barriers. A key technology required for content screening is public-key watermarking, that is, a marking scheme where breaking a single player or a relatively large subset of players does *not* compromise the security of the entire system. Such a system, potentially efficient for content screening, has been detailed in [4]. If breaking a single player does not pose a significant security threat, the main target of the adversary is finding a signal processing primitive that removes the watermark or prevents a detector to find it. Several attack mechanisms surveyed in [5] have been largely successful in setting up robustness benchmarks for watermarking technologies. However, none of the attack technologies that do not rely on having access to the watermark detector, remove watermarks without any hope that an irreversible or preventing action is possible.

1.2   The Replacement Attack

In this manuscript, we propose an attack which aims at reducing the correlation of a watermarked signal with its watermark by replacing each original watermarked block of the multimedia signal with another perceptually similar block which is computed as a combination of other signal blocks that are perceptually similar but not tainted with the same watermark bits as the original marked block. We call this type of an attack: a **replacement attack**. The rationale behind this attack is the fact that the replacing block, if at certain minimal distance from the original marked block, conveys little correlation with respect to the watermark embedded in the replaced block as it is created from data that is independent with respect to this watermark. Thus, the newly created content preserves the perceptual similarity with respect to the original clip, while irreversibly cleared of the correlation with the originally embedded watermark. The strategy of this new attack paradigm is simple:

1	partition the content into overlapping low-granularity signal blocks,
2	for each block B find a subset S of K most perceptually similar blocks,
3	compute a block R as a combination of blocks from S, such that the Euclidean distance between R and B is minimal, and
4	replace B with R.

In step 2, perceptually similar blocks are originally searched within the original media clip. The search is constrained to a part of the media clip which is assumed to be marked with a different secret compared to block B. If the computed replacement block R is at an Euclidean distance which is higher than some predefined fidelity constraint (e.g., $|B - R| < 4\text{dB}$), the adversary can alternatively seek replacement blocks in an external multimedia library. The distance between R and B must not be small, because the replaced block in that case preserves certain correlation proportional to the similarity. For example, if $B = R$ then the attack does not affect the existence of the watermark. Thus, if R is at a distance which is closer than a certain lower bound, it is recomputed as to increase the similarity beyond that bound.

Finding perceptually similar blocks of certain music or video content is a challenging task. With no loss of generality, in this paper we restrict our focus to audio, although video is in many cases a much better source of repetitive content within a single recording. For example, within a common scene both background and objects experience geometric transformations significantly more frequently than changes in appearance. In general, repetition is often a principal part of composing music and is a natural consequence of the fact that distinct instruments, voices and tones are used to create a soundtrack. Thus, it is likely to find similarities within a single musical piece, an album of songs from a single author, or in instrument solos. In this paper, we explore the challenges of the replacement attack and show how it can be launched on audio content.

2   Logistics of the Replacement Attack

The replacement attack is not limited to a type of content or to a particular watermarking algorithm. For example, systems that modulate secrets using spread-spectrum [6] and/or quantization index modulation (QIM) [7] are all prone to the replacement attack. In order to launch the attack successfully, the adversary does not need to know the details of the watermark codec. The adversary needs to reduce the granularity of integral blocks of data such that no block contains enough information from which a watermark can be identified individually. Note that watermark detection involves processing large amount of data (for example, reliable and robust detection of audio watermarks requires at least several seconds of audio [8]). Thus, blocks considered for replacement must be at least one order of magnitude smaller than watermark length. For both audio and video, this requirement is not difficult to satisfy as typically blocks of $256 - 2048$ transform coefficients for audio or bitmaps of up to 64×64 pixels for video are considered for pattern matching.

In the remainder of this section, we assume that coefficients of the marked signal are replaced only with other coefficients of the same signal. It is straightforward to redefine the attack such that coefficients from external signal vectors are considered as a substitution base.

The **host signal** to be marked $\mathbf{x} \in \mathcal{R}^N$ can be modeled as a vector, where each element $x_i \in \mathbf{x}$ is a zero-mean independent identically distributed normal random variable[1] with standard deviation σ_x: $x_i \sim \mathcal{N}(0, \sigma_x)$. The replacement

---

[1] This model is adopted for the purpose of analyzing the watermark detector. Reality shows that the model is not memoryless as parts of the signal tend to repeat, slightly distorted, both in music and video.

attack is not restricted to a particular signal model; we use the Gaussian assumption to analyze certain properties of the attack. A **watermark** is defined as an arbitrary pseudo-randomly generated vector $\mathbf{w} \in \mathcal{R}^N$, where each element $w_i \in \mathbf{w}$ is a random variable with standard deviation $\delta \ll \sigma_x$. For example, if direct sequence spread-spectrum is used for watermark modulation then $\mathbf{w} \in \{\pm\delta\}^N$. We assume that the watermark $\mathbf{w}$ is mutually independent with respect to $\mathbf{x}$. The **marked signal** $\tilde{\mathbf{x}}$ is created as $\tilde{\mathbf{x}} = \mathbf{x} + \mathbf{w}$. The replacement attack receives as input the marked signal $\tilde{\mathbf{x}}$ and outputs its modification $\tilde{\mathbf{x}}'$.

2.1   Attack Steps

Signal Partitioning. In the initial step of the attack, the watermarked content $\tilde{\mathbf{x}}$ is partitioned into a set $\mathcal{B}$ of overlapping blocks, where each block B_p represents a sequence of m samples of $\tilde{\mathbf{x}}$ starting at $\tilde{x}_{(B_p)}$. (B_i) denotes the index of the first sample in the i-th block B_i. For an overlap ratio of η, the total number of blocks equals $n = \lceil \frac{N-m}{1-\eta} \rceil$. The higher the overlap, the larger the search-space for the replacement attack. We want to select the overlap such that:

1. consecutive blocks do not have similar perceptual characteristics – this upper bound on block overlap aims at reducing the search space – and
2. for two consecutive blocks B_p and B_{p+1} starting at $\tilde{x}_{(B_p)}$ and $\tilde{x}_{(B_{p+1})}$ respectively, the block starting at $\tilde{x}_a$, $a = [(B_p) + (B_{p+1})]/2$ is not perceptually similar to B_p or B_{p+1}.

Similarity Function. This is the core function of the replacement attack. It takes as an input a pair of blocks B_p and B_q and returns a real number $\phi(B_p, B_q) \geq 0$ that quantifies their similarity. Block equality is represented as $\phi(B_p, B_q) = 0$. The adversary can experiment with a number of different functions. In this section, we restrict similarity to the root-mean-square distortion between blocks:

$$\phi(B_p, B_q) = \frac{1}{\sqrt{m}}||B_p - B_q|| = \sqrt{\frac{1}{m}\sum_{i=0}^{m-1}\left[\tilde{x}_{i+(B_p)} - \tilde{x}_{i+(B_q)}\right]^2}. \quad (1)$$

Search for the Substitution Base. This step is repeated for each block (target B) of the original media clip. The goal is to find a subset S of K perceptually similar blocks to B. An additional constraint is that the subset S is searched in part of the signal which is marked with watermark bits different with respect to the watermark present in the target. Usually, watermark bits are replicated within certain vicinity of the target [8], which excludes several neighboring blocks to the target from the search process. The following principles guide the search process.

1. **Lower bound on similarity** – the computed block R replacing B must be at a certain minimal distance from B, i.e. $\phi(B, R) \geq \alpha$. This requirement

stems from the fact that replacing a signal block with another, exceptionally similar block has only nominal impact on watermark existence. Parameter α depends on the watermark amplitude as well as the type of watermark modulation (e.g., direct-sequence spread spectrum or QIM). It is discussed further in Subsection 2.2.

2. **Upper bound on similarity** – the upper limit ensures that the resulting clip has a preserved high fidelity with respect to the marked copy. If the search procedure cannot find a subset of blocks that can linearly combine to create a replacement block R that is sufficiently similar to B, $\phi(B, R) \leqslant \beta$, then $R = B$, i.e. replacement does not occur. Note that the search procedure is not limited to the host media clip – the subset of similar blocks can be extracted from a large library of media clips.

Based on the above principles, the algorithm for computing the replacement block R takes the following steps. In the first step, the algorithm finds two pools of blocks, S' and S. The first pool S' contains all blocks from the substitution database which are at distance $(\forall B_i \in S')\phi(B_i, B) < \alpha$. Frequently, with the exception of electronically generated music, this pool is empty as it is hard to find exceptionally similar blocks in music performed by humans. The second pool S contains K most similar blocks to B that are at distance $(\forall B_i \in S)\phi(B_i, B) \geq \alpha$. Parameter K should be significantly smaller than the length of a block. For 256- to 2048-long audio blocks, values within $10 \leqslant K \leqslant 50$ result in good balance for fidelity and performance. Although parameter K can, in general, be variable across blocks, in our experiments we consider only constant K. The complexity of finding S is linearly proportional to the size of the replacement database.

1	**for each** block B
2	find $S' \subset \mathcal{B} \vert (\forall B_i \in S')\phi(B_i, B) < \alpha$
3	find $S \subset \mathcal{B} \vert (\forall B_i \in S)\phi(B_i, B) \geq \alpha$
4	create matrix $\mathbf{s}$ such that each row in $\mathbf{s}$ is a distinct block from S
5	compute $R' = \mathbf{s}(\mathbf{s}^T\mathbf{s})^{-1}\mathbf{s}^T B$
6	depending on $\phi(R', B)$ and S', set R according to rules (i-iv)
7	replace B with R
8	**end for**

In the next step, the replacement block R is computed from the selected blocks in S such that its similarity with respect to R is maximized. More formally, we construct a matrix $\mathbf{s} \in \mathbb{R}^{K \times m}$ where each row of this matrix represents one block from S. We aim to compute a vector A such that $\|\mathbf{s}A - B\|$ is minimized. The least-squares solution to this set of overdetermined linear equations, commonly called pseudo-inverse of $\mathbf{s}$, equals $A = (\mathbf{s}^T\mathbf{s})^{-1}\mathbf{s}^T B$. A temporary replacement block R' is now computed as $R' = \mathbf{s}A$. Four cases can occur:

(i) the temporary replacement block R' satisfies the requirements, e.g., $\alpha \leqslant \phi(B, R') \leqslant \beta$, in which case the replacement equals $R = R'$, *(ii)* R' is too distorted and subset S' is empty, e.g., $\phi(B, R') > \beta$ and $S' = \varnothing$, in which case no replacement occurs $R = B$ for preserved signal fidelity,

(iii) R' is too distorted and S' is not empty, e.g., $\phi(B, R') > \beta$ and $S' \neq \varnothing$, in which case R' and a randomly chosen block T from S' are mixed as $R = (1 - q)T + qR'$ such that $\phi(R, B) = \alpha$, and

(iv) R' is too similar to B, e.g., $\phi(B, R') < \alpha$, in which case R' and a randomly chosen block T from S are mixed as $R = (1-q)T+qR'$ such that $\phi(R, B) = \alpha$.

The mixing parameter q enforces the desired similarity $\phi(B, R) = \alpha$ in the last two cases if:

$$q = \frac{\varepsilon^2 - \sqrt{\alpha^2(\vartheta^2 + \varepsilon^2) - \vartheta^2\varepsilon^2}}{\vartheta^2 + \varepsilon^2}, \tag{2}$$

where $||R' - B||^2 = m\vartheta^2$ and $||T - B||^2 = m\varepsilon^2$ under the assumption that $T - B$ and $R' - B$ are mutually independent[2].

Block Substitution. In the final step, each block B of the original watermarked signal is replaced with the corresponding computed replacement R to create the output media clip $\tilde{\mathbf{x}}'$.

2.2 Determining α for Spread-Spectrum Watermarks

Lets assume that vector $\mathbf{x}+\mathbf{w}$ is deemed similar to and replaced by vector $\mathbf{y}+\mathbf{v}$, where $\mathbf{x}$ and $\mathbf{y}$ are original signals marked with two distinct watermarks $\mathbf{w}$ and $\mathbf{v}$, where $\mathbf{w}, \mathbf{v} \in \{\pm\delta\}^m$. All vectors are assumed to have the same length as a single block: m. In addition, we assume that the watermarks are spread-spectrum sequences, which means that watermark $\mathbf{w}$ is detected in a signal $\mathbf{z}$ by matched filtering: $C(\mathbf{z}, \mathbf{w}) = \mathbf{z}^T\mathbf{w}$. If $\mathbf{z}$ has been marked with $\mathbf{w}$, $\mathrm{E}[C(\mathbf{z}, \mathbf{w})] = m\delta^2$, otherwise $\mathrm{E}[C(\mathbf{z}, \mathbf{w})] = 0$, with variance $\mathrm{Var}[C(\mathbf{z}, \mathbf{w})] = m\sigma_z^2$. Watermark is detected if $C(\mathbf{z}, \mathbf{w})$ is greater than a certain detection threshold τ. In order to have symmetric probability of a false alarm and misdetection, τ is commonly set to $m\delta^2/2$. From the requirement for two blocks to be eligible for substitution:

$$E[||(\mathbf{y} + \mathbf{v}) - (\mathbf{x} + \mathbf{w})||^2] = E[||\mathbf{y} - \mathbf{x}||^2] + 2m\delta^2 - 2E[C(\mathbf{v}, \mathbf{w})] \geqslant m\alpha^2, \tag{3}$$

we can compute the expected resulting correlation $\mathrm{E}[C(\mathbf{y} + \mathbf{v}, \mathbf{w})]$ under the assumption that vectors $\mathbf{v}$ and $\mathbf{w}$ are independent with respect to $\mathbf{x}$ and $\mathbf{y}$ [3]:

$$E[C(\mathbf{y} + \mathbf{v}, \mathbf{w})] \leqslant \frac{1}{2}E[||\mathbf{y} - \mathbf{x}||^2] + m\left(\delta^2 - \frac{\alpha^2}{2}\right) \tag{4}$$

Assuming that there exists true repetition of the original content $\mathbf{y} = \mathbf{x}$, then setting $\alpha \geqslant \delta\sqrt{2}$ would set the expected minimum correlation to zero after

---

[2] In case *(iv)* the two vectors are not mutually independent as R' is dependent upon T. To address this issue, we select T as the block from S which has the smallest absolute value of the corresponding coefficient in the vector A that builds R'.

[3] $\mathrm{E}[C(\mathbf{y}, \mathbf{v})] = \mathrm{E}[C(\mathbf{x}, \mathbf{v})] = \mathrm{E}[C(\mathbf{y}, \mathbf{w})] = \mathrm{E}[C(\mathbf{x}, \mathbf{w})] = 0$.

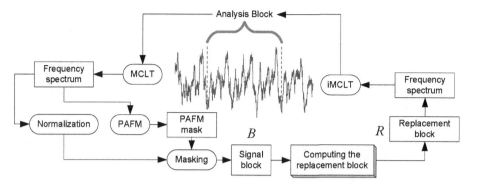

Fig. 1. Block diagram of the signal processing primitives performed as pre- and post-processing to the replacement attack.

substitution. If $\mathbf{y} \neq \mathbf{x}$, then α needs to be additionally increased to compensate for the effect of $E[||\mathbf{y} - \mathbf{x}||^2]$ on resulting correlation. Quantifying this compensation analytically is difficult as it depends upon the self-similarity of the targeted content.

3   A Replacement Attack for Audio

In this section, we demonstrate how the generic principles behind the replacement attack can be applied against an audio watermarking technology. We first describe how an audio signal is partitioned and pre-processed for improved perceptual pattern matching. Next, we analyze the similarity function we used for our experiments. The effect of the replacement attack on direct-sequence spread-spectrum watermark detection is presented in the following sections.

3.1   Audio Processing for the Replacement Attack

Since most psycho-acoustic models operate in the frequency spectrum [9], we launch the replacement attack in the logarithmic (dB) frequency domain. The set of signal blocks $\mathcal{B}$ is created from the coefficients of a modulated complex lapped transform (MCLT) [9]. The MCLT is a 2× oversampled DFT filter bank, used in conjunction with analysis and synthesis windows that provide perfect reconstruction. We consider MCLT analysis blocks with 2048 transform coefficients and an $\eta = 0.25$ overlap. Each block of coefficients is normalized and psycho-acoustically masked using an off-the-shelf masking model [9]. Similarity is explored exclusively in the audible part of the frequency spectrum. Because of psycho-acoustic masking, the actual similarity function in Eqn.1 is not commutative. A replacement block is always masked with the psycho-acoustic mask of the replaced block. Figure 1 illustrates the signal processing primitives used to prepare blocks of audio content for substitution.

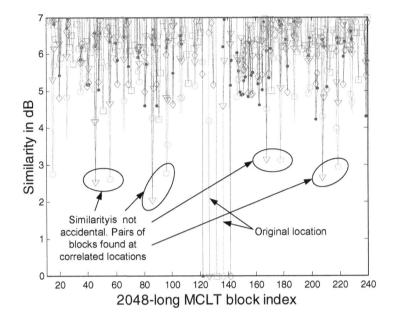

Fig. 2. Music self-similarity: a similarity diagram for five different 2048-long MCLT blocks within a techno clip with 240 MCLT blocks. Zero-similarity denotes equality. The abscissa x denotes the index of a particular MCLT block. The ordinate denotes the similarity $\phi(x, B_i)$ of the corresponding block x with respect to the selected five blocks with indices $B_i|i = \{122, 127, 132, 137, 142\}$.

Watermark length is assumed to be greater than one second. In addition, we assume that watermark chips may be replicated along the time axis at most for one second[4] [8]. Thus, we restrict that for a given block its potential substitution blocks are *not* searched within one second.

3.2   Analysis of the Similarity Function

We performed several experiments in order to evaluate the effectiveness of the replacement attack. The first set of experiments aims at quantifying similarity between blocks of several audio clips marked with spread-spectrum watermarks at $\delta = 1$dB. In all examples, block similarity is computed over the 2–7kHz sub-band as watermark codecs commonly hide data in a sub-band that is not strongly distorted by compression and medium quality low- and high-pass filtering [8]. Figure 2 shows the values of the similarity function $\phi(B_i, B_j)$ for five 2048-long MCLT blocks at positions $i = \{122, 127, 132, 137, 142\}$ against a database of 240 blocks $j = \{1 \ldots 240\}$ within one audio clip (techno music). We observe that throughout the database four different pairs of blocks (circled in the subfigure) are found as similar below 4dB to the pair of blocks with indices 127 and 137.

---

[4] Higher level of redundancy may enable effective watermark estimation.

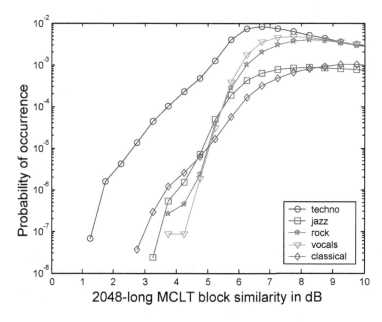

Fig. 3. Music self-similarity: probability density function of the similarity function $\phi(B_i, B_j)$ within an audio clip – five different types of music are considered: rock, classical, jazz, vocals and techno. A certain value x on the abscissa represents a histogram bin from $x - 0.25$ to $x + 0.25$ dB.

All similar pairs of blocks preserve the same index distance as the target pair. This points to the fact that in many cases content similarity is not a result of coïncidence, but a consequence of repetitive musical content.

Figure 3 illustrates the probability that for a given 2048-long MCLT block B_i, there exists another block B_j within the same audio clip that is within $\phi(B_i, B_j) \in [x - 0.25, x + 0.25]$dB, where x is a real number. This experiment was conducted for five different types of audio content: techno, jazz, rock, vocals, and classical music. For this benchmark set of distinctly different musical pieces, we conclude that the average $\phi(B_i, B_j)$ for two randomly selected blocks within an audio clip is in the range of 6–8dB. The probability of finding a similar block should rise proportionally to the size of the substitution database, especially if it consists of clips of the same genre/performer. Finally, note that electronically generated music (in our benchmark a techno song) is significantly more likely to contain perceptually correlated blocks than music that is performed by humans.

The second set of experiments explores the distortion that the replacement attack introduces. We consider three cases. In the first case, in the left subfigure of Figure 4, we present the probability that the replacement block R' is at distance $\phi(B, R')$ if R' equals the most similar block found in the substitution database (e.g., $K = 1$). The right subfigure presents the same metric for the case when $K = 10$ and R' is computed as described in Subsection 2.1. Finally, Table 1 quantifies the improvement in the average distortion $\phi(B, R')$ as K increases

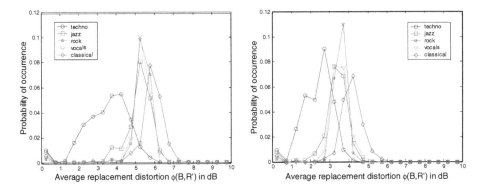

Fig. 4. Probability density function of the similarity function $\phi(B, R')$ for two different cases: $K = 1$ (left) and $K = 10$ (right).

Table 1. Improvement in signal distortion due to the replacement attack as parameter K is increased. Results are reported on the dB scale. Average block length is $\bar{m} \approx 400$.

$\phi(B, R')$	Techno	Jazz	Rock	Vocals	Classical	Average $\phi_K(B, R') - \phi_{K=1}(B, R')$
K=1	3.5714	5.2059	5.3774	5.3816	5.8963	N/A
K=10	2.3690	3.2528	3.5321	3.5193	4.0536	1.741
K=20	2.2666	3.0576	3.3792	3.3664	3.7968	1.914
K=30	2.2059	2.9255	3.3061	3.2762	3.5613	2.032
K=50	2.1284	2.6595	3.1702	3.1209	3.0635	2.253
K=100	1.9512	2.1331	2.8631	2.7439	1.8719	2.775

from 1 to 100. We conclude that the replacement attack in our experimental setup induces between 1.5–3dB distortion noise with respect to the marked copy – a change in fidelity that most users are willing to sacrifice for free content.

4   Effect of the Attack on Watermark Detection

In order to evaluate the effect of a replacement attack on spread-spectrum watermarks, we conducted two experiments. For both experiments, we used spread-spectrum watermarks that spread over 240 consecutive 2048-long MCLT blocks (approximately 11sec long), where only the audible frequency magnitudes in the 2–7kHz subband were marked. We did not use chip replication as its effect on watermark detection is orthogonal with respect to the replacement attack.

Figure 5 shows how normalized correlation of a spread-spectrum watermark detector is affected by the increase of the parameter K. We performed the following experiment. We marked the first 240 2048-long MCLT blocks of five different songs (ranging from 3 to 5 minutes in duration) with a direct sequence spread spectrum watermark. The watermark amplitude was set to $\delta = 1$dB. During the attack, we replaced each target block B with its computed replacement block R following the recipe presented in Subsection 2.1. For the purpose of demonstrating the change of the correlation due to increase in K, we did not apply

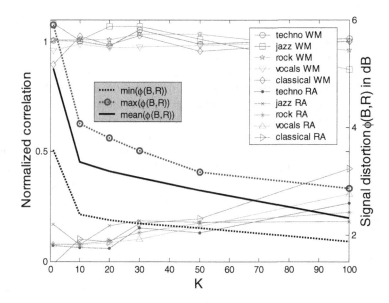

Fig. 5. Response of a spread-spectrum watermark detector to the replacement attack. The abscissa quantifies the change in parameter K from 1 to 100 for fixed watermark amplitude of $\delta = 1$dB. The left ordinate shows the increase of the normalized correlation as K increases. The results are obtained for five full songs in different genres. The right ordinate shows the corresponding minimal, maximal, and average distortion with respect to the set of benchmark clips due to the replacement attack.

steps (*iii-iv*). When these steps are applied the minimal distortion per block is limited to αdB.

In Figure 5, we show two results. First, we show the average normalized correlation value (left ordinate) across 10 different tests for watermark detection within marked content $E[C(\mathbf{z}, \mathbf{w})] = 1$ (curves marked WM) and within marked content attacked with our attack for several values of $K = \{1, 10, 20, 30, 50, 100\}$ (curves marked RA). Second, we show on the right ordinate the signal distortion caused by the replacement attack: the minimal, average, and maximal distortion across all five audio clips. We can conclude from the diagram that for small values of K, its increase results in greatly improved distortion metrics, while for large values of K, the computed replacement vectors are too similar with respect to the target blocks which results in lower effect on the normalized correlation.

The power of the replacement attack is most notably observed by comparing the effect of adding a white Gaussian noise (AWGN) pattern $\mathbf{n} = \mathcal{N}(0, \sigma_n)$ of certain standard deviation $\sigma_n \in \{2 \ldots 3\}$dB to a replacement attack of equivalent distortion. Whereas the dramatic effect of replacement can be observed in Figure 5, AWGN affects the correlation detector only negligibly. In the latter case, the expected correlation value remains the same $E[C(\tilde{\mathbf{x}} + \mathbf{n}, \mathbf{w})] = E[C(\tilde{\mathbf{x}}, \mathbf{w})]$, with increased variance $Var[C(\tilde{\mathbf{x}} + \mathbf{n}, \mathbf{w})] = Var[C(\tilde{\mathbf{x}}, \mathbf{w})] + m\sigma_n^2$. Finally, additive noise of 2–3dB in the 2–7kHz subband is a relatively tolerable modification.

Another important issue is the fact that the distortion introduced by the replacement attack is linearly proportional to the watermark amplitude. Clearly, with the increase of watermark amplitude δ, the search process of the replacement attack becomes harder for two reasons: (i) block contents become more randomized and (ii) the substituted blocks are more correlated with the original blocks. On the other hand, we have empirically concluded that watermark amplitude affects the reduction of the normalized correlation minimally. Although stronger watermarks may sound like a solution to the replacement attack, high watermark amplitudes cannot be accepted because of two reasons: first, the requirement for high-fidelity marked content and second, strong watermarks can be efficiently estimated using an optimal watermark estimator [4], i.e. estimate $\mathbf{v} = \text{sign}(\mathbf{x} + \mathbf{w})$ makes an error per bit $\varepsilon = \Pr[v_i \neq w_i] = \frac{1}{2}\text{erfc}(\frac{\sigma_x}{\delta\sqrt{2}})$ exponentially proportional to δ.

5   Conclusion

For any watermarking technology and any type of content, one powerful attack is to re-record the original content, e.g., perform again the music or capture the image of the same original visual scene. In this paper, we emulate this attack using a computing system: the replacement attack aims at replacing small pieces of the marked content with perceptually similar but unmarked[5] substitution blocks created using a library of multimedia content. The hope is that the substitutions have little correlation with the original embedded mark. Inspired by predictive coding of speech and video [15,10], we present an algorithm for computing the replacement blocks using a least-squares linear combination of K signal blocks most similar to the target block.

Although the attack is generic and can be applied to all marking strategies, we demonstrate how it can be launched for audio content and a traditional watermarking modulation technology: direct sequence spread-spectrum. Our preliminary results demonstrate that the attack has similar effect on other marking mechanisms such as quantization index modulation.

From the presented experimental results, we conclude that an implementation of the replacement attack that considers a relatively small substitution database can create replacement blocks that are only within 1.5–3dB distance with respect to the target signal blocks. Such an attack removes approximately 80–90% of the correlation between the watermark and the marked/attacked content. Similar adversarial effects can be obtained against QIM-based watermarking schemes.

We identify two possible prevention strategies against a replacement attack. For example, a data hiding primitive may identify rare parts of the content at watermark embedding time and mark only these blocks. However this reduces significantly the practical capacity of the scheme and increases dramatically the complexity of the embedding process. In the case of spread-spectrum watermarks, longer watermarks and increased detector sensitivity may enable watermark detection at lower thresholds (e.g., $\tau < m\delta^2/10$). Unfortunately, such a

---

[5] Or marked with a different watermark.

solution comes at the expense of having significantly longer watermarks which results in a significantly lowered robustness with respect to de-synchronization attacks.

References

1. Andy Patrizio, "DVD piracy: It can be done," November 1st, 1999, http://www.wired.com/news/technology/0,1282,32249,00.html.
2. "Secure Digital Music Initiative," http://www.sdmi.org.
3. "The DVD Copy Control Association," http://www.dvdcca.org.
4. Darko Kirovski, Henrique Malvar, and Yacov Yacobi, "A dual watermarking and fingerprinting system," Tech. Rep. MSR-TR-2001-57, Microsoft Research, June 2001.
5. Fabien A. P. Petitcolas, Ross J. Anderson, and Markus G. Kuhn, "Attacks on copyright marking systems," In [11], pp. 218–238.
6. Ingemar J. Cox, Joe Kilian, Tom Leighton, and Talal Shamoon, "A secure, robust watermark for multimedia," In [12], pp. 183–206.
7. Brian Chen and Gregory W. Wornell, "Quantization index modulation: a class of provably good methods for digital watermarking and information embedding," *IEEE Transactions on Information Theory*, vol. 47, no. 4, pp. 1423–1443, May 2001.
8. Darko Kirovski and Henrique Malvar, "Robust covert communication over a public audio channel using spread spectrum," In [14], pp. 354–368.
9. Henrique Malvar, "A modulated complex lapped transform and its application to audio processing," in *International Conference on Acoustics, Speech, and Signal Processing*, Phoenix, Arizona, USA, March 1999, pp. 1421–1424.
10. Mehmet Kıvanç Mıhçak, *Personal Communication*.
11. David Aucsmith, Ed., *Information Hiding: Second International Workshop*, vol. 1525 of *Lecture Notes in Computer Science*, Portland, Oregon, USA, 1998. Springer-Verlag, Berlin, Germany.
12. Ross J. Anderson, Ed., *Information hiding: first international workshop*, vol. 1174 of *Lecture Notes in Computer Science*, Isaac Newton Institute, Cambridge, UK, May 1996. Springer-Verlag, Berlin, Germany.
13. Ping Wah Wong and Edward J. Delp, Eds., *Security and Watermarking of Multimedia Contents II*, vol. 3971, San Jose, California, U.S.A., 24–26 Jan. 2000. The Society for Imaging Science and Technology (IS&T) and the International Society for Optical Engineering (SPIE), SPIE.
14. Ira S Moskowitz, Ed., *Information hiding: fourth international workshop (IH'2001)*, vol. 2137 of *Lecture Notes in Computer Science*, Pittsburgh, Pennsylvania, U.S.A., 2001. Springer-Verlag, Berlin, Germany.
15. Jerry D. Gibson, Toby Berger, David Lindbergh, and Richard L., III Baker, *Digital Compression for Multimedia : Principles and Standards*, Morgan Kaufmann Publishers, San Francisco, CA, USA, January 1998.

FAIR: Fair Audience InfeRence

Rob Johnson[1,*] and Jessica Staddon[2]

[1] University of California at Berkeley
rtjohnso@cs.berkeley.edu
[2] Palo Alto Research Center
staddon@parc.com

Abstract. Given the recent changes in the policy governing Internet content distribution, such as the institution of per listener royalties for Internet radio broadcasters, content distributors now have an incentive to under-report the size of their audience. Previous audience measurement schemes only protect against inflation of audience size. We present the first protocols for audience measurement that protect against both inflation and deflation attempts by content distributors. The protocols trade-off the amount of additional information the content distributors must distribute to facilitate audience inference with the amount of infrastructure required and are applicable to Internet radio, web plagiarism, and software license enforcement.

1 Introduction

Internet content distributors often want to prove to a third party that they have a large number of visitors or listeners. Such information is usually used to set advertising rates, so content distributors have an incentive to inflate these numbers. Various schemes for preventing content distributors from reporting artificially inflated audience sizes have been proposed [22,13,18].

With the advent of per listener royalty fees for Internet radio [15] and the growth of web content plagiarism [11], content distributors now have an incentive to report artificially small audiences, but none of the prior schemes for audience measurement prevent such behavior. We present two new audience measurement protocols which prevent content distributors from reporting artificially deflated audience sizes. Besides the application to Internet radio, these protocols have a variety of uses, as we describe in Section 1.3.

Our protocols achieve accurate audience measurement by leveraging the ability of the auditor to anonymously request content. Anonymity can be achieved with services such as [1]. Our first protocol (see Section 2) requires essentially no additional infrastructure. The content distributor simply maintains a Bloom filter [4] that is computed as a function of the IDs (anonymized to preserve privacy) of all clients who have requested the content. The filter is small in applications such as micro-broadcasting. The protocol offers protection against

---

* Rob Johnson was employed at PARC while this research was conducted.

J. Feigenbaum (Ed.): DRM 2002, LNCS 2696, pp. 190–207, 2003.

Table 1. The main features of the schemes presented in this paper. The number of clients is denoted by n

Scheme	Protocol 1	Protocol 2
Deflation protection	Yes	Yes
Inflation protection	No	Yes
Privacy preserving	Yes	No
Communication overhead	$O(n)$	$O(1)$
Counts cumulative audience	Yes	Yes
Counts current audience	Yes	No

deflation because each client can verify that their ID was one of the inputs to the filter, however inflation cannot be detected.

The second protocol (see Section 3) uses encryption to offer protection against both inflation and deflation. Assuming a keying infrastructure is in place, a trusted party randomly allocates to each client a subset of a global set of keys. The content distributor makes the content publicly available (e.g. by posting a file on the web) in encrypted form using an encryption key known to all its clients. If the keys are allocated according to a well-chosen distribution, then the auditor can estimate the number of clients based only on the encryption key the content distributor is using. This protocol requires essentially no additional communication (that is, other than the encrypted content) on the part of the content distributor, but doesn't completely preserve the privacy of the clients. Table 1 summarizes the main features of our protocols.

1.1 Related Work

One of the first methods for counting the number of visitors to a web site is due to Franklin and Malkhi [13]. Naor and Pinkas [22] present a protocol with stronger security guarantees [13]. Ogata and Kurosawa [23] identify flaws in the Naor and Pinkas scheme, and propose their own. The Naor-Pinkas model has been generalized and analyzed extensively [5,18,6,26]. In a similar vein, Kuhn [17] presents a scheme by which an auditor can efficiently verify the number of unique signatures on a document, with applications to digital petitions and web metering.

The methods currently used to measure audience size are far more primitive than anything proposed in the above papers. The simplest audience measurement technique counts the number of entries in the server's log files [8]. Since it is easy for the server administrator to delete or insert entries into the log files, these numbers cannot be trusted. In the specific case of counting the number of visitors that see an advertisement, the trustworthiness of the measurements can be improved by having the advertising agency serve the ad directly [12]. In this arrangement, the ad agency can under-report the number of ads it serves, thus lowering the advertising fees it pays. Reiter, Anupam, and Mayer [24] propose a scheme for detecting this sort of fraud. Conversely, Mayer, Nissam, Pinkas and

Reiter [2] describe general attacks for inflating the number of ads that appear to be served through a given web page.

The size of a particular website's audience can also be gauged by consumer surveys and focus groups [19,25]. These numbers can be fairly accurate, but this method is expensive. Some audience measurement services combine log analysis and consumer surveys [19,9]. Similarly, audience size can be measured by having web surfers keep a diary of the sites they visit, although these numbers are prone to accidental error as much as malicious mis-reporting [10,25].

All the audience measurement techniques above are designed for determining advertising rates and thus are only concerned about attempts by the content distributor to inflate the audience size. In all the schemes above except the survey and diary methods, the content distributor can easily deflate the size of her audience. In the context of advertising, content distributors have no incentive to do so, hence this has not been a problem. This is not the case when the audience size is being measured to determine royalty fees. Ours are the first schemes we know of that attempt to prevent the content distributor from deflating her audience size.

Finally, we note that secure voting (see for example, [7]) is also concerned with accurate audience measurement. However, voting protocols tend to be fairly heavyweight due to the requirements of that setting (e.g. public verifiability) hence we don't believe those techniques are directly applicable to the content distributor setting.

1.2 Goals and Limitations

We are primarily interested in efficient and easily implemented schemes whereby Internet content distributors can prove to an auditor that their audience is small. Depending on the nature of the content provided, it may be appropriate to measure the number of client requests (or hits) received during a given time interval, or it may be better to track the number of active clients (or streams, in unicast applications) during a given time period. It is also desirable that the auditor learn nothing about the audience members, i.e. they maintain their anonymity.

In most of the scenarios we consider, it makes sense to assume that content distributors and clients are aligned against the auditor, hence we need to protect against attempts by the distributor and the clients to conduct their transactions "under the table", and other collusion attacks. We offer such protection by monitoring content distributor/client interactions to check for protocol compliance. The auditor cannot monitor every transaction but, on the relatively anonymous Internet, he can pose as a regular client. The auditor can then verify that the content distributor obeys the protocol in a small number of randomly chosen transactions. In traditional web metering schemes, each client of a content distributor gives a token to the content distributor. After the distributor has received enough tokens, it combines them (e.g. using a secret sharing scheme) and presents the result to an auditor. The content distributor cannot forge tokens and hence cannot inflate her audience size. The content distributor can obviously throw away tokens in order to appear to have a smaller audience. In our schemes, the auditor poses anonymously as a client, giving the content distributor some (undetectably) marked tokens. If the content distributor tries to cheat by throwing away one of the marked tokens, she will be caught. Since the content distributor cannot distinguish the marked tokens from regular ones, she cannot safely throw away any tokens, and hence cannot cheat.

Since our protocols require the auditor to pose as a regular client, they require a network which supports anonymous connections by default. Ideally, the underlying network would support perfect anonymity and unlinkability for all connections. The current Internet offers relative anonymity and, by virtue of dynamically assigned addresses and dial-up connections, relative unlinkability. Emerging peer-to-peer technologies may support perfect anonymity in the near future. Thus we analyze our protocols in the context of perfect anonymity, and believe they will degrade gracefully in the imperfect world of the current Internet. Some DRM applications may not allow perfect anonymity, since each client may have a fixed public/private key pair that it uses to communicate with content distributors. Note that this scenario doesn't preclude anonymity, just unlinkability. Both of the protocols described in this paper depend primarily on anonymity, not unlinkability, so they may still be usable in these DRM applications.

The client anonymity we require can also be used against the content distributor. The auditor (or any other client) may artificially inflate the audience size by repeatedly requesting the content as a new client. Our protocols do not explicitly protect against this. One possible remedy is to insert a trusted party between the distributor and the clients with anonymous communication only between the trusted party and the distributor. If the content distributor suspects this attack is underway, the trusted party's logs can be examined. Of course, requiring a trusted party for the sole purpose of protecting against this attack is suboptimal, however if the protocol is such that a trusted party is already required (as is true of the protocol in Section 3) then this approach is worth considering.

1.3   Applications

There are a number of settings in which audience measurement protocols that are secure against deflation are necessary.

INTERNET RADIO. The Internet has given rise to hobbyist Internet radio broadcasters which have extremely small audiences. For example, according to live365.com, there are over 1000 Internet radio stations with less than 100 listening hours per month; e.g. these stations have an average of less than one listener tuned in for 3 hours each day. An audience measurement protocol may be used to prove this fact to an organization such as the RIAA.

DISTRIBUTION OF LICENSED CONTENT. Consider a web site that holds a limited distribution license for content (e.g. movies, music files or software). Our protocols can be used to ensure that the distributor does not exceed the license.

WEB ADVERTISING As described in Section 1.1, some web advertisers serve their ads directly, and hence can under-report the number of ads they serve in order to reduce the fees they must pay to carrying websites. Our audience counting schemes can detect this type of fraud.

SCREEN-SCRAPING. Websites that provide a useful service, such as Yahoo's real-time stock prices, often get "screen-scraped" by other web services [11]. The scraping service simply fetches the information from the original service, parses the desired data out of the returned web page, repackages it in a new format, and finally presents it to the client. As long as the screen-scraping service does not overuse the original service provider, this behavior can be tolerated. If the scraping service agrees to use one of our request counting protocols, then the originating web service provider can audit the scraping service to ensure that it is not abusing the original service provider.

2   Estimating Audience Size with Minimal Infrastructure

This protocol is very easy to adopt and can be adapted to support either total request counting or current client set counting. Its main drawback is that the bandwidth required is linear in the size of the audience, but this protocol is quite efficient for scenarios in which the audience is small, as is the case for several of our intended applications (e.g. Internet radio micro-broadcasters).

The protocol uses Bloom filters [4], so we give a brief introduction to them here. A Bloom filter is a lossy representation of a set and consists of a bit-vector b of length m and s independent hash functions $h_1, \ldots, h_s : \{0, 1\}^* \to \mathbb{N}$ [1]. In the literature of Bloom filters, m is called the *width* of the filter. Initially, the bit vector is all zeros. To insert an element x into the set represented by the Bloom filter b, set the bits $b[h_1(x) \bmod m] = \cdots = b[h_s(x) \bmod m] = 1$ (if a bit is already set to 1 then it remains 1). To test whether x is an element of the set represented by Bloom filter b, test that $b[h_1(x) \bmod m] = \cdots = b[h_s(x) \bmod m] = 1$. Note that this test can lead to false positives; this is why the Bloom filter is termed "lossy". If $b[h_i(x)] = 0$ for some i, then x cannot be in the set. Bloom filters do not support item removal.

Let $w(b)$ denote the Hamming weight of b. The probability that a bit is 1 in a Bloom filter of width m after n insertions using s hash functions is $1 - (1 - \frac{1}{m})^{ns}$. So given a filter b, we can estimate the number of insertions which have been performed on b by $I(b) = \frac{\ln(1 - w(b)/m)}{s \ln(1 - 1/m)}$. To minimize the probability of a false positive, s should be chosen so that $s = (\ln 2)m/n$, which gives a false positive rate of $\left(\frac{1}{2}\right)^{(\ln 2)m/n} \approx (0.6185)^{m/n}$. So, for example, if $m/n = 8$, the false positive rate using $s = 5$ is 0.0216. Finally, if b_1 and b_2 are two Bloom filters of the same width, then we say $b_1 \leq b_2$ if $b_1[i] \leq b_2[i]$ for all i.

The protocol is illustrated in Figure 1. Each content distributor maintains a Bloom filter of width $m = cn$, where n is the average number of requests seen by

---

[1] The hash functions need not be cryptographically secure. They are just used to map the universe of objects down to integers.

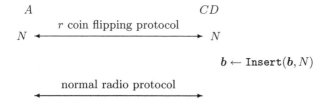

Fig. 1. The join counting version of the Bloom-filter protocol. The content distributor is denoted by CD. The client, A, must be anonymous, and N is the result of executing a coin flipping protocol for r coins

the content distributor each week and c is a parameter agreed upon in advance. In practice, $c = 8$ works well. When a client sends a request to the content distributor, the content distributor and client engage in a coin flipping protocol to agree on an r bit nonce N and the content distributor inserts N into the Bloom filter. Any standard coin flipping protocol will work [14]. They then proceed with their normal protocols. Each week, for example, the content distributor sends the Bloom filter to the auditor and then starts again with a fresh filter. The auditor checks that the Bloom filter it receives, b, has $w(b) \leq 2m/3$ and computes an estimate of the number of requests seen by the content distributor via $I(b) = \frac{\ln(1-w(b)/m)}{s\ln(1-1/m)}$. The requirement that $w(b) \leq 2m/3$ is a technical constraint necessary to guarantee that the estimate $I(b)$ is sufficiently accurate (see Theorem 1). To audit the content distributor for compliance, the auditor anonymously sends k requests to the content distributor and then checks that all their nonces, $N_1, \ldots, N_k$, are present in the Bloom filter that the content distributor submits for that interval.

For small content distributors, this scheme is very efficient. Using the ratio $m/n = 8$ mentioned above, the content distributor must send the auditor about 1 byte per join. So, for example, a content distributor that receives 20 requests each day would only have to send a 140 byte message to the auditor each week. Thus this scheme is completely feasible for small to medium content distributors. Even a relatively large content distributor with around 150 requests per day would only have to send a 1K weekly message to the auditor. In the context of Internet radio broadcasters, these overheads are very small since the average audio stream takes at least 2K/s.

Using $I(b)$ as an estimate of the size of the content distributor's audience gives good accuracy. The following theorem implies that if we use $I(b)$ as an estimate of the number of requests received by the content distributor then, with extremely high probability, the actual number of requests will differ from our estimate by at most $\alpha\sqrt{m}$ for a small value of α.

Theorem 1. *Fix $n_{max} < \frac{m\ln s}{s}$ and $W < (1 - \frac{1}{s})m$. Let X be a random variable representing the set of nonces received by the content distributor. We model X as taking on values at random from the set $\{\{x_1, \ldots, x_n\} | x_i \in \mathbb{Z}/2^r\mathbb{Z}, 0 \leq n < n_{max}\}$. Let $B[X]$ denote the Bloom filter representation of X, and $w(X) = w(B[X])$. Then*

$$\Pr[||X| - I(\boldsymbol{B}[X])| \geq \alpha\sqrt{m} \mid w(X) = W] = O\left(\sqrt{m}\exp\left(\frac{-(\alpha-1)^2}{2}\right)\right).$$

Proof. By Bayes' Theorem,

$$\Pr[|X| = n \mid w(X) = W] = \frac{\Pr[w(X) = W \mid |X| = n]\Pr[|X| = n]}{\sum_{i=0}^{M}\Pr[w(X) = W \mid |X| = i]\Pr[|X| = i]}.$$

Since we are estimating $|X|$ from $w(X)$, we assume that $|X|$ is uniformly distributed[2]. Letting $K = \sum_{i=0}^{M}\Pr[w(X) = W \mid |X| = i]$ and simplifying gives

$$\Pr[|X| = n \mid w(X) = W] = \frac{\Pr[w(X) = W \mid |X| = n]}{K}.$$

Except for the factor of K, the LHS of this equation is just the well-known occupancy distribution derived from tossing n balls into m bins. Let $\mu(i) = E[w(X) \mid |X| = i] = (1 - (1 - \frac{1}{m})^{is})m$. When $\mu(i) < (1 - \frac{1}{s})m$ (or, equivalently, when $i < \frac{m\ln s}{s}$), then $\frac{d\mu}{di} > 1$.

By Kamath, Motwami, Palem, and Spirakis' Occupancy Bound [16],

$$\Pr[|w(X) - \mu(|X|)| \geq \theta\mu(|X|)] \leq 2\exp\left(\frac{\theta^2\mu(|X|)^2(m - 1/2)}{m^2 - \mu(|X|)^2}\right).$$

By combining this bound with the Bayesian equation above and unenlightening algebraic manipulation, one can derive that

$$\Pr[||X| - I(W)| \geq \alpha\sqrt{m} \mid w(X) = W] \leq \frac{4\sqrt{m}}{K}\sum_{i=\alpha}^{\infty}\exp\left(\frac{-(i-1)^2}{2}\right)$$

$$= O\left(\sqrt{m}\exp\left(\frac{-(\alpha-1)^2}{2}\right)\right)$$

The only tricky part of the derivation is to use that $|i - I(W)| \leq |W - \mu(i)|$, which holds because $\frac{d\mu}{di} > 1$. $\square$

In practice, $I(\boldsymbol{b})$ is a much better estimate of the number of requests than this theorem predicts. Figure 2 shows the width of the 99.9% confidence interval for several choices of m. As the figure shows, as long as $w(\boldsymbol{b}) \leq 2m/3$ as required by our protocol, then with 99.9% confidence, $|I(\boldsymbol{b}) - |X|| \leq \frac{4\sqrt{m}}{5}$. So for example, using a Bloom filter $\boldsymbol{b}$ with $m = 640$, if $w(\boldsymbol{b}) = 320$, then with 99.9% confidence, the actual number of insertions performed on the filter is between 80 and 100.

In general, the content distributor can attempt to cheat during an auditing period by reporting a Bloom filter $\boldsymbol{b}' < \boldsymbol{b}$, where $\boldsymbol{b}$ is the correct Bloom filter containing all requests for the auditing period. The auditor detects this cheating if there exist i and j such that $\boldsymbol{b}'[h_i(N_j)] = 0$. The following Proposition describes the content distributor's optimal strategy and bounds his chances of success.

---

[2] This is a common but controversial assumption in Bayesian analysis. The controversy arises because the validity of the analysis depends on this assumption, but the assumption cannot be verified statistically. For the purposes of bounding the tail probabilities, the uniform distribution is a relatively pessimistic choice, hence we believe it is a safe one. A similar situation arises in Section 3.

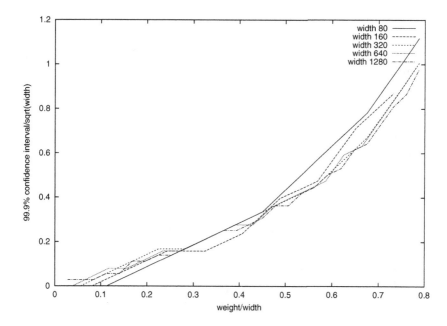

Fig. 2. The accuracy of using $I(x)$ to estimate the number of insertions performed on a Bloom filter. Note that the confidence intervals have been normalized to $\sqrt{m}$. Since our protocol requires that content distributors submit Bloom filters $\boldsymbol{b}$ with $w(\boldsymbol{b}) \leq \frac{2m}{3}$, we can conclude that with 99.9% confidence, the actual number of requests received by the content distributor differs from $I(\boldsymbol{b})$ by at most $\frac{4\sqrt{m}}{5}$

Proposition 1. *Suppose the content distributor is allowed to service L requests, but receives $n > L$ requests. Let $\{J_1, \ldots, J_n\}$ be the set of nonces generated by servicing the requests, and $\boldsymbol{b}$ be the Bloom filter generated from $\{J_1, \ldots, J_n\}$. Then the content distributor's optimal strategy is to report a Bloom filter $\boldsymbol{b}'$ containing the largest subset $S \subseteq \{J_1, \ldots, J_n\}$ such that $I(w(\boldsymbol{b}')) \leq L$. If $w(\boldsymbol{b}) - w(\boldsymbol{b}') = D$ and the auditor sent k requests to the content distributor, then*

$$\Pr[\text{content distributor succeeds}] \leq \frac{\binom{n-k}{D/s}}{\binom{n}{D/s}}$$

Proof. The content distributor gains nothing by reporting a Bloom filter $\boldsymbol{b}' \not\leq \boldsymbol{b}$, since it does not decrease his chances of being caught. If there exist i, j such that $\boldsymbol{b}'[h_i(J_j) \bmod m] = 0$, then setting $\boldsymbol{b}'[h_{i'}(J_j) \bmod m] = 1$ for $i' \neq i$ does not decrease the content distributor's chances of being caught. Hence the content distributor's optimal strategy is to report a Bloom filter $\boldsymbol{b}'$ containing some subset $S \subseteq \{J_1, \ldots, J_n\}$.

To decrease the weight of the Bloom filter by D, one must remove at least D/s items, since each item can decrease the weight of the filter by at most s. Since the content distributor cannot distinguish the auditor's requests, his best strategy is to select the largest S such that $w(\boldsymbol{B}[S])$ is below the allowed

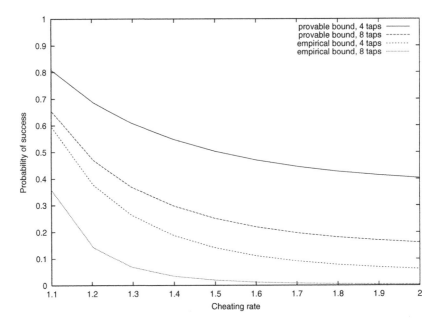

Fig. 3. The probability that a content distributor can fool the auditor, assuming $m = 1024$, $s = 5$, and the content distributor is allowed to report Bloom filters with weight at most 512, which corresponds to 128 requests. The top two curves are provable bounds: a content distributor cannot fool the auditor with probability better than these curves indicate. The bottom two curves are empirical bounds: based on computer simulations, we believe that a content distributor cannot fool the auditor with greater probability than these curves indicate. So for example, if a content distributor receives $1.3*128$ requests, and the auditor sent 8 auditing requests, then the content distributor's chances of successfully convincing the auditor that he only received 128 requests is less than 10%

threshold. We may assume that for any $J_j \in \{J_1, \ldots, J_n\} \setminus S$, there exists an i such that $h_i(J_j \mod m) = 0$ since otherwise the content distributor could add J_j to S without affecting the weight of $\boldsymbol{B}[S]$. So cheating successfully requires selecting (at least) D/s items from $\{J_1, \ldots, J_n\}$ without selecting one of the k requests sent by the auditor. The probability of doing this is $\frac{\binom{n-k}{D/s}}{\binom{n}{D/s}}$. $\square$

Again, the bounds in this proposition are not as tight as possible. In practice, the content distributor will have to omit considerably more than D/s requests in order to reduce the weight of the reported Bloom filter below the allowed threshold. To get a better idea what the real chances of cheating successfully are, we wrote a computer program to simulate a content distributor trying to cheat by finding the optimal subset S described in the above proposition. Based on our experiments, the content distributor has to remove at least $D/2$ items from $\{J_1, \ldots, J_n\}$ in order to decrease the weight of his Bloom filter by D. Figure 3 compares the probability of successfully cheating estimated from the above proposition and the probability of success derived from our experiments. As the graph shows, the actual probability of cheating is much lower than the proposition indicates.

This scheme preserves audience anonymity. The content distributor and client use a coin flipping protocol to agree on the nonce to be placed in the Bloom filter. Since this nonce is generated randomly, it cannot reveal anything about the identity of the client. This strong guarantee of privacy has a downside: a malicious client can send many requests to the content distributor, artificially inflating the audience size. Since this scheme provides total listener anonymity, the content distributor cannot identify the attacker. Also, a content distributor and a group of cooperative clients can agree to always generate the same nonce, hence all the clients would appear to be just one client, deflating the content distributor's audience.

We have described this scheme in terms of request-counting, but it can also be used to count current audience size. Suppose the auditor wants to know the current audience size at each minute. Then the content distributor simply inserts the IDs for all its active clients into a Bloom filter every minute and sends this off to the auditor. To audit, the auditor anonymously requests content from the content distributor and verifies that it is counted among the active streams. Although the reporting overheads are obviously increased in such a scheme, they are still quite low. For example, an Internet radio station with 20 listeners will have to send the auditor about 20 bytes of data every minute, which is quite modest. The above accuracy and security analysis apply directly to this scheme, too.

Finally, this scheme can be further improved by using compressed Bloom filters [20] to reduce the false positive rate without increasing the size of messages sent to the auditor.

3   Estimating Audience Size with Constant Overhead

In the following protocol, the auditor is able to infer the audience size from a constant number of bits that are associated with the (encrypted) content. The protocol offers security against both inflation and deflation of audience size. It is most naturally applicable to the distribution of fairly static content, for example, consider a web site that provides software or movies in encrypted form available for download and decryption with payment. When used with real-time content, the content distributor must be using the network as a broadcast channel in order for the auditor to be assured the measurements are accurate. The drawback of the protocol is that it requires a keying infrastructure. As in Section 2, the basic protocol is essentially a metering scheme in that it counts *hits* (or, joins). In Section 3.2, we discuss extensions to the basic protocol that allow demographic information to be extracted from the content and the current audience size (i.e., not just the cumulative audience) to be estimated.

In this protocol, each client stores a set of encryption keys issued by a trusted party (TP). In the initial phase of the protocol, the TP sends all the keys to the

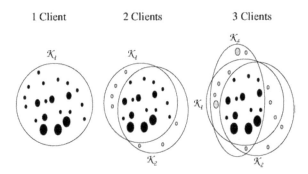

Fig. 4. The black ovals represent keys in the set T when there are 1, 2 and 3 clients. The larger ovals correspond to keys that are more likely to be assigned to any given client. As the number of clients grows the proportion of large ovals in T increases. Hence, the key that's selected from T reflects the audience size

content distributor. When a client requests the content, the TP gives some subset of the keys to the client and sends the ID number of each of the client's keys to the content distributor. To distribute content to the current set of clients, the content distributor forms the intersection of the clients' key sets, T, and chooses a key from T for encrypting the content. Because the TP assigns keys to clients probabilistically, the auditor (who may be the same as the TP) when requesting the content anonymously[3] (e.g. by visiting the distributor's web site), can infer the audience size from the encryption key in use.

The TP assigns keys to clients as follows. First, the entire set of keys is partitioned into t sets, $S_1, \ldots, S_t$. Each client receives any particular key with a fixed, independent probability. For keys in the same set S_i, this probability is the same. By choosing the sets $\{S_i\}_{i=1}^t$ to be of decreasing size (as i increases), but with increasing associated probabilities, the TP can control the proportion of keys in T that are in any S_i given the audience size. More precisely, if the audience is small, T is dominated by keys from S_1, but as the audience grows, the proportion of keys in T that are in S_1 will be far less than the proportion that are in S_i for $i > 1$. Hence, because the content distributor doesn't have any a priori knowledge of the composition of the sets $\{S_i\}_i$, the distributor is unable to distinguish between the keys in T and so the choice of $k \in T$ is a reflection of the distribution of T, and by inference, the audience size. Figure 4 demonstrates how T, may change over time. For illustrative purposes, keys with higher probabilities are indicated by larger ovals.

The following makes the protocol more precise.

---

[3] Receiving the content anonymously also allows the auditor to determine that the content distributor isn't distributing keys to clients (to maintain the appearance of a small audience) or abusing the protocol in some other way. For applications in which the surreptitious distribution of keys to clients by the content distributor is a real concern, a simplified version of the analysis in Section 2 can be performed to calculate the frequency with which the auditor should request the content.

BASIC PROTOCOL. This protocol takes as input a positive integer m representing the number of keys in the system, a positive integer t, and positive integers $s_1, \ldots, s_t$ such that $s_1 + s_2 + \ldots + s_t = m$. The keys are partitioned into t sets, $S_1, \ldots, S_t$, such that for each i, $|S_i| = s_i$, where $s_1 > s_2 > \ldots > s_t$. For each $i = 1, \ldots, t$ there is a probability p_i that the TP will assign a key $k_j \in S_i$ to any given client (keys are assigned independently), where $p_1 < p_2 < \ldots < p_t$. Numbers $\epsilon_1, \epsilon_2, 0 < \epsilon_1, \epsilon_2 < 1$, are also input to provide a gauge of the accuracy of the audience measurements. These parameters imply an upper bound, n_{max}, on the number of joins that can be accurately measured by the system. The variable n is used to denote the actual number of joins. The protocol consists of the following steps:

1. The TP randomly generates m keys, $k_1, \ldots, k_m$, and sends them to the content distributor.
2. Upon contacting the content distributor, a client, u_i, receives a set of keys $\mathcal{K}_i \subseteq \{k_1, \ldots, k_m\}$ from the TP. For $j = 1, \ldots, m$, $k_j \in \mathcal{K}_i$ with probability p_r if $k_j \in S_r$. The TP sends the content distributor the ID numbers of the client's keys[4].
3. To distribute content to clients $u_{j_1}, \ldots, u_{j_r}$, the content distributor chooses a key $k \in T = \mathcal{K}_{j_1} \cap \ldots \cap \mathcal{K}_{j_r}$ and encrypts the content (or perhaps, a key that is used to encrypt the content) with k. A fresh key should be chosen regularly.
4. Periodically, the auditor requests content and notes the key, k, that the content distributor is using in Step 3. There exists $i \in \{1, \ldots, t\}$ such that $k \in S_i$. The auditor calculates the distribution of the random variable that measures the proportion of keys in T that are in S_i as a function of n, $(\frac{|T \cap S_i|}{|T|}|n)$, to within a confidence level of $1 - \epsilon_1$. Using this distribution, the auditor determines a range $[n_1, n_2]$ such that for each $n \in [n_1, n_2]$, $P(k \in S_i|n) \geq \epsilon_2$, and estimates[5] the audience size as being in this range.
   - To increase the likelihood of inferring audience size correctly, the auditor can monitor the content through several key changes.
   - If the auditor has contacted the content distributor previously and received a different set of keys, the auditor should check that k is also in

---

[4] We suggest that the TP send the keys rather than the client, so that the client cannot cause the audience size to appear larger than it is by sending only a subset of their keys to the content distributor.

[5] Note that the probability that directly infers audience size is $P(n = x|k \in S_i)$. Since the distribution on n is unknown we cannot calculate this probability precisely. However, provided some information on the distribution of n is available, this probability can be derived from the one we know by using: $P(n = x|k \in S_i) = \frac{P(k \in S_i|n=x)P(n=x)}{P(k \in S_i)} \geq P(k \in S_i|n = x)P(n = x)$. For example, if $P(n = x) \geq \alpha$ for all x, then we have an upper bound: $P(n = x|k \in S_i) \geq \alpha P(k \in S_i|n = x)$, and if n is uniformly distributed (as is assumed in Section 2 to achieve analysis benefits that don't seem to occur for this protocol), we have an equality: $P(n = x|k \in S_i) = c_i P(k \in S_i|n = x)$ where $c_i = \sum_{y=1}^{n_{max}} P(k \in S_i|n = y)$. Hence, we believe $\{P(k \in S_i|n = x)\}_x$ is sufficient to infer the value of n as being in $[n_1, n_2]$.

that key set. Alternatively, the auditor can request the content as several different clients and perform the same checks. If any of these checks fail, the content distributor is not following the protocol.

This protocol relies on the content distributor's inability to distinguish between the keys in the intersection, T. The content distributor can gain such an ability in the following ways. First, a key that is *not* known to any of a large set of clients is less likely to be in S_t than a key in T. However, provided the distributor follows the protocol and encrypts the content so that all of the audience can decrypt it, the distributor is unable to make use of this information. The other information the content distributor learns about the keys comes from bills (e.g. licensing royalties). For example, if the distributor is charged less when using key k than when using key k', the distributor knows the index j_k such that $k \in S_{j_k}$ is less than the index $j_{k'}$ such that $k' \in S_{j'_k}$. To remedy this, we suggest that the system be refreshed with every bill (e.g. once a month).

There is also the possibility that the content distributor attempts to cheat in a similar way as in our first protocol, namely by removing some users' key sets from the calculation of the intersection, T, in order to get a larger set from which to draw the encryption key. We argue that it is unlikely this attack will be successful. First, cheating in this way can have the effect of preventing some users from accessing the content (which should generate complaints). Second, it is difficult to guarantee that a small audience will be inferred by the auditor because the key allocation algorithm is probabilistic. That is, if the content distributor chooses a key that is not known to several of the clients then there is still some probability that this key is in S_i for large i, in which case a large audience will be inferred. To guarantee that a small audience will be inferred, the content distributor has to use a key that's not known to several clients, in which case the distributor may indeed only be able to reach a small audience.

Finally, the content distributor can potentially benefit from collusion with clients or other content distributors. If the TP is using the same global set to allocate keys to clients of different content distributors (which is a desirable practice because it can allow clients to "surf" multiple distributors without needing to repeat the initialization phase) then the distributors (and users) may be able to distinguish between keys that they wouldn't have been able to otherwise. However, as mentioned earlier, this may be only of limited value because a key that causes a small audience to be inferred does so because it is only likely to be stored by a small number of clients.

3.1   Analysis

In this section we develop equations that allow the auditor to execute the protocol. First, we find an accurate approximation to the distribution of $(\frac{|T \cap S_i|}{|T|}|n)$.

Lemma 1. *Let $0 < \delta < 1$. For $i = 1, \ldots, t$ and $n = x$, $P(k \in S_i | n = x)$ is at least as large as*

$$\frac{(1-\delta)s_i p_i{}^x}{(1+\delta)(s_1 p_1{}^x + \ldots + s_{i-1}p_{i-1}{}^x + s_{i+1}p_{i+1}{}^x + \ldots + s_t p_t{}^x) + (1-\delta)s_i p_i{}^x} \quad \text{and at most as large as}$$

$\frac{(1+\delta)s_i p_i{}^x}{(1-\delta)(s_1 p_1{}^x + \ldots + s_{i-1}p_{i-1}{}^x + s_{i+1}p_{i+1}{}^x + \ldots + s_t p_t{}^x) + (1+\delta)s_i p_i{}^x}$ *with probability at least* $1 - \epsilon_1$, *when*

$(\frac{e^\delta}{(1+\delta)^{1+\delta}})^{s_t p_1{}^{n_{max}}} \leq \frac{1-(1-\epsilon_1)^{1/t}}{2}$ *and* $e^{-\delta^2 s_t p_1{}^{n_{max}}/2} \leq \frac{1-(1-\epsilon_1)^{1/t}}{2}$.

Proof. For $i = 1, \ldots, t$, when the number of clients is x, the random variable $|T \cap S_i|$ is binomially distributed with size s_i and probability $p_i{}^x$. Hence, the expected value of $|T \cap S_i|$ is $s_i p_i{}^x$. Applying Chernoff bounds (see, for example, [21]), it follows that, $|T \cap S_i| \in [(1-\delta)s_i p_i{}^x, (1+\delta)s_i p_i{}^x]$ with probability at least $(1-\epsilon_1)^{1/t}$ when both $(\frac{e^\delta}{(1+\delta)^{1+\delta}})^{s_i p_i{}^{n_{max}}} \leq (\frac{e^\delta}{(1+\delta)^{1+\delta}})^{s_t p_1{}^{n_{max}}} \leq \frac{1-(1-\epsilon_1)^{1/t}}{2}$ and $e^{-\delta^2 s_i p_i{}^{n_{max}}} \leq e^{-\delta^2 s_t p_1{}^{n_{max}}/2} \leq \frac{1-(1-\epsilon_1)^{1/t}}{2}$. Hence, $P(k \in S_i | n = x) = \frac{|T \cap S_i|}{|T|} = \frac{|T \cap S_i|}{|T \cap S_1| + \ldots + |T \cap S_t|}$ is in the interval stated in the lemma with probability at least $(1 - 2\frac{1-(1-\epsilon_1)^{1/t}}{2})^t = 1 - \epsilon_1$. $\square$

From the above lemma, it follows that the auditor needs to find x values such that $\frac{(1-\delta)s_i p_i{}^x}{(1+\delta)(s_1 p_1{}^x + \ldots + s_{i-1}p_{i-1}{}^x + s_{i+1}p_{i+1}{}^x + \ldots + s_t p_t{}^x) + (1-\delta)s_i p_i{}^x} \geq \epsilon_2$ to complete the protocol. In addition, n_{max}, s_i and p_i must be chosen to satisfy Lemma 1, for example, by using the bounds in the following corollary.

Corollary 1. *To satisfy step 4 of the basic protocol it suffices (but isn't generally necessary) to choose* $n_{max} \leq \frac{\ln(\frac{c(\epsilon_1, \delta, t)}{s_t})}{\ln p_1}$ *and* $s_i \geq \frac{c_i(\epsilon_1, \delta)}{p_i{}^{n_{max}}}$ *for all i, where $c(\epsilon_1, \delta, t)$ and $c_i(\epsilon_1, \delta)$ are defined below. Provided these inequalities are met, the expected number of keys that a client must store is at least* $\Sigma_{i=1}^{t} \frac{c_i(\epsilon, \delta)}{p_i{}^{n_{max}-1}}$.

Proof. The constant $c_i(\epsilon_1, \delta)$ in the upper bound on s_i comes from solving the following two inequalities used in the proof of Lemma 1:
$(\frac{e^\delta}{(1+\delta)^{1+\delta}})^{s_i p_i{}^{n_{max}}} \leq \frac{1-(1-\epsilon_1)^{1/t}}{2}$ and $e^{-\delta^2 s_i p_i{}^{n_{max}}/2} \leq \frac{1-(1-\epsilon_1)^{1/t}}{2}$. It follows that
$c_i(\epsilon_1, \delta) = \max\{\frac{2\ln(\frac{1-(1-\epsilon_1)^{1/t}}{2})}{-\delta^2}, \frac{\ln(\frac{1-(1-\epsilon_1)^{1/t}}{2})}{\ln(\frac{e^\delta}{(1+\delta)^{1+\delta}})}\}$.

The bound on n_{max} follows similarly with
$c(\epsilon_1, \delta, t) = \min\{\frac{2\ln(\frac{1-(1-\epsilon_1)^{1/t}}{2})}{-\delta^2}, \frac{\ln(\frac{1-(1-\epsilon_1)^{1/t}}{2})}{\ln(\frac{e^\delta}{(1+\delta)^{1+\delta}})}\}$.

The lower bound on the expected number of keys per client follows by substituting the lower bound for s_i into the quantity, $\Sigma_{i=1}^{t} p_i s_i$. $\square$

For illustrative purposes[6], we conclude this section with a small example.

SINGLE THRESHOLD EXAMPLE. The following example shows how the basic protocol can be used to determine that a threshold number of clients has been

---

[6] In general, it is unwise to choose $p_2 = 1$ and $t = 2$ because the content distributor then knows that any key, k, that's not stored by all the clients, is in S_1 with probability 1. However, even in this example it's arguable that using key k yields a successful attack, since we expect k to only be stored by around 7 clients ($.6 n_{max}$) which is already very close to the 6 client audience that the auditor will infer from the usage of k.

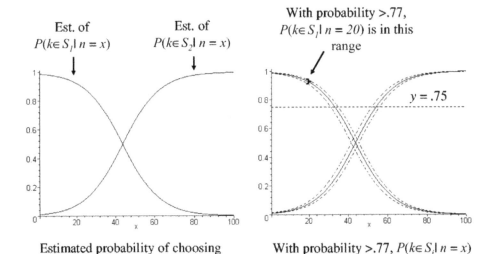

Est. of
$P(k \in S_1| n = x)$

Est. of
$P(k \in S_2| n = x)$

With probability >.77,
$P(k \in S_1| n = 20)$ is in this
range

$y = .75$

Estimated probability of choosing
$k \in S_i$ given $n = x$, for $i = 1,2$.

With probability >.77, $P(k \in S_i| n = x)$
is within the dashed lines, for $i = 1,2$.

Fig. 5. In the left-hand side of the figure we graph, $\frac{p_i^x s_i}{p_1^x s_1 + p_2^x s_2}$ for $i = 1, 2$ (where $p_1 = .6$, $p_2 = 1$, $s_1 = 37000$, $s_2 = 370$) as estimates for $P(k \in S_1|n = x)$ and $P(k \in S_2|n = x)$. $P(k \in S_1|n = x)$ and $P(k \in S_2|n = x)$ are within the distance indicated by the dashed lines of their respective estimates with probability at least .75

achieved. Let $s_1 = 37000$, $p_1 = .6$, $s_2 = 370$, $p_2 = 1$ and $n_{max} = 13$. Because $|T \cap S_2| = 370$ with probability 1, we need only find a confidence interval for $|T \cap S_1|$ and this will imply confidence intervals for $|T \cap S_1|/|T|$ and $|T \cap S_2|/|T|$. Setting $\delta = .2$, by the proof of Lemma 1 we need the following inequality to hold: $(.98)^{s_1 p_1^{13}} < \frac{\epsilon_1}{2}$. Solving for ϵ_1 yields, $\epsilon_1 \geq .75$. If we choose $\epsilon_2 = .75$, then with at least .75 confidence, it follows by solving the inequality, $\frac{(1-\delta)37000(.6)^x}{(1-\delta)37000(.6)^x+370} \geq .75$ for x, that $P(k \in S_1|n \leq 6) \geq .75$. Similarly, by solving, $\frac{370}{(1+\delta)37000(.6)^x+370} \geq .75$ we get, $P(k \in S_2|n \geq 12) \geq .75$. Hence, if $k \in S_1$ the auditor returns the interval $[1,6]$ for n and if $k \in S_2$ the interval $n \geq 12$ is returned. This is depicted in Figure 5 [7].

In this example, we expect a client to store 22, 570 keys. If the keys are each 64 bits long, this represents .17 megabytes of keying material. While this is significant, it is a fraction of the space required by most media players (for example, it's about .09 of the download size of WinAmp.com's "full" player). Viewed differently, after listening to streaming music at a data rate of 28.8 kilobits per second for less than 20 minutes, the keying material is less than .0425 of the audio data that's been downloaded.

Since a client will typically have more than half of the 37, 370 keys in this example, the TP can tell the content distributor the keys the client *doesn't* have more efficiently than listing the keys the client does have, in step 2 of the

---

[7] Note that the confidence intervals hold up to $n = 13$ only.

protocol. Since the key IDs are less than 16 bits long, we expect this step to require the transmission of at most 29 kilobytes of data. Using compression, this can probably be reduced to only 10 kilobytes. Again, this is only necessary when the client first requests the content.

3.2   Extensions

MULTIPLE CONTENT DISTRIBUTORS. The basic protocol is easily modified to allow the trusted party to use a single set of keys for multiple content distributors. In step 2, each user sends keys that are computed as the output of a one-way function applied to each of the keys received from the TP concatenated with the CD's ID. Because the CDs have distinct IDs it is computationally infeasible for them to determine which of their received keys are the same.

PRIVACY AND DEMOGRAPHICS. Note that this protocol is not completely privacy preserving because the auditor learns something about the clients, namely, that they have key k. However, if there is sufficient separation between the auditor and the TP it will be difficult for the auditor to make use of this information. In addition, we note that it may be possible to use this aspect of the scheme to embed demographic information. For example, although men and women should with high probability receive the same number of keys in S_i, the particular keys they tend to receive may be partly a function of their sex. Hence, the auditor may be able to infer the predominant sex of the audience from the content distributor's choice of encryption key in S_i.

MEASURING THE CURRENT AUDIENCE. The protocol described above is best suited to estimate *cumulative* audience size, for example, the number of hits received by a web site over a certain period of time. In some settings, this may be the only possible measure of audience size. For example, in multicast applications, the content distributor typically only is informed of new additions to the multicast group and is unlikely to know when a member leaves [3]. Hence, by observing the content distributor's behavior, or by querying directly, it may only be possible to learn the cumulative audience. In this case, behavioral patterns may be used to infer current audience size from cumulative data.

It may also be possible to modify the basic protocol to measure audience size directly. The key idea is that if the auditor can observe the content for long enough[8] to gain an accurate estimate of the entire contents of T, then the *current* audience may be inferred. The entire contents of T are necessary because the content distributor gains some ability to distinguish keys from every new client. For example, if k is stored by several clients but k' is only known to a few, then k' may be a cheaper key for the content distributor to use because it may imply a smaller audience in the basic protocol ($k' \in S_i$, $k \in S_j$, where $i < j$). Hence, if the audience shrinks and k' ends up being a key all the current clients know, the content distributor may seek to mislead the auditor by only using k'. However,

---

[8] This requirement may be easy to meet because the auditor may need to observe the content for a long time in order to preserve anonymity.

if the content distributor is required to change keys frequently (e.g., a different key for every few songs) and the auditor listens long enough to determine that k' is the only key in use, an alarm will be raised as the probability that the content distributor would be left with only k' at some point is very low. One problem with this is that a key that is known to clients who are no longer in the audience may be selected as the encryption key.

4   Open Problems

Each of our protocols requires some a priori knowledge of the maximum audience size. Although this seems like a reasonable assumption for the applications we consider, it would be useful to design a scheme that can efficiently adapt to unanticipated surges in audience size. Ideally, such a protocol would provide content access to only the current set of clients while preserving privacy and enabling efficient auditing. In addition, we believe the general problem of measuring current audience size in a manner that's secure against both inflation and deflation hasn't been adequately explored.

Acknowledgements

The authors thank Ian Smith for suggesting this problem and Prateek Sarkar, David Goldberg, Dirk Balfanz and Dan Greene for helpful discussions.

References

1. Anonymizer.com. Company web page. http://www.anonymizer.com.
2. Vinod Anupam, Alain Mayer, Kobbi Nissim, Benny Pinkas, and Michael K. Reiter. On the security of pay-per-click and other Web advertising schemes. *Computer Networks (Amsterdam, Netherlands: 1999)*, 31(11–16):1091–1100, 1999.
3. R. Baudes and S. Zabele. RFC 1458: Requirements for multicast protocols, May 1993. Status: INFORMATIONAL.
4. B. Bloom. Space/time trade-offs in hash coding with allowable errors. *Communications of the ACM*, 13(7):422–426, July 1970.
5. A. De Bonis and B. Masuci. An information thoeretical approach to metering schemes. *Proccedings of ISIT 2000*, 2001.
6. A. De Bonis C. Blundo and B. Masuci. Bounds and constructions for metering schemes. *To appear in Communications in Information and Systems 2002*, 2002.
7. D. Chaum. Elections with unconditionally-secret ballots and disruption equivalent to breaking rsa. *Advances in Cryptology Eurocrypt '88*, 330:177–182, 1988.
8. Steve Coffey. Internet audience measurement: A practitioner's view. *Journal of Interactive Advertising*, 2001.
9. comScore Networks. net-score product description. http://www.comscore.com/.
10. Ipsos-RSL Broadcast Division. An introduction to the ipsos-rsl broadcast division. http://www.rslmedia.co.uk/broadcast/experience.html.
11. T. Dyck. Yahoo chief scientist describes web attacks. *EWeek*, July 2002.

12. FAST/ARF. Principles of online media audience measurement. http://www.fastinfo.org/measurement/pages/index.cgi/audiencemeasurement.
13. Matthew K. Franklin and Dahlia Malkhi. Auditable metering with lightweight security. In *Financial Cryptography*, pages 151–160, 1997.
14. Shafi Goldwasser and Mihir Bellare. Lecture notes on cryptography. Summer Course "Cryptography and Computer Security" at MIT, 1996–1999, 1999.
15. Catherine Greenman. Royalty fees threaten web stations. *New York Times*, April 2002.
16. A. P. Kamath, R. Motwani, K. Palem, and P. Spirakis. Tail bounds for occupancy and the satisfiability threshold conjecture. *Random Structures and Algorithms*, 7:59–80, 1995.
17. Markus G. Kuhn. Probabilistic counting of large digital signature collections, 2000.
18. B. Masuci and D. R. Stinson. Efficient metering schemes with pricing. *IEEE Transactions on Information Theory*, 47:2835–2844, 2001.
19. Inc. MeasureCast. An analysis of streaming audience measurement methods. http://www.measurecast.com/docs/Audience_Measurement_Methods.pdf.
20. M. Mitzenmacher. Compressed bloom filters. *ACM Symposium on Principles of Distributed Computing*, pages 144–150, 2001.
21. R. Motwani and P. Raghavan. Randomized algorithms, Cambridge University Press, 2000.
22. Moni Naor and Benny Pinkas. Secure and efficient metering. *Lecture Notes in Computer Science*, 1403:576–589, 1998.
23. Wakaha Ogata and Kaoru Kurosawa. Provably secure metering scheme. *Lecture Notes in Computer Science*, 1976:388–398, 2000.
24. Michael K. Reiter, Vinod Anupam, and Alain Mayer. Detecting hit shaving in click-through payment schemes. In *Proceedings of the 3rd USENIX Workshop on Electronic Commerce*, pages 155–166, 1998.
25. Nielsen Media Research. Audience measurement services – the global leader for actionable internet information. http://www.nielsen-netratings.com/marketing/advertising/audience_measurement/.
26. B. Preneel V. Nikov, S. Nikova and J. Vandewalle. Applying general access structure to metering schemes, 2002.

Theft-Protected Proprietary Certificates

Alexandra Boldyreva[1] and Markus Jakobsson[2]

[1] Dept. of Computer Science & Engineering, University of California at San Diego
9500 Gilman Drive, La Jolla, California 92093, USA
aboldyre@cs.ucsd.edu
http://www-cse.ucsd.edu/users/aboldyre
[2] RSA Laboratories, 174 Middlesex Turnpike, Bedford MA 01730, USA
mjakobsson@rsasecurity.com
http://www.markus-jakobsson.com

Abstract. The notion of *proprietary certificates* [8] was recently introduced in an attempt to discourage sharing of access rights to subscription-based resources. A proprietary certificate is a certificate on a public key – the so-called *proprietary* key – that contains some information related to another (so-called *collateral*) certificate and has the property that if the owner of the proprietary public key reveals the corresponding (so-called proprietary) secret key, then the collateral secret key (corresponding to the public key in the collateral certificate) is automatically released. Thus, if a service provider requires all users to use proprietary certificates linked with collateral certificates corresponding to resources the users always wish to keep private – such as access to 401(k) accounts, the user's criminal history, etc – then this will discourage the access rights sharing. However, the original solution for proprietary certificates overlooks the possibility of *accidental* sharing, namely, sharing caused by theft of the proprietary secret key which would lead to immediate loss of the collateral secret key, making wide-scale deployment of proprietary certificate approach unlikely. In this paper we discuss what steps can be taken towards making proprietary certificates approach more practical. While our solution preserves all the properties the original solution of [8] achieves, most importantly, protection against *intentional* rights sharing, it satisfies an additional property, namely, *theft protection*.

1 Introduction

1.1 Proprietary Certificates

One of the main goals of Digital Rights Management (DRM) is to protect digital content from illegal or inappropriate use. In various PKI applications, digital certificates can provide a partial solution to this problem. Namely, in order for a service provider to restrict access to appropriate users, it can verify each user's identity and authenticity of the user's public key by having the user present a valid digital certificate. However, this does not fully solve the problem. A registered user can share access rights to the resource (thus violating DRM

J. Feigenbaum (Ed.): DRM 2002, LNCS 2696, pp. 208–220, 2003.

policies) by lending his or her certificate and the corresponding secret key to another party.

The problem of preventing access rights sharing has been addressed in the literature. The high level idea of the existing solutions is to force a user who shares a secret key which gives access to some service to additionally share some other sensitive information, e.g. a credit card number. In most solutions (see, for example, [6,15]) a service provider or a certification authority must be trusted since it learns this sensitive information.

A solution proposed recently by Jakobsson, Juels and Nguyen [8] attempts to solve the problem of access rights sharing without a trusted third party requirement. The authors introduce a *proprietary certificate*, which is a way of implementing digital certificate that discourages unwanted sharing of resources. A proprietary certificate may be used where a standard certificate may otherwise be employed but where the service provider wishes to discourage resource sharing. For example, it may be used for verifying and granting access rights to subscribers of a stock quote service while discouraging them from sharing their access with non-subscribers.

Subscribers are discouraged from sharing access rights with others by "linking" the secret key associated with the user's certificate (called the *proprietary* secret key and certificate) to a second secret key corresponding to another certificate (called the *collateral* secret key and certificate). The certificates which can serve as collateral ones are those which correspond to the accounts that are supposedly very important and long-lived such as bank accounts, 401(k) plans, health or criminal records, etc.

The link between the proprietary and collateral secret key guarantees that anybody with knowledge of the proprietary secret key can compute the corresponding collateral key. Thus, users who allow others access to the resource associated with the *proprietary* key are punished by automatically relinquishing control over the resource associated with the *collateral* key. If the collateral key grants access to the user's bank account or appending to his criminal record, this would clearly make sharing undesirable on a large scale.

More precisely, [8] considers a set of *users* and *certification authorities (CAs)* and proposes a certification protocol run between a user and CA in order to produce a proprietary certificate. We note, that CAs is in many cases can be functionally similar or identical to *service providers*, as the latter may often register users by pseudonyms or public keys – whether used internally or globally. For this reason, we will use the terms *service provider* and *certification authority* interchangingly onwards. At a high level, the approach of [8] is to include in proprietary certificates a ciphertext of a special form, where the secret key allowing the ciphertext to be decrypted is a proprietary secret key. Decrypting the ciphertext, in turn, results in the collateral secret key. In order not to require CAs to know proprietary and collateral secret keys of the users the solution of [8] uses fair encryption methods of Poupard and Stern [12]. We review fair encryption in Section 2.2 and discuss the solution of [8] and the properties it achieves in more detail in Section 3.

1.2   Vulnerabilities of Proprietary Certificates

While the original construction for proprietary certificates [8] achieves its stated goals, it overlooks the possible scenario in case of theft of the proprietary secret key that would lead to immediate loss of the collateral secret key. Hence, theft of the proprietary key grants the intruder full access rights to all resources associated with both the proprietary and corresponding collateral keys. In other words, their approach punishes not only *intentional* sharing, but also *accidental* sharing. This would, with a big likelihood, make large-scale deployment of such a scheme unlikely, given the threat of device loss and theft, burglaries, and computer viruses.

1.3   Our Goals

In this paper, we suggest measures which can help to overcome the weakness of the proprietary certificates approach and to make it more practical. We try to balance the requirements to punish intentional sharing with the desire to avoid penalizing accidental sharing, which is a seemingly contradictory problem. We propose a proprietary key certification protocol where the resulting proprietary certificate has an additional *theft protection* property. Theft-protected proprietary certificates meet all the properties of proprietary certificates and satisfy an additional theft-protection property. Namely, derivation of a collateral secret key from the proprietary secret key and the proprietary certificate is possible only after some predefined time delay. During this time delay, however, no information about a collateral secret key can be obtained, even by the party with knowledge of a proprietary secret key. Thus, the advantage is that the legitimate user has time to take measures in case of accidental exposure of a proprietary secret key.

Such approach would be useful for the settings where it is reasonable to assume that the collateral secret key is stored more securely than the proprietary secret key and that the owner of the device containing proprietary keys would know of a potential compromise of them. For example, if the proprietary keys reside on a palmtop computer or a cellular phone, loss of such device would indicate secret key compromise. Similarly, if the proprietary keys reside on a desktop computer, it would be prudent to assume key exposure if the office containing the computer is burglarized or if security software detects viruses, hacker activities or intrusion. For various less obvious techniques which help to detect secret key compromise see [9].

If the user reports theft of his key within this time period, the access keys for the proprietary and collateral services may be cancelled and re-newed, preventing both the accidental and intentional "share holder" from accessing either resource. Potentially the user can repeatedly share re-newed keys, however, various policies can be enacted to avoid this – a user who time after time cancels and re-keys an account may not get a renewed key after some time. This will satisfy both requirements, as it would provide security against theft and losses, while still discouraging sharing.

1.4   The Solutions

Technically speaking, the core of our solutions can be described as implementing time delays for the routine for deriving collateral secret keys from proprietary secret keys and certificates. We provide the solutions for time delays measured in real time or delays measured in CPU time. Our solution for the real time delay requires that the proprietary CAs support additional interaction with the parties regarding release of information related to collateral keys. In contrast, the CPU time delay solution does not require such communication, since the derivation of the collateral key can be done locally by any party with knowledge of the proprietary secret key and certificate. While CPU time is relative to processor speed, our solution withstands efforts to speed up the derivation of collateral keys by the use of parallelization of computation. Both of our solutions use fair encryption, and the CPU delay solution uses the notion of time-lock puzzles introduced by Rivest, Shamir and Wagner in [13]. We review the latter in Section 2.3 and describe our solutions in detail in Section 4.

In Section 5 we discuss various techniques of how service providers can help detecting secret keys compromise, and describe how additional features, such as user alerts can be implemented on top of our basic protocols, and used according to suitable policies.

1.5   Business Model

It is clear that subscription services benefit from the establishment of proprietary certificates to discourage their users from sharing access to the resources with others. Honest users, in turn, may also benefit from such an arrangement by a reduction of subscription fees and improved access, where the latter is due to the decreased access by non-registered users. Turning to the collateral accounts, there are two distinct situations. A first type of collateral account has the property of being *intrinsically* valuable to its owner, or where limited access rights are vital. Examples of this type is a 401(k) account or an account with append access to criminal records. These accounts will exist independently of the use of proprietary certificates. A second type of account is *artificially* made to become valuable. For this second type, one needs to provide an incentive to create and maintain accounts. We suggest the possibility of a class of service providers *whose sole business* is to support collateral accounts. Thus, such parties would certify users after having received a deposit or other security from them, and would either charge the user for the service (the interest, say), or receive periodical payments from the proprietary service providers. Note that users may establish *one* such "collateral account" and use it as collateral for several service providers.

2   Building Blocks

Here we outline the existing primitives and notions we will use in our work. Since our solutions support two main key types used in proprietary and collateral certificates we first recall the structure of RSA and discrete-log based keys. Next we review the notion of fair encryption [12] that is used in [8] and our solutions. Finally we outline time-lock puzzles introduced in [13], which we use for our CPU-time-delay solution.

2.1   Types of Keys

RSA keys Let k be the security parameter. In order to create an RSA type key pair a user picks at random two k-bit primes p, q and computes $N = pq$. He then picks a random number $e \in Z_N$ coprime to $\phi(N)$, where $\phi(\cdot)$ is a Euler's totient function. The public key of the user is (N, e). The user also computes d such that $ed \equiv 1 \bmod \phi(N)$. The secret key of the user is (N, d). Usually $k = 512$. These types of keys are used in the standard RSA encryption and signature schemes [11] and in many others schemes and protocols.

Discrete-log (DL) keys Let k be the security parameter. In order to use discrete log (DL)-based keys, a user picks at random a k-bit prime p and a prime q such that q divides $p-1$. He then picks a random generator g of the group of order q. He picks a random element x of Z_q and computes $y = g^x$. The public key of the user is (p, q, g, y) and the corresponding secret key is (p, q, g, x). Often all users use the same values p, q, g. Usually $k = 1024$. These types of keys are used in El Gamal encryption and signature schemes [7], Cramer-Shoup encryption scheme [4], Schnorr signature schemes [14], etc.

2.2   Fair Encryption

Following the definition given in [2], a *verifiable encryption* is a two-party protocol between a prover P and a verifier V who initially have access to some public key pk_1, some public value p and some binary relation R. At the end of the protocol the verifier obtains a ciphertext under pk_1 of some value x and accepts if the relation R between x and p holds and rejects otherwise. The properties of the protocol is that V can accept "invalid" x only with negligible probability and that V learns nothing about x.

A *fair encryption* is a verifiable encryption where the relation is true if x is a secret key sk_2 corresponding to the public key $pk_2 = p$. In other words, the prover convinces the verifier that a given ciphertext is a valid encryption of the secret key sk_2 corresponding to pk_2 which can be decrypted using sk_1, the secret key corresponding to pk_1 such that the verifier does not learn anything about sk_2. Poupard and Stern [12] give efficient solutions for the fair encryption of the RSA- and discrete-log-type secret keys using the Paillier encryption scheme [10]. As noted in [8], the protocols of [12] are applicable for the case when pk_1 is RSA-type key since the Paillier encryption (resp. decryption) can be performed under RSA public (resp. secret) keys (wlog we assume that Paillier public key G is equal $N + 1$, where N is a public modulus of pk_1). [8] provides the solution for fair encryption of both types of secret keys under the discrete-log-type public keys. Their solution for fair encryption of RSA type keys under the DL-type keys has a an additional requirement that a user's RSA modulus N be a product of two *safe* primes p, q, where $(p-1)/2$ and $(q-1)/2$ are both large primes.

Therefore, there exist solutions for fair encryption of both types of secret keys under the both types of public keys. All the protocols of [12,8] can be made non-interactive, so in this paper we will assume so. We will use the notation $\mathcal{FE}_{pk_1}(sk_2)$ to denote the fair encryption of the secret key sk_2 under the public key pk_1.

2.3   Time-Lock Puzzles

Rivest et al. [13] provide a solution for the problem of encrypting a message in such a way so that no one can decrypt it until a pre-defined amount of time has passed. It might seem that the problem has a trivial solution, namely, one should encrypt the message using some symmetric encryption scheme using some not very long key. Then in order to decrypt this ciphertext one would need to do exhaustive key search which would take some time depending on the length of the key. As [13] notes, this solution is not satisfactory. First, a brute-force key search is parallelizable and second, the actual running time of the decryption process will depend on the order in which the keys are examined.

We now sketch the solution of [13]. Assume A wants to encrypt a message M with a time-lock puzzle for a period of T seconds. A picks at random two large primes p, q and computes $n = pq, \phi(n) = (p-1)(q-1)$. She then computes $t = TS$ where S is the number of squarings modulo n per second that can be performed by the potential decryptor. Then A picks a long random key K for some secure symmetric encryption scheme and encrypts M using K. Let us call the resulting ciphertext C_M. She then computes $C_K = K + a^{2^t} \bmod n$ for some random $a, 1 < a < n$. Since A knows $\phi(n)$, she can do this efficiently. The time-lock puzzle will contain (n, a, t, C_K, C_M). In order to extract M anybody would need to compute a^{2^t} and the only way to do this without knowing $\phi(n)$ is to perform t sequential squarings. The time delay ensured by this solution is not really absolute real time but some time period depending on the CPU power of the decryptor. We will refer to this as CPU time delay.

3   Proprietary Certificates

Let CA_1, (resp. CA_2) be the distinct certification authorities issuing the certificates for the proprietary (resp. collateral) services. Let C_1, (resp. C_2) be the proprietary (resp. collateral) certificates of some user. Assume that C_1, C_2 are publicly available. We now review the desirable properties of the system; for more details see [8].

- *Non-transferability.* Any user who learns secret key of C_1 would be able to compute the secret key of C_2, thus, reducing the likelihood of transferring proprietary certificates.

- *Cryptosystem agility.* Proprietary and collateral services can use different cryptosystems. For example, the secret key of C_1 can be RSA type and the secret key of C_2 can be discrete-log based key.
- *Locality*: CA_1 does not need to interact with CA_2 directly. However, the "light" version of interaction such as broadcast of information by CA_2 is necessary. See the discussion below.
- *Efficiency*: The certificate C_1 should not be substantially larger than a regular certificate of its type without proprietary properties.
- *Security.* Any party does not learn any information about the secret key of C_2. No party besides CA_1 learns what other certificates the user has. CA_1 learns only what public key and certificate the user uses to access collateral service.

The paper [8] shows how to extend the regular certificate to make it proprietary one, namely being linked to the collateral certificate. As it was suggested in [8], fair encryption can be used for the implementation of proprietary certificates. More precisely, the standard certification process of the public key of the user is modified as follows:

In order to certify the public key pk_1, the certification authority CA_1 (which acts as a proprietary one) asks the user to present the certificate of the another key pk_2 issued by CA_2 which he uses for some other service (to be considered as collateral) and the value $F = \mathcal{FE}_{pk_1}(sk_2)$ which is the fair encryption of his collateral secret key sk_2 under pk_1. If CA_1 agrees to use this certificate as collateral (if the potential loss of the collateral secret key would prevent the user from sharing his proprietary secret key), she then verifies validity of the collateral certificate by checking the signature of CA_2 and validity of the fair encryption. The properties of fair encryption ensure that CA_1 does not learn any information about the user's collateral secret key while being able to verify whether this ciphertext is valid. CA_1 also needs to be sure that pk_2 is still a valid key. It is assumed that CA_2 broadcasts the updates to the list of valid public keys. Thus CA_1 needs to check that pk_2 is still on that list. No direct interaction between CA_1 and CA_2 is required. If verification is successful, then CA_1 includes F and the encryption of pk_2 under pk_1 in the certificate in addition to standard information such as the user's identity information and pk_1. If the user shares sk_1 with another party, then that party can decrypt F and obtain sk_2. It is shown in [8] that this approach allows us to achieve the properties sketched above.

As we mentioned in the introduction, the weakness of the above approach comes from the fact that accidental exposure of a proprietary secret key due to theft or intrusion would immediately lead to a loss of the collateral key. Such scenario is possible since the proprietary keys are supposedly less valuable than collateral ones and, therefore, can be stored on less secure devices. Therefore, direct use of proprietary certificates would be risky since it imposes additional insecurity on the collateral secret key: no matter how well its storage is protected, its security can be violated through exposure of the less secure proprietary key.

As a result of this problem it is unlikely that the proprietary certificates approach be of wide practical use.

4   Making Proprietary Certificates Theft Protected

In this paper we discuss what steps can be taken towards making proprietary certificates approach more practical. At the first glance, the problem of key lending prevention and the problem of theft protection might seem contradictory. Indeed, the former requires the entity with possession of the proprietary secret key to be able to compute the collateral secret key while the latter would ask to prevent this possibility. However, we show that a compromise is possible.

While our approach is based on the proprietary certificates solution of [8] and preserves all the properties it achieves, our solution has one more additional property, namely, *theft protection*. The theft-protection property is a modified non-transferability property we discussed above. Namely, we require that in case of involuntary proprietary key exposure the user has time to detect the fact of theft and to contact proprietary and collateral service providers. During this time delay no entity, even the one with knowledge of the proprietary secret key should be able to derive the collateral secret key. After that delay (but not before), however, the entity with possession of the proprietary secret key should be able to obtain the collateral secret key as has been required before by the non-transferability property.

As we discussed in the introduction, we assume that the users are able to detect key theft within some period of time. The necessary time delay should be determined depending on the factors such as how fast the user can detect intrusion, contact service providers, etc.

We now provide our main solutions. We show how to implement the certification protocol run by a user and a proprietary CA in order to produce a theft-protected proprietary certificate. We prove that the resulting certificates meet the requirements of proprietary certificates and also have theft-protection property. Namely, we first show that even possessing the proprietary secret key no information about the collateral secret key can be obtained during some preset time delay and secondly we show how the collateral secret key can be derived after the delay.

The first of our solutions describes the implementation of CPU time delay, which does not require additional participation of the CA. Our second solution presents the realization of real time delay. In this case, however, additional involvement of the CA is required.

4.1   Implementing a CPU Delay

We use the idea of time-lock puzzles from [13], as outlined in Section 2.3, in order to implement a CPU delay for the link between the proprietary and collateral secret keys.

Let $\mathcal{U}$ denote the user that wants to certify the proprietary public key pk_1 with the proprietary certification authority CA_1. We assume that $\mathcal{U}$ holds proprietary and collateral public and secret key pairs $(pk_1, sk_1), (pk_2, sk_2)$ and the certificate on the collateral key C_2 signed by CA_2 that contains standard information such as U's identity info ID_U and the collateral public key pk_2.

We let $\mathcal{FE}$ denote the fair encryption algorithm and $\mathcal{SE}$ be some semantically-secure symmetric encryption algorithm with some appropriately chosen key length k. We may use a symmetric cipher such as AES with a 128-bit key in CBC mode [5,1].

Let T be the desirable time delay in seconds, and let S be the approximate number of squarings required to unlock the puzzle, where all squarings are performed modulo some composite n, chosen by CA_1.

By combining time-locks and encryption under the proprietary public key, we obtain the desired functionality.

Certification protocol. In order to produce a theft-protected proprietary certificate C_1 on a public key pk_1, the following interactive protocol is executed by $\mathcal{U}$ and CA_1:

1. $\mathcal{U}$ computes $F = \mathcal{FE}_{pk_1}(sk_2)$ (see Section 2.2 for details). He then sends (ID_U, pk_1, F, C_2) to CA_1.
2. CA_1 verifies ID_U, C_2 and whether F is a valid fair encryption of the collateral secret key (we refer to [8] for a description of these steps). If it is incorrect, then CA_1 aborts; otherwise she continues as follows:
   (a) She picks two large random primes p, q and computes $n = pq$.
   (b) She picks a random k-bit string K and computes $E_F = \mathcal{SE}_K(F)$, where k is large enough such that exhaustive search done in polynomial time is not possible.
   (c) She computes values a, b as a function of pk_1. (We provide the details of how a, b are computed below for RSA and DL keys). Wlog we assume that $n > a$.
   (d) She computes $E_K = K + a^{2^t} \bmod n$, where $t = TS$.
   (e) Finally, she composes the certificate C_1 which contains $(ID_U, pk_1, E_F, E_K, n, t, b)$ and a valid signature on this data and returns C_1 to $\mathcal{U}$.
3. CA_1 sends $\phi(n)$ to $\mathcal{U}$ securely (encrypted under pk_1 using any secure encryption scheme).

We now specify how the values a, b above are computed.

Use of RSA keys. First, we will consider the case when $\mathcal{U}$ holds RSA-type proprietary keys. Assume his proprietary public key is (N, e) and the corresponding secret key is (N, e), see Section 2.1 for details. Then CA_1 picks some random number $a \in Z_N^*$ and computes $b = a^e \bmod N$.

Use of DL keys. Now, consider the case when $\mathcal{U}$ has discrete-log-type proprietary keys. Suppose his proprietary public key is (p, g, q, g^x) and his secret key is x, refer to Section 2.1. Then CA_1 picks some random $r \in Z_q$ and computes $b = g^r$ and $a = y^r = g^{rx} \bmod p$. If CA_1 holds discrete-log-type keys as well, then we can simplify this by making use of the CA's keys. If CA_1 has the public key (g, q, g^y) and the corresponding secret y, she can put $b = g^y$, which is a part of CA's public key and compute $a = (g^x)^y = g^{xy} \bmod p$.

Claims. We now show that the above protocol has the desired properties. First of all, note that due to the properties of the proof of correctness of fair encryption the CA does not get any information about sk_2. Next note that since the CA knows the factorization of n, she can compute a^{2^t} efficiently, namely, she can compute $s = 2^t \bmod \phi(n)$, $E_K = K + a^s \bmod n$. Next, we claim that not knowing sk_1 it is not possible to compute any information about sk_2 due to semantic security of $\mathcal{FE}$. Hence, security property is satisfied.

Now suppose that some party P learned $\mathcal{U}$'s proprietary secret key sk_1. In any case the only way for P to compute sk_2 is to decrypt E_F in order to get F and to decrypt it using sk_1. P cannot do exhaustive key search for K within polynomial time because the key is long. Note that for any types of the $\mathcal{U}$'s keys P can compute a as a function of b and sk_1. For the RSA-type keys P computes $a = b^d \bmod n$. For DL-type keys P computes $a = b^x \bmod p$. As [13] shows, the only way for P to decrypt E_F is by computing a^{2^t} and then K. And since P does not know the factorization of n, he can do so only by performing sequential squarings which take time at least T. After that P can decrypt E_F, F and obtain sk_2. P can also compute pk_2 and find the corresponding collateral certificate C_2, since we assumed that all certificates are public. Thus, the theft-protection property is preserved. It is easy to see that the protocol satisfies the rest of the properties of theft-protected proprietary certificates.

$\mathcal{U}$ can verify that E_F, E_K are composed correctly using $\phi(n)$ as follows. He computes $s = 2^t \bmod \phi(n)$, $K = E_K - a^s \bmod n$, decrypts E_F and compares the result with F.

It remains to mention that it is not possible to pre-compute the value of a from b without the knowledge of the proprietary secret key.

4.2   Implementing a Real-Time Delay

Herein, we consider an approach in which a party has to interact with a CA in order to complete the derivation of the collateral secret key.

Certification protocol. As with regular proprietary certificates, during the process of certification of a public key, the user sends to the proprietary CA his proprietary public key, some proof of identity, and the collateral certificate. In addition, he sends a fair encryption F of the collateral secret key under the proprietary public key, one component of which is a proof of correct contents.

As before, the proprietary CA verifies the validity of all information, including the certificate associated with the collateral key, and the fair encryption. Now, however, she does *not* include F in the certificate, but rather stores it privately along with user's information in her database. We also assume that the CA and users agree on the use of a secure (unforgeable under chosen-message attack) signature scheme which uses keys of the same type as the one of the proprietary keys.

Derivation of collateral secret. If some party P obtains the user U's proprietary secret key sk_1, he would contact the CA which in turn would send P the random challenge value r. P computes a signature on r using sk_1 and sends it to the CA along with a public key pk_p for which P knows the secret key.

The CA searches for pk_1 in her database and verifies the validity of the signature. If it is correct, she waits the necessary time period and then returns the fair encryption F of the collateral key (as collected above), encrypted under pk_p. We stress that the CA needs to send F securely, or other parties could obtain it, allowing them to derive the collateral key of party U *immediately* after they obtain U's proprietary key (thus, the delay would only hold for the first request, in the worst case).

Upon receiving F, P (who knows sk_1) can decrypt F and obtain the collateral secret key.

Claims. The above shows that the party P with knowledge of the proprietary secret key can obtain the collateral secret key after the real time interval. It is clear that P cannot do it prior to this time, as he does not know F then. No party which does not know the proprietary secret key cannot obtain F since he cannot forge a valid signature. Thus, the theft protection property is preserved. It is easy to check that all the other properties are satisfied. We omit the details.

5   Alarm Techniques and Policies

Proprietary side alarms. It is clear that the trusted third party – the proprietary CA in the protocol of Section 4.2 – may sound an alarm once she receives a request for a fair encryption. By the proposed structure, it is clear that he will know what proprietary key has been compromised (in other words: the requests are not blinded with respect to what account they correspond to). We argue that it may not be in her best interests always to sound the alarm, though, as this provides cheaters with a "rescue mechanism". By making the alarm probabilistic, we can maintain the deterrence against sharing, while still allowing warnings to be generated when appropriate. We can use any policy, potentially made dependent on the status of the account in question, to determine when to alert users and collateral account holders.

Collateral side alarms. In the scenario in which the delay is governed by a CPU intensive task there would not be anybody to sound such an alarm, given that the party who is trying to retrieve the collateral key does not need to interact to do so. Let us therefore also consider the use of alarms on the collateral accounts as well as on the proprietary accounts. (These may be used for certificates with real time delay as well as those with CPU delay).

A collateral-side alarm can be achieved by requiring *two* keys to access a collateral account, one long and one short. Both have to be used to gain access to an account. The *long* key would be the one we have referred to as the collateral secret key. The *short* key, which may be as short as a few bits, does not have a public counterpart (and so, a guess cannot be verified). We refer to the short key as the *secret string*. This is not embedded in any certificates, whether proprietary or collateral, but merely used as a "trip wire". It is known by its owner, and by the CA corresponding to the associated account. When a user attempts to log in, he would not be given access permission of the collateral key is incorrect (whether the collateral string is or not). If both are right, he is given access. Otherwise, it is up to local policies whether to give access, and whether to sound the alarm. These, and other actions, may be probabilistic, and may be governed by arbitrary policies.

Acknowledgments

This work has greatly benefitted from discussions with Stanislav Jarecki. We also wish to thank Ari Juels and Chanathip (Meaw) Namprempre for their helpful feedback. Alexandra Boldyreva was supported in part by SDSC Graduate Student Diversity Fellowship, NSF Grant CCR-0098123 and NSF Grant ANR-0129617.

References

1. M. BELLARE, A. DESAI, E. JOKIPII AND P. ROGAWAY, "A concrete security treatment of symmetric encryption: Analysis of the DES modes of operation," *Proceedings of the* 38th *Symposium on Foundations of Computer Science*, IEEE, 1997.
2. JAN CAMENISCH, IVAN DAMGÅRD, "Verifiable Encryption, Group Encryption, and Their Applications to Group Signatures and Signature Sharing Schemes," *Advances in Cryptology – ASIACRYPT '00*, LNCS Vol. 1976, T. Okamoto ed., Springer-Verlag, 2000.
3. DARIO CATALANO, ROSARIO GENNARO, NICK HOWGRAVE-GRAHAM AND PHONG Q. NGUYEN, "Paillier's cryptosystem revisited," *ACM Conference on Computer and Communications Security* 2001.
4. R. CRAMER AND V. SHOUP, "A practical public key cryptosystem provably secure against adaptive chosen ciphertext attack," *Advances in Cryptology – Crypto '98*, LNCS Vol. 1462, H. Krawczyk ed., Springer-Verlag, 1998.
5. "DES modes of operation," *National Institute of Standards and Technology, U.S. Department of Commerce*, 1980.
6. C. DWORK, J. LOTSPIECH AND M. NAOR, "Digital signets: Self-enforcing protection of digital information," *Proceedings of the* 28th *Annual Symposium on Theory of Computing*, ACM, 1996.
7. T. ELGAMAL, "A public key cryptosystem and signature scheme based on discrete logarithms," *IEEE Transactions on Information Theory*, vol 31, 1985.
8. M. JAKOBSSON, A. JUELS AND P. NGUYEN, "Proprietary Certificates," *Proceedings of the The Cryptographers' Track at the RSA Conference 2002*, LNCS Vol. 2271, Springer-Verlag, 2002.

9. M. JUST AND P. VAN OORSCHOT, "Addressing the problem of undetected signature key compromise," *NDSS*, 1999.

10. P. PAILLIER, "Public-key cryptosystems based on composite degree residuosity classes," *Advances in Cryptology – Eurocrypt '99*, LNCS Vol. 1592, J. Stern ed., Springer-Verlag, 1999.

11. "PKCS-1," RSA LABS, http://www.rsasecurity.com/rsalabs/pkcs/pkcs-1/.

12. G. POUPARD AND J. STERN, "Fair encryption of RSA keys," *Advances in Cryptology – Eurocrypt '00*, LNCS Vol. 1807, B. Preneel ed., Springer-Verlag, 2000

13. R. RIVEST, A. SHAMIR AND D. WAGNER, "Time-lock puzzles and timed-release crypto," *LCS technical memo MIT/LCS/TR-684, February 1996.*

14. CLAUS P. SCHNORR, "Efficient signature generation by smart cards," *Journal of Cryptology, 4:161–174, 1991.*

15. S. STUBBLEBINE, P. SYVERSON AND D. GOLDSCHLAG, "Unlinkable serial transactions: protocols and applications," *TISSEC 2(4): 354-389, 1999.*

Author Index